D0303558

WOMEN AND DEPRESSION

Women and Depression: Recovery and Resistance takes a welcome look at women's experiences of living well after depression. Lafrance argues that the social construction of femininity is dangerous for women's health and, ultimately, central to their experiences of depression. Beginning with a critical examination of the ways in which women's depression is a product of the social, political, and interpersonal realities of their everyday lives, the analysis moves on to explore an often ignored aspect of women's experience – how women manage to 'recover' and be well after depression.

The book draws on extensive in-depth interviews with women who have been depressed, as well as on previous research and on analyses of how health practices are represented in the media. In this way Lafrance critically examines how women negotiate and actively resist hegemonic discourses of femininity in their struggles to recover from depression and be well. Threaded throughout the analysis is the exploration of a variety of subjects related to women's distress and health, including:

- negotiating identity
- the medicalization of women's misery
- women's narratives of resistance
- the material and discursive context of women's self-care

In exploring the taken-for-granted aspects of women's experiences, Lafrance sheds light on the powerful but often invisible constraints on women's well-being, and the multiple and creative ways in which they resist these constraints in their everyday lives. These insights will be of interest to students and scholars of psychology, sociology, women's studies, social work, counselling, and nursing.

Michelle N. Lafrance is Associate Professor of Psychology at St Thomas University in Canada. Her research and teaching interests are in the area of women's mental health.

WOMEN AND PSYCHOLOGY
Series Editor: Jane Ussher
School of Psychology, University of Western Sydney

This series brings together current theory and research on women and psychology. Drawing on scholarship from a number of different areas of psychology, it bridges the gap between abstract research and the reality of women's lives by integrating theory and practice, research and policy.

Each book addresses a 'cutting edge' issue of research, covering such topics as post-natal depression, eating disorders, theories and methodologies.

The series provides accessible and concise accounts of key issues in the study of women and psychology, and clearly demonstrates the centrality of psychology to debates within women's studies or feminism.

The Series Editor would be pleased to discuss proposals for new books in the series.

Other titles in this series:

FEMININITY AND THE PHYSICALLY ACTIVE WOMAN
Precilla Y.L. Choi

GENDER, LANGUAGE AND DISCOURSE
Anne Weatherall

THE SCIENCE/FICTION OF SEX
Annie Potts

THE PSYCHOLOGICAL DEVELOPMENT OF GIRLS
AND WOMEN
Sheila Greene

JUST SEX?
Nicola Gavey

WOMAN'S RELATIONSHIP WITH HERSELF
Helen O'Grady

GENDER TALK
Susan A. Speer

BEAUTY AND MISOGYNY
Sheila Jeffreys

BODY WORK
Sylvia K. Blood

MANAGING THE MONSTROUS FEMININE
Jane M. Ussher

THE CAPACITY TO CARE
Wendy Hollway

SANCTIONING PREGNANCY
Harriet Gross and Helen Pattison

ACCOUNTING FOR RAPE
Irina Anderson and Kathy Doherty

THE SINGLE WOMAN
Jill Reynolds

WOMEN AND DEPRESSION

Recovery and Resistance

Michelle N. Lafrance

Routledge
Taylor & Francis Group

LONDON AND NEW YORK

First published 2009 by Routledge
27 Church Road, Hove, East Sussex BN3 2FA

Simultaneously published in the USA and Canada
by Routledge
270 Madison Avenue, New York NY 10016

Routledge is an imprint of the Taylor & Francis Group, an Informa business

© 2009 Psychology Press

Typeset in Times by Garfield Morgan, Swansea, West Glamorgan
Printed and bound in Great Britain by TJ International Ltd, Padstow, Cornwall
Paperback cover design by Terry Foley

This publication has been produced with paper manufactured to strict environmental
standards and with pulp derived from sustainable forests.

British Library Cataloguing in Publication Data
A catalogue record for this book is available from the British Library

Library of Congress Cataloging in Publication Data
Lafrance, Michelle N., 1972–
Women and depression : recovery and resistance / Michelle N. Lafrance. – 1st ed.
p. ; cm. – (Women and psychology)
Includes bibliographical references.
ISBN 978-0-415-40430-3 (hardback) – ISBN 978-0-415-40431-0 (pbk.) 1. Depression in
women. I. Title. II. Series.
[DNLM: 1. Depressive Disorder–therapy. 2. Women's Health. WM 171 L183w 2009]
RC537.L325 2009
616.85'270082–dc22
2008029205

ISBN: 978-0-415-40430-3 (hbk)
ISBN: 978-0-415-40431-0 (pbk)

FOR MY MOTHER, MARILYN LAKE
AND
IN LOVING MEMORY OF MY DEAR
FRIEND AND MENTOR, JOHN McKENDY,
WHO SHONE LIGHT, LOVE AND
PEACE ON ALL THOSE HE ENCOUNTERED

CONTENTS

ACKNOWLEDGEMENTS

I am grateful to the many people who supported me and the completion of this project. First and foremost, I would like to thank the women who participated in my research and shared their stories of recovery from depression and their experiences of self-care. I would also like to thank Jane Ussher for inviting me to embark on this project, and for her inspiration and assistance throughout the process. I am also deeply grateful to Janet Stoppard, whose critical reflection on women's lives and distress inspired this work and whose friendship, support, and mentorship have been invaluable to me. Words cannot express my gratitude to John McKendy for his constant support, encouragement and enthusiasm. The parts of this text I am most proud of are those we worked on together. Those he left behind carry forward his passion for ideas and his passion for peace.

I would like to acknowledge Nicola Gavey, Deborah van den Hoonaard, Mavis Kirkham and Doug Vipond whose ideas and comments helped to strengthen this manuscript. I am also grateful to Anita Saunders and Christina Drost who offered valuable assistance in the compilation of information, and comic relief when pressures rose. Special thanks to Sue McKenzie-Mohr and Shannon Glenn who have engaged in these ideas with me over the years, and to Marilyn Erb (Lake), George Lafrance, Howard Erb and Micheal Carr for their constant encouragement and affection.

This work was also made possible by funding received through the Social Sciences and Humanities Research Council of Canada, MindCare New Brunswick, and the New Brunswick Innovation Foundation.

CHAPTER 1

INTRODUCTION

Studying women's experiences of recovery from depression

This book is about women's stories of moving out of depression and striving to become and live well. I came to this subject through my interest in women's mental health and a discontent with the fact that the bulk of research in this area focuses on pathology and illness rather than health and well-being. I believe that while an understanding of women's suffering is essential, attention to the ways in which women become and live well is also vitally important. Thus, with a view to better understanding women's health more broadly, I wanted to explore the ways in which women talk about 'recovering' from depression and nurturing their own health and well-being in their everyday lives (I take up the term 'recovery' at the end of the chapter). Further, I wanted to examine women's health narratives for their personal, social, and political meanings and implications.

Feminist scholars have firmly situated women's depression as a consequence of patriarchal society (Jack, 1991; Stoppard, 2000; Stoppard & McMullen, 2003; Ussher, 1991, 2006). And, while very many women do become depressed, many also 'recover' and emerge from their despair. Thus, at the heart of this book is a concern for the ways in which women describe and experience 'recovery' from depression. Starting from a feminist, social constructionist perspective, I explore women's narratives of recovery and well-being through an analysis of interviews I conducted with women in two related research projects. In the first, I interviewed women who self-identified as having 'recovered' from or overcome depression in some way. In describing recovery from depression, these women recurrently pointed to both the importance of beginning to attend to their own needs and pleasure, and their difficulties in doing so. In talking to these women, I began to wonder about the possibility of other ways in which women might come to attend to their own health and well-being, other than through the pathway of crisis and depression. I then conducted a second study in which I interviewed another group of women who self-identified as taking care of themselves in their everyday lives. Through an analysis of these sets of interviews, in conjunction with an examination of the literature on women's mental health and of representations of women's health practices in the media, I explore women's narratives of health and healing, and the ways in which they position themselves and are positioned in discourse.

RECOVERY FROM DEPRESSION: A NEGLECTED TOPIC OF INQUIRY

Recovery from depression is the anchoring theme of this book. I chose to investigate recovery experiences from depression in particular because depression is the most common mental health problem among women (Bebbington, 1996; Weissman, Bland, Joyce, Newman et al., 1993). Not only is depression a leading cause of disability among women worldwide, but it ranks as one of the most important health problems for women overall (Murray & Lopez, 1996; World Health Organization (WHO), 2000a). Further, women outnumber men in terms of prevalence at a fairly consistent rate of about two to one (Beaudet, 1996; Bebbington, 1996; Eaton, Anthony, Gallo, Cai et al., 1997; Jenkins, Kleinman, & Good, 1991; Kessler, McGonagle, Swartz, Blazer, & Nelson, 1993; Maier, Gänsicke, Gater, Rezaki et al., 1999).[1] This gender gap appears to emerge at the time of puberty when rates of depression among girls rise precipitously (Nolen-Hoeksema & Girgus, 1994). In adulthood, the risk of depression is estimated to range from 5 per cent to 12 per cent for men, and from 10 per cent to 25 per cent for women (American Psychiatric Association, 2000). Thus, substantial numbers of women experience depression. Moreover, depressive experiences are associated with significant impairments across physical, emotional, cognitive, occupational and social functioning. Depression can therefore, be understood as a 'woman's problem' (Marecek, 2006); one that is often profoundly and pervasively debilitating.

An extensive and wide-ranging body of literature has been dedicated to understanding the causes of depression. Across this literature, the models currently receiving the most attention are rooted in either biomedical or psychological frameworks, including neurochemistry, genetic inheritance, hormones, attributional style, cognitive coping style, interpersonal relationships, and negative life events (Blehar, 2006; Gotlib & Hammen, 2002; Keyes & Goodman, 2006; Mazure, Keita, & Blehar, 2002). While integrative 'biopsychosocial' and 'diathesis-stress' models have been proposed, the literature remains largely comprising efforts to establish the dominance of one or more of these domains in the explanation and treatment of depression. For instance, while some are dedicated to demonstrating the role of neurochemical dysregulation, others work on elaborating the ways in which depression depends on patterns of thinking. Meanwhile, feminist scholars have critiqued such narrow conceptualizations as decontextualized and pathologizing. Instead, they have offered new understandings of women's distress based on the material and social conditions of women's everyday lives (Nicholson, 1998; Stoppard, 2000; Stoppard & McMullen, 2003; Ussher, 1991).

While depression continues to be the focus of concentrated attention and debate, researchers have largely ignored the experience of recovery from depression. Those who have attended to recovery tend to focus on identifying predictors of recovery and recurrence in clinical and non-clinical samples (Eaton et al., 1997; Kendler, Walters, & Kessler, 1997; Kessler et al., 1993; Lewinsohn, Zeiss, & Duncan, 1989; Mueller, Leon, Keller, Solomon et al., 1999; Solomon, Keller, Leon, Mueller et al., 1997; Solomon, Keller, Leon, Mueller et al., 2000; Viinamäki, Tanskanen, Honkalampi, Koivumaa-Honkanen et al., 2006). When participants in these studies recover without treatment, researchers acknowledge recovery only insofar as to label it 'spontaneous remission' (Frank, Prien, Jarrett, Keller et al., 1991; Gardner, 2003). When recovery occurs among those who receive intervention, researchers conceptualize it in terms of 'treatment outcome' or 'treatment effectiveness'. Therefore, these investigators appear to view recovery almost exclusively as an outcome that can be adequately expressed in terms of a number (for instance, 'percentage recovered' or 'time to recovery'). Considering that recovery is presumably the goal of treatment interventions, it is surprising that researchers should fail to consider it as a process in its own right.

I propose that there are several reasons for this significant gap in the literature, all of which stem from the way in which researchers conceptualize depressive experiences. Intense and prolonged sadness has taken on widely different meanings across culture, time, and place (Jackson, 1986; Jenkins et al., 1991; Marecek, 2006). In the West, it is currently viewed as the hallmark of individual pathology; signs of a clinical disorder. Defined by the American Psychiatric Association in the *Diagnostic and Statistical Manual of Mental Disorders* (2000), depression is signified by the presence of a standard constellation of symptoms including depressed mood, diminished interest or pleasure, fatigue, feelings of worthlessness or guilt, problems concentrating, suicidal thoughts, and changes in weight, sleep, and activity level. A person who experiences a certain set of these symptoms over a period of two weeks or more can be diagnosed with 'Major Depressive Disorder' by a mental health professional. This diagnostic term invites a decontextualized understanding of despair whereby subjective experiences of suffering become viewed as objective signs of pathology. Displaced from view, then, is an appreciation of the ways in which depressive experiences are embedded in the landscape of people's lives. Further, the construction of depression as a 'disorder' invites the assumption that it is a separate entity that invades the life of an otherwise healthy person (Davidson & Strauss, 1995). Within this formulation, health is assumed to be the natural state, one that unfolds automatically unless otherwise impeded. Consequently, '[i]f it is assumed that health is something that is passively given at the outset, or taken away by illness, then it follows that the process of restoring health be viewed as a similarly passive affair' (Davidson & Strauss, 1995, p. 48). Thus, it appears to be taken-for-granted in mainstream models that recovery from depression is nothing more than the removal of the presumed cause. When depression and recovery are understood in these ways, it follows that research should be directed toward an exploration of the causes and treatments of pathology, leaving recovery a somewhat irrelevant and invisible focus of study (Davidson & Strauss, 1995).

A second and related reason why recovery has been overlooked is that sustained recovery from depression (in terms of mainstream understandings of symptom remission) is a relatively rare occurrence. Research conducted by the National Institute of Mental Health (NIMH) provides perhaps the most extensive picture to date on the course of depression (Keller, 1996; Mueller & Leon, 1996; Mueller et al., 1999; Solomon et al., 1997). Participants in this longitudinal study were individuals who sought treatment for an affective disorder at one of five US university medical centres between 1978 and 1981. Participants were evaluated on intake with the Schedule for Affective Disorders and Schizophrenia (SADS) and 495 individuals were diagnosed with major depression. Follow-up evaluations were conducted with the Longitudinal Interval Follow-up Evaluation (LIFE) every six months for the first five years and annually thereafter. Rates of recovery indicated a positive course. Most participants recovered in the first year (69 per cent), after two years, the cumulative probability of recovery was 82 per cent, after three years 85 per cent, and after five years 90 per cent (Keller et al., 1982; cited in Keller, 1996). After ten years, only 7 per cent remained ill with no recovery (Mueller & Leon, 1996).

While the statistics from this series of studies appear encouraging, further investigation of the long-term course of depression suggests that a pattern of recovery and recurrence is the rule rather than the exception. One quarter of those in the NIMH study who recovered in the first year of follow-up relapsed within 12 weeks of recovery (Keller, 1996). At 15 years' follow-up, the researchers paid particular attention to 380 individuals who had recovered at some point from an index episode of major depressive disorder and 105 individuals who had recovered and subsequently remained well for at least five years. Although the vast majority of participants in the total sample recovered from depression, 85 per cent of the 380 experienced a recurrence, as did 58 per cent of those who remained well for at least five years. Based on these and other epidemiological findings, mainstream scholars tend to conceptualize depression as a recurrent disorder, one from which many may not 'recover' once and for all. Therefore, when depression is understood in this medicalized, symptom-based way, then the study of recovery may appear to be a misguided endeavour since few may qualify as 'properly recovered'.

4

A third reason for the fact that recovery has been largely overlooked in research is that the term itself does not appear to resonate with those who have been depressed. From a medical perspective, recovery implies both sustained symptom remission, and a returning to one's previous state of health. It *means* 'getting back to how you were before the illness started, being restored to your former state . . . It involves being the same as before' (Whitwell, 1999, p. 621). However, even among those who experience symptom remission, many report ongoing struggles with low mood or daily functioning (Boland & Keller, 1996; Coryell & Winokur, 1992). Further, people do not tend to simply return to the way they were before, but are often fundamentally altered by their experiences (Ridge & Zicbland, 2006; Whitwell, 1999). That is, even though people may *feel* better, they often report feeling changed in multiple ways by their profound experiences of emerging from despair (Ridge & Ziebland, 2006; Schreiber, 1996a; Steen, 1996). These findings have led some to question the utility of the very concept of recovery *vis-à-vis* 'mental illnesses' such as depression. Indeed, some have gone so far as to suggest that recovery from mental illness is, in fact, 'a myth' (Whitwell, 1999). However, I would argue that the problem with the concept of recovery lies not in people's experiences, but in our preconceived notions about what recovery *means,* including the ways in which it is understood and studied. Instead, I would argue that new ways of understanding people's experiences of recovery, healing, and well-being are required.

By arguing for a re-conceptualization of recovery, I am not suggesting that modifications to the symptom criteria for recovery are required (e.g., Fava, Ruini, & Belaise, 2007; Frank et al., 1991), nor do I mean to dismiss people's experiences of ongoing pain and distress. Rather, my aim is to highlight the problems inherent in any attempt to make lived (personal) experience fit into preconceived (expert-based) notions. Perhaps what is missing from current formulations is an understanding of recovery from the perspective of those who have experienced it. If individuals do not identify with the word 'recovery', is this because they do not experience well-being after depression, or because a symptom-based understanding of recovery does not adequately describe their lived experiences? If individuals are not considered to have recovered, are they then by default chronically ill? Do continued struggles with stress or sadness preclude individuals from claiming to be recovered? Are experiences of distress and well-being best understood by reducing them to the dichotomy of 'sickness' and 'health'? Or, are other ways of understanding depression and recovery needed?

One way to address these types of questions is to ask people to talk about their experiences of living well after depression. However, given that the dominant methodological approach in psychology is positivist, empiricist, and quantitative, psychologists have rarely explored such questions in their research. Therefore, a final reason why recovery has not been the subject of in-depth investigation is that the types of questions that would lead to a richer understanding of people's experiences of recovery are not easily addressed with the research methods normally adopted. If we want to look 'inside the numbers' and explore not only rates of symptom remission and recurrence, but people's stories of healing and the meanings they ascribe to them, then alternative approaches to research are required.

RESEARCH ON RECOVERY

Drawing on first-person narratives and qualitative methods, a small, but growing body of literature on recovery has recently emerged (Anonymous, 1989; Anthony, 1993, 2004; Corrigan, Giffort, Rashid, Leary, & Okeke, 1999; Davidson, Harding, & Spaniol, 2005; Davidson & Strauss, 1992; Deegan, 1988; Lapsley, Nikora, & Black, 2000; Pettie & Triolo, 1999; Young & Ensing, 1999). Focusing on experiences such as schizophrenia, this literature was born out of the consumer/survivor movement of the 1970s in which recipients of mental health services spoke out against the marginalization, mistreatment, and abuse they endured as patients. Mainstream understandings of 'mental illness' were critiqued as pathologizing and limiting for consumers of mental health services, theorists, and clinicians alike. Consumers advocated for more empowering models of intervention and a consideration of the needs of the 'person behind the patient' (Fisher, 1994; Frese & Davis, 1997). Within this Zeitgeist, recovery emerged as a guiding vision for research and services in mental health, one that can open our eyes to new possibilities for what it might mean to live with and beyond 'mental illness' (Anthony, 1993). From this perspective, recovery is not limited to symptom-based notions, but is understood as a complex and deeply personal experience that is 'best understood as a process, not an outcome' (Frese & Davis, 1997, p. 244). It has been conceptualized as the process of developing a new and valued sense of self and purpose (Deegan, 1988) and as living a satisfying, hopeful, and contributing life within and beyond the constraints of one's problems (Anthony, 1993; Corrigan et al., 1999).

A handful of researchers have explored recovery from depression in particular, and these studies were all conducted in North America, Australia, or Europe (Fullagar, 2008; Peden, 1993; Ridge & Ziebland, 2006; Schreiber, 1996a, 1996b, 1998; Skärsäter, Dencker, Bergbom, Häggström, & Fridlund, 2003; Steen, 1996; Vidler, 2005). Using qualitative methodologies and grounded in people's first-hand accounts, this body of work tends to revolve around the common aim of describing the phenomenological experience and meaning of the process of becoming well after depression. For instance, Rita Schreiber (1996a, 1998) developed a grounded theory of the process through which women recover from depression; one that involves several stages and culminates in a woman's redefinition of self.

6

In conducting research through a postmodern lens, I aim to expand understandings of women's experiences of recovery from depression – not by attempting to discover an essential process of recovery, but rather by exploring the multiple ways in which women describe their experiences, and the discursive effects of these various ways of accounting. How do women talk about their experiences of recovery and healing? What implications do these different ways of understanding have for women's sense of identity? How do they shape women's experiences of distress and direct their actions? By beginning analysis from women's own accounts and tracing the influences of power throughout, I hoped to provide new insights about women's pain, healing, and their lives in general.

THE RESEARCH PROJECTS

With a view to exploring potentially emancipatory ways of understanding women's health and healing, I conducted two studies from a critical-realist perspective (for a discussion of this and other epistemological positions, see Appendix A): one on women's stories of recovery from depression and the other on women's accounts of the ways in which they nurture themselves in their everyday lives. In the first study, I interviewed 19 women who self-identified as having recovered from or overcome depression in some way (Lafrance, 2003). I recruited participants in a city in Eastern Canada through advertising in the local newspaper and posting flyers in public spaces (e.g., grocery stores, libraries, laundromats). Among the women I spoke with, some described having been depressed as many as four times in their lives, while about half indicated having experienced one depressive period. Participants also varied in their experiences with formal intervention (including medication, hospitalization, electroconvulsive therapy (ECT), and counselling) and the degree to which this was experienced as helpful. For some women, it had been many years since they were depressed; others considered themselves in the beginning stages of recovery.

As I will discuss further in Chapter 3, a recurrent theme in these women's accounts was the importance of learning to take care of themselves and engage in practices they had previously denied themselves in favour of caring for others. In order to flesh out this finding, I conducted a second study in which I interviewed 14 women about the ways in which they attend to their own health and well-being in their everyday lives. I advertised for this second study by giving an address to the participants of a grassroots workshop for women called 'Nurturing Ourselves'. This annual, two-day workshop attracts several hundred women from across a semi-rural province in Eastern Canada. Participants are invited to 'nurture themselves' by taking part in a range of activities including personal finance, yoga, journaling, dance, and physical activity. While there is a fee for participation, the organizers waive the fees for those unable to pay and many participants are sponsored by a variety of government-funded agencies. As a result, women from a range of socioeconomic backgrounds regularly participate. I was able to interview 12 women who participated in the Nurturing Ourselves workshop. Since this workshop tends to attract women over 30 and I wanted to talk with women from a range of ages, I later recruited two younger participants through selective advertisement (for more information on the research participants and the interview process, see Appendix B).

On average, interviews lasted between two and three hours, and all were tape recorded and transcribed verbatim (see Appendix C for the transcript notation). I analysed the interview tapes and transcripts using a discourse analytic approach. Broadly speaking, discourse analysis is a family of approaches to working with language and text (Marecek, 1999). Within psychology, discourse analytic methods can be roughly divided into two perspectives (Parker, 1997; Wetherell, 1998; Wood & Kroger, 2000). The first approach focuses on a fine-grained analysis of the action orientation of talk and is affiliated with ethnomethodological and conversation analytic traditions (Potter & Wetherell, 1987; Wood & Kroger, 2000). This approach tends to focus on the details of what people do with their talk and the rhetorical strategies people use to make and counter claims. The focus of this level of analysis is on 'interpretative repertoires', which Potter and Wetherell (1987) define as 'recurrently used systems of terms used for characterizing and evaluating action, events and other phenomena' (p. 149). An interpretative repertoire is a 'recognizable routine of arguments, descriptions and evaluations distinguished by familiar clichés, common places, tropes and characterizations of actors and situations' (Edley & Wetherell, 2001, p. 443). This line of discourse analysis can be thought of as a 'bottom-up' approach where the fine detail of talk is explored for the effects of people's accounts (Edley & Wetherell, 1997).

The second approach draws on the work of Foucault and involves a more 'top-down' analysis of how discourses constitute particular phenomena and with what political, social, and personal consequences (Parker, 1992, 1997; Willig, 1999a, 1999b). Parker (1997) explains that in concert with Foucault's ideas about power/knowledge, 'discourse analysts study the way in which various forms of language work, and . . . are concerned with the ways in which these forms of language serve social, ideological, and political interests' (p. 285). Therefore, while the first approach to discourse analysis focuses on discursive practices, the second focuses on discursive resources. This is not to suggest that there is no overlap between these traditions, and many have called for a more integrated approach (Harper, 1999; Wetherell, 1998; Wood & Kroger, 2000). As Edley and Wetherell (1997) have argued,

While the distinction between 'top-down' and 'bottom-up' has been useful for clarifying key theoretical and methodological issues, it is also, in our view, time to move on. Our broad aim is to build forms of discursive psychology which draw more eclectically on both styles of work and which study the ways in which people are both the master, and the slave of discourse (Barthes, 1982). In line with the arguments of Billig (1991) and Sampson (1993), the contradictions need to be *embraced* rather than trying (in vain) for resolution. The two approaches are most usefully understood as reflecting two sides of a central paradox: people are simultaneously the products and the producers of discourse. We are both constrained and enabled by language.

(p. 206)

In the present analysis, I drew on both 'top-down' and 'bottom-up' approaches. Drawing on and integrating both approaches served my aim of grounding my interpretation in the particularities of participants' language while extending the analysis to the broader level of social, political, and institutional forces (Edley & Wetherell, 1997, 2001; Harper, 1999).

Starting from a critical-realist perspective, this multilayered analysis also included attention to materiality, or the 'extra-discursive' (Sims-Schouten, Riley, & Willig, 2007; Stoppard, 1997, 1998, 2000; Ussher, 1996, 1997; Yardley, 1996, 1997a, 1997b). That is, I attended to both the material realities of women's lives that they described (e.g., abuse, poverty, the work of care-giving) and the structure, function, and effect of their talk. While this approach would be critiqued by those coming from a relativist stance who propose that discourse is the only valid unit of analysis (Edwards, Ashmore, & Potter, 1995), for me, the risk of undermining the realities of women's lives is too great. As Sims-Schouten et al. (2007) have pointed out,

analysing participants' talk without considering their material existence does not always do justice to the participants' lived experience. For example, considering a mother's justification to return to work because of financial reasons as *purely* rhetorical (e.g., Himmelweit & Sigala, 2003) may be deemed inappropriate to a participant who is struggling to feed her family.

(p. 104)

Therefore, throughout my analysis, I approached women's accounts as both descriptive and performative. I attended to both content and form in endeavouring to produce an analysis that attends to discursive practices, discursive resources, as well as the embodied and material realities of speakers' lives (Sims-Schouten et al., 2007; Stoppard, 2000; Ussher, 1996, 1997).

9

In beginning the analysis, I read and reread the interview transcripts while listening to the interview tapes. I paid particular attention to patterns both within and across the transcripts of the content, details, features, and effects of talk. I explored what participants said, how they said it, and the functions and implications of their accounts. I looked for consistency and variability in participants' language and traced the use of various discursive features (such as the use of metaphor or grammar) within each transcript as well as across all participants' transcripts. I then created files of codes in order to track each emerging pattern, noting which participants did and did not draw on each discursive feature, in what context, and with what effect.

In exploring the text, I also paid particular attention to the 'subject positions' that emerged in participants' accounts. Individuals construct their experience through the discourses available in a particular cultural context. At the same time, however, the discourses drawn on contain a range of subject positions that in turn shape speakers' subjectivity. 'Such positionings constitute ways-of-being through placing the subject within a network of meanings and social relations which facilitate as well as constrain what can be thought, said and done by someone so positioned' (Willig, 2000, p. 557). For instance, the ways in which depression is constructed (e.g., as the result of a chemical imbalance, personality structure, or a traumatic experience) position speakers in different ways, thereby directing the actions a person might take (e.g., drug therapy, counselling), as well as a person's very sense of self (e.g., a person who needs to take medication to regulate mood, a 'depressive person', etc.). Therefore, individuals can position themselves *within* discourse and can also be positioned *by* discourse (Davies & Harré, 1990; Harré & Van Langenhove, 1991). By paying close attention to the ways in which participants are positioned by the accounts they construct, I aimed to explore the discursive consequences of various ways of accounting for women's subjectivity and sense of self.

CHAPTER OUTLINE

In the chapters that follow, I explore women's accounts of recovery from depression, and their stories of well-being and self-care. I will draw on both research studies described above, as well as the wealth of literature on women's depression and health. By drawing on extensive in-depth interviews with women, literature review, and analyses of representations of women's health practices in the media, I will endeavour to critically examine the ways in which women talk about recovering from depression and living well in their everyday lives.

In Chapter 2, I begin the analysis, as the women in the recovery study did, with a focus on stories of depression. Here, I will explore some common themes recurring throughout women's accounts of their experiences of depression and despair: stories of trauma, abuse, and poverty, difficulties in relationships, and the struggles and challenges of women's everyday lives. While participants explained depression in a variety of ways, their accounts were notably gendered and in this chapter I will focus on the ways in which hegemonic constructions of femininity are implicated in women's distress. In particular, I will argue that the socially revered 'good' woman identity directs women to be pleasing and self-sacrificing, contentedly denying their own needs and pleasures in the interest of nurturing others. At the same time, women's care-giving and domestic work are often taken-for-granted and rendered invisible as potential sources of distress. Faced with the option of being the 'good' woman or the bad – the mother or monster, Madonna or whore – women's expressions of distress are often silenced. Moreover, the dominant understanding of depression as a biomedical problem serves to further eclipse the material realities of women's oppression while frequently subverting their expressions of distress as 'not real'. Thus, this chapter will explore the ways in which discourses of femininity and biomedicine form an interlocking set of ideologies and institutions that both create and silence women's pain.

In Chapter 3, I explore participants' accounts of recovery and argue that while women's talk of depression was entwined in discourses of femininity, their talk of recovery involved the rupture or resistance of these discourses. That is, while women can be seen to be *silenced* in depression, recovery can be understood as a process through which women *talk back*. Women's accounts of becoming well centred on the importance of having their distress validated, relinquishing an exclusively other-orientation, and beginning to attend to their own needs, desires and interests. Two central patterns of accounting were identified that supported these aims. In the first, participants reasserted the legitimacy of depression within the medical model. In the second, and sometimes overlapping pattern of accounting, participants talked of recovery as a personally transformative experience. They described recovery as a process through which they resisted or rejected the suffocating confines of the 'good' woman identity and began to pay closer attention to their own health and happiness. Thus, women tended to describe recovery as either a re-naming of their experiences in medical terms, and/or as a re-authoring of their identities within a narrative of personal transformation. In either case, the importance of self-care (as opposed to self-negation) for women's well-being came to the fore.

In Chapter 4, I take up the issue of women's self-care. I will first problematize the concept as one that supports the hegemony of various pillars of power (e.g., individualism, capitalism, patriarchy, and medicalization) by inviting individuals to regulate and discipline themselves (Foucault, 1977). At the same time, however, women's self-negation is common and it has been repeatedly implicated in the creation and compounding of women's distress (Jack, 1991; Stoppard, 2000; Ussher, 1991, 2006). Therefore, although I approach the concept of self-care with suspicion, I will argue that facilitating women's abilities to attend to their own needs remains worthwhile. In this chapter, I will explore the material and discursive constraints to women's self-care, including a lack of time, money, freedom, safety, as well as the negative meanings of self-care for women's identities. When women talk about attending to themselves, they often appear to struggle with the implication that they are 'selfish', 'bad' women. Thus, taking up practices of self-care appears to place women in a double-bind whereby they describe self-care as central to their well-being, but threatening to their identities as women. I will explore the various discursive strategies deployed by women that enable them to negotiate this bind and legitimize attention to their own needs. The analytic findings discussed across chapters will be revisited in the final chapter where I will explore the ways in which they might be useful to women, health care providers, educators, and researchers.

TERMINOLOGICAL TROUBLES: A FINAL WORD ON WORDS

This book centres on two facets of women's health experiences: 'recovery' from depression and 'self-care'. Notably, neither the term 'recovery' nor 'self-care' appears to adequately reflect the experience referenced, and neither was unequivocally adopted by the women I spoke with. For instance, many participants struggled with or rejected the term 'recovery' as it implies returning to the way one was before depression, no longer being affected by depressive experiences, and a medicalized understanding of depression and well-being – implications rejected in part or in sum by the women I interviewed. Further, 'self-care' commonly refers to the application of medical treatments to the self. In contrast to this medicalized formulation, I use the term 'self-care' to refer to the antithesis of women's taken-for-granted self-sacrifice and the exclusive orientation to others that women so often described as central to their depressive experiences. Therefore, the concepts of 'recovery' and 'self-care' suggested here appear to remain without appropriate referents, and as such, they remain largely marginalized and invisible facets of women's experiences. Although I have adopted the terms, I do so with an acknowledgement that women's experiences do not fit comfortably within the language available. One aim of this project, then, was to shed light on stories that have remained largely untold and unheard, with a view to better understanding women's overall health and well-being.[2]

Notes

1 It should be noted that most of this research has been conducted in Western countries, including the United States, Canada, Western Europe, and Australia.

There is little data from non-Western countries, but what exists suggests that the gender gap in rates of depression may not be universal (Culbertson, 1997; Marecek, 2006).

2 The language of 'health' and 'well-being' can be further deconstructed and problematized. Given the colonization of 'health' by medicine, these words inevitably evoke a medical discourse as well as problematic notions of individual imperatives (for instance, the male sexual drive discourse; Gavey, 2008, personal communication). In this analysis, I want to explore women's accounts of their experiences of 'health' and 'well-being', but am leery of the medicalized and individualized implications these terms bring up. However, in order to be intelligible in the analysis, I must use *some* referents. Therefore, I have chosen to adopt the language of health and well-being while acknowledging the problems inherent in its use.

CHAPTER 2

NARRATIVES OF DEPRESSION

Before the depression I was up, confident, secure, high self-esteem, high self-concept. Um ... I can remember saying to my husband and I said this often 'My life is so:: good' ... ... then of course during the depression it was just the very very opposite. Nothing. Just this empty vessel this, you know, a bunch of bones walking around. Just a bunch of bones walking around that's just how you felt.

(Deborah)

I couldn't, I couldn't think straight. I just sat there and spun my wheels and I guess too and it got to be to the point, I didn't even want to come home. [...] Wouldn't answer the phone. <Would not do anything with anybody>. Got t-wouldn't even shower, wouldn't even shower and that's not me either, I took a lot of pride in my appearance but I just, I just felt so:: rock bottom. That I just, hhh I was nothing, I was no good for anything, I was a failure.

(Emily)

Just a big cloud would just come over me and it would be like a, a ... just a I called it a funk. I would like fall into this funk and it I ((sighs)) Oh God that's an awful awful memory I rem-remember just not being able to do anything, **just** I couldn't sit, I couldn't lay down, I couldn't have a bath, I couldn't walk around, I couldn't eat, I couldn't, I <couldn't do anything>. I didn't **want** to do anything. For the first time in my life I understood how ... people could consider suicide. For the first time in my life I understood. God it was awful.

(Heather)

Without exception, when I invited women to talk about recovery, they began with their stories of depression. They told of profound and debilitating sadness, of being unable to think, feel, or relate to others or themselves. They described being at 'rock bottom' and being lost in a 'black hole' of hopelessness. They talked of loss, pain, emptiness, and isolation. They talked of suicide.

These stories of despair were the ground in which participants' narratives of recovery were rooted. As their accounts made clear, it is impossible to comprehend their experiences of relief and recovery without first understanding the depths from which they emerged. Therefore, this analysis begins as participants' accounts did, with an exploration of women's experiences of depression.

Within mainstream formulations, the accounts of the women cited above would be considered reflections of the symptomatology of clinical depression – checkmarks on a symptom list that add up to a diagnosis. From this view, 'depression' is understood as a discrete entity, a thing that can be measured with objective diagnostic tools. Regarded as a constellation of somatic, psychological, and behavioural symptoms, depressive experiences become sanitized, disentangled from messy, complicated, and uncontrollable realities of people's everyday lives. When depression is constructed as individual pathology, attention is drawn to the woman in isolation, removed from the cultural and social context of her life (Marecek, 2006). Suffering is extracted from the lived experience of the sufferer. Accordingly, dominant theories have focused on individual 'factors' such as neurotransmitters, hormones, or cognitive coping styles to explain women's misery. Obscured from view, then, is not only the phenomenology of depression – the subjective and embodied experiences of what it *feels like* to be depressed, but also the cultural, social, political, economic, and interpersonal realities of women's lives (Stoppard, 2000).

But, if instead of beginning from the standpoint of the diagnostician, we align our view with that of depressed women, a very different picture begins to emerge. When women talk about being depressed, they talk of their lives, and in particular they talk of their lives as women. Among the women I interviewed, some spoke of having been physically or sexually abused as children or adults, and many of these also described living in poverty. Some spoke of their yearnings to be in a relationship, or their pain when relationships ended. Many spoke of their struggles to be 'good enough' – good enough mothers, wives, girlfriends, daughters. All spoke about being depressed as the worst times of their lives.

In this chapter, I want to explore the ways in which the women I interviewed began their accounts of recovery – with stories of depression. Here, the term 'depression' will not be used in the essentialist sense described above, but rather in a non-specific sense to refer to the subjective experiences of being depressed that women described. The aim of this analysis is to examine some common themes across women's narratives of depression, not to identity causal pathways, but to develop a contextualized understanding of women's distress that attends to both the material and discursive conditions of their lives. I will explore three central themes that recurred in participants' talk of depression, namely, stories of the traumatic and chronic life events of abuse and poverty, difficulties in relationships, and women's everyday lives. By focusing on these three themes, I do not mean to suggest that other issues were irrelevant to women's accounts of depression. Participants drew on a range and combination of understandings, including chemical and hormonal imbalances, abuse and rape, job loss and transition, menopause, relationship dissolution, illness of family members, and the stresses and struggles of their everyday lives. Regardless of how they accounted for depression, however, women's stories of despair were notably gendered. I will explore the gendered nature of women's depression narratives through an analysis of these three dominant themes, focusing variously on the content (what they said), form (how they said it), and discursive effects of their accounts. Whereas the following chapters will elaborate on a finer-grained analysis of discourse, my aim in this chapter is to report more generally on these three main patterns across the interviews.

TRAUMATIC AND CHRONIC EXPERIENCES: VIOLENCE BY MEN AGAINST WOMEN AND WOMEN'S EXPERIENCES OF POVERTY

The psy-disciplines (e.g., psychology, psychiatry, psychotherapy) are notorious for holding a myopic view of people's distress. Two of the most dominant theories of depression today, neurochemical models and cognitive models, point to women's brain chemistry and thinking patterns to explain their despair. Vast amounts of time, energy and money have been invested in research aimed at testing and validating these models, and these are largely regarded as the golden standards of empirically validated treatments for depression. Perhaps the women I spoke with exhibited 'dysfunctional neurochemistry' or 'ruminative cognitive styles'. I don't know – this was not the focus of my inquiry. But, what I do know is that when given the opportunity to speak and be heard, too often, women spoke of trauma, victimization, and depression in the same breath.

> Because of my uncle, it started the whole cycle. Um I was a very timid child to begin with. I mean that was just my nature. Um and when I was seven and I was molested I didn't understand what was going on. But it doesn't- I remember I remember so::: .hhh ... ... remember everything about it and

16

how it made me fee:l and that's where it started. And actually um it made you sexually aware before you were able to handle it and I felt dirty and rotten. And the person, it was my uncle who was a **pi**llar of the community. And I couldn't talk to him and no one would understand because I didn't understand. And when I got older and older I learned about incest in school. And then my uncle was the head of this um church and he was thought of very very very highly by **everybody** and it was like then it has to be me. I'm bad I'm evil I'm rotten I mean I ruined him! ((laughs)) ah ... ... and that wasn't something I could ever get out of my head. Or ever accept that I wasn't ba:::d because you had so many years and all those years of growing up believing you were evil and rotten and hating yourself and despising yourself and I withdrew into a shell.

(Susan)

.hhh well ahh hhh uh, it might help you to understand a little more if I told you what precipitated the major depressive episodes that I had. Um, my first one started in about 1960 so I would have been umm twenty-five years old. And it was because I was married to an alcoholic. And um so I stayed with him for another probably eight and a half years before. But but the thing that people don't understand is when you're married to an alcoholic um a lot of us what happens is that you- they tell you they're going- they won't do this again or they won't do that again won't do something else and so you let it go until eventually you don't have the confidence to make any choices in your life. And the other thing was because my son was adopted he ah was from my ex-husband's **fa**mily. It was his sister's boy. And we adopted him so every time I would threaten to separate, he would say he was going to take my son from me. And I was afraid he **could** because of the blood rela**ti**onship so I never dared to go to anybody. I didn't ever approach anybody to find out (about) a lawyer or anything else. So um during the course of that probably from 1960 o::n when when my depression started was ah my husband committed adultery on a constant basis. He beat me. Ahhh he tried to kill me. And, ah. ((sighs)) how can I tell you this. I tried to commit suicide three times. [...] And then he started an affair when he did get back he started an affair with my best friend. My closest friend. And that was pretty destructive to my personality. Um, then when he tried to kill me that just sort of, when he shot at me that just sort of finished it, you know. And I was at that point becoming totally unable to communicate with anybody. I just sat. Stared at the wall. So finally my husband in desperation took me up to the Emergency Ward in the hospital in [city] and ah they put me in the day hospital because I was losing my:: ability to communicate almost. So they put me in the day hospital rather than as an inpatient so I spent sixteen weeks there um all kinds of intensive psychotherapy.

(Lynn)

In these excerpts, Susan and Lynn describe the profound psychological and emotional effects of sexual and physical violence. Susan described being left feeling 'dirty', 'rotten', and 'evil', unable to understand her experience in any way other than to be at fault. Lynn described the gradual but persistent erosion of self she suffered at the hands of a man who left her literally fearing for her life. The sequelae of the abuse these women suffered appear compounded by the multiple barriers to escape they faced. Susan described being without voice as a small child, particularly in comparison to the power held by her uncle who was 'a pillar of the community'. As an adult, she suffered further silencing. Her efforts later in life to talk to about the abuse resulted in ostracism from her family and when she reported the abuse to authorities, she was raped by the police officer assigned to her case. Lynn also suffered substantial barriers to speaking out and escape – fear of losing her son and the threat of being beaten or killed. Without resources, safety, or even a validating ear, both women endured years of victimization. Trapped in trauma, these women described suffering an erosion of self, intense despair and depression.

Although often de-emphasized in the mainstream literature, the link between violence against women and depression is well established (Herrera, Koss, Bailey, Yuan, & Lichter, 2006; Mazure, Keita, & Blehar, 2002; McGrath, Keita, Strickland, & Russo, 1990); markedly higher rates of depression are found among women who have been physically or sexually abused as children or adults (Hamilton & Jensvold, 1995; Herrera et al., 2006; Koss, Koss, & Woodruff, 1991; McGrath et al., 1990). For instance, a meta-analysis of 18 studies on depression and partner violence found that the average rate of depression among women who had been physically abused by intimate partners was 48 per cent, with reports ranging from 39 per cent to 83 per cent (Golding, 1999). Similarly high rates of depression have been found among survivors of childhood sexual abuse and sexual violence in adulthood (Frank & Stewart, 1984; Saunders, Kilpatrick, Hanson, Resnick, & Walker, 1999). In addition to depression, women who have been abused often report a range of serious difficulties including posttraumatic stress disorder, suicide attempts, anxiety, stress-related syndromes, pain syndromes, substance use and addiction problems, and poor subjective health (Koss, Koss, & Woodruff, 1990; WHO, 2000b). Thus, when we attend to the stories of women who have been violated, depression comes into view, not as individual pathology, but as a reasonable reaction to unreasonable situations.

While it is essential to understand the consequences of violence on individual women's lives, we must also attend to the systemic ways in which violence against women occurs. It has been well documented that girls and women make up the overwhelming majority of victims of childhood sexual abuse, and sexual and intimate partner abuse in adulthood (Kessler, Sonnega, Bromet, Hughes, & Nelson, 1995; Koss, Goodman, Browne, Fitzgerald, Keita, & Russo, 1994; WHO 2001). Therefore, instances of violence cannot be regarded as merely isolated events in the lives of individual women, but as one consequence of living as women in patriarchal society. With men accorded more value and power than women, they are situated in a web of interlocking ideological and institutional forces that secure their dominance across political, economic and social spheres, including those of family and interpersonal relations (White & Frabutt, 2006). Thus, individual violence is best understood as both a reflection and embodiment of gendered social and cultural contexts, and nowhere is men's power over women more tangibly exerted than through violence. Worldwide, at least one in three women is physically or sexually abused in her lifetime (Heise, Ellsberg, & Gottemoeller, 1999). Violence against women takes many forms, including childhood sexual abuse, battering and partner abuse, rape, sexual coercion, female genital mutilation, forced prostitution, and sexual slavery. Accordingly, the World Health Organization (2001) has declared that '[v]iolence against women constitutes a major social and public health problem, affecting women of all ages, cultural backgrounds, and income levels' (p. 15). While not all women who are depressed have experienced violence, and not all women who have been the targets of abuse become depressed, it is clear that a consideration of violence against women must figure prominently in understandings of depression among women.

For many of the women I interviewed, violence was described as resulting in physical and emotional pain, as well as poverty. Women's economic marginalization worldwide means that they very often depend on men for financial security. Therefore, leaving a heterosexual relationship, even an abusive one, can mean the prospect of a dramatic decline in income, if not abject poverty (WHO, 2000b). Further, the constraints of poverty are all the more intense for those caring for dependants. Joanne recounted escaping from her abusive husband, leaving her and her children with little more than the shirts on their backs. Lynn told of how her husband emptied her bank account, leaving her with no money to support herself and her child.

> I left. Finally got- I saved up money squirreled away money ... and I enlisted my in-laws and they helped me get over here find a place and I went over here and I went to welfare ... and I got them to agree for a welfare cheque. I found a place to rent and [...] went back home and spent another month pretending nothing was going on and packed all my kids up enough clothes to keep them going for a week, put them in the car and took them over here. That was that. We left with enough clothes for them to keep going for a week. That was it. Yeah. Oh, that was fun. Yeah. [...] We moved into an apartment we didn't have a stitch of furniture. Nothing.
>
> (Joanne)

> We had left [city] and gone to [city] um and my husband had taken off again. He was sober but he had taken off again. [...] I didn't know where the heck he was and I had no money and he emptied the bank account and my son and I were in this high rise apar(h)tment and no money no nothing.
>
> (Lynn)

These women, like others who told stories of abuse, described the economic insecurity that so commonly accompanies violence against women. Violence is but one of the many pathways that lead to women's over-representation among the poor. Pay inequity, the concentration of women in work that is socially undervalued and underpaid, the lack of affordable and quality childcare, lower levels of education, and the prohibition against women's work and study in some cultural contexts converge to ensure women's economic marginalization. Indeed, poverty has been described as having 'a woman's face – of 1.3 billion people in poverty, 70% are women' (United Nations Development Program (UNDP), 1995, p. 4). Poverty is an often chronic oppression that taxes the body and soul. Not surprisingly, 'poverty is one of the most consistent predictors of depression in women' (Belle & Doucet, 2003, p. 101). Therefore, in understanding women's preponderance among the depressed, instead of asking 'what is wrong with women?' (e.g., their neurochemistry or thought patterns), we are better to ask 'what is wrong with women's lives?' (Miedema, Stoppard, & Anderson, 2000).

INTERPERSONAL RELATIONSHIPS

One facet of women's lives that has been associated with their experiences of depression is the challenge they often face in heterosexual relationships (Jack, 1991), and this theme appeared prominently in the interviews I conducted. Younger women in particular talked about their desire to find and secure romantic relationships and their feelings of insecurity in this domain. For instance, both Alexandra and Cynthia talked about their poor sense of self and concomitant troubled relationships with men.

> I was doing a lot of sleeping with men because I kind of felt that that was how I was going to get ... some attention or how I was going get ... somebody to love me because it was kind of like the basis of where the depression started.
>
> (Alexandra)

> I guess as a child and a young person, maybe I didn't see myself as responsible for my own happiness? .hhh and I depended on someone else. [...] and mostly- it's funny because mostly it was men that I looked to to make me happy. You know and maybe that's a common female thing. Um, so it was always an external thing, [...] There was nothing <in me> that could make me feel good. I wasn't worthy. Um, terrible, terrible image, self-image problems. [...] You know, and terrible ter- body image problems.
>
> (Cynthia)

Repeated throughout many women's narratives of depression were stories of feeling ugly, wrong, and unlovable as children and young women. Like Alexandra and Cynthia, these women often sought validation and affection through relationships with men, a path that left many clinging to bad relationships ultimately resulting in their feeling even more unsatisfied and empty. For instance, Cynthia's account above continued with her description of her experience of a bad dating relationship and subsequent marriage.

> As a teenager I started going out with this guy that I eventually married and I remember one time I was so surprised at myself Michelle because one time we were having an argument and he said he was leaving, this was the first time he ever said '>Well I'm leaving, I'm getting out of here blaa blaa blaa<' and I was practically down on my

knees begging him to stay. ... And as I was doing it- **at the same time** I was doing it but I was thinking <I have never done this before in my whole life>. You know I have never begged anybody like that and then that's how our relationship kind of to(h)ok off from there. [...] Part of me, I don't know, I didn't want to be without the boyfriend? I didn't want to ... ah be alone? Outside appearances were really- even though he wasn't treating me well you know and everybody in town knew he was a jerk. ((laughs)) You know, but and what they must have thought of me for going out with that jerk, you know, but that didn't register with me. I just wanted- but at the same ti:::me there was this little voice saying- and I just kind of smothered that little person, that was saying you know 'what, this is new, what's going on here Cynthia? You know, you are not this-' and I was seventeen or eighteen years o:ld you know and this wasn't the, ... this wasn't the person that I, that I knew I should be or wanted to be? And then this went on, this continued on for almost another ten years because [ex husband] and I didn't break up until I was twenty-seven, twenty-six, twenty-seven.

ML: *How do you understand ... that.*

.hhh hhhhhh .... I think, I think that it's kind of a continuation of my fa- m- m- my and my father's relationship and I think it is thinking, like every guy I meet it's my last chance. And he was my- he was my only chance, he was my last chance, there was no one else. I got kinda tunnel vision?

ML: *Chance for?*

((sighs)) To have a relationship, to have a guy in my life, to have you know, I don't think I really knew what to do with hi(h)m because he and I certainly did not have the same type of, um ... you know we didn't have the same likes or dislikes, we had **nothing** in common really. You know but it was just to have this this boyfriend and just this need for ... hhh you know, just to have a **guy** in my life.

(Cynthia)

In this excerpt, Cynthia describes being of two minds – of two selves: the self that wanted to cling to the man at all costs, and the self that she knew she 'wanted to be'. While she described recognizing the voice of her authentic self questioning her pleas of desperation for her boyfriend to stay, ultimately this voice was silenced. She said, 'I just kind of smothered that

22

little person'. Although she described her boyfriend as 'a jerk', who 'wasn't treating (her) well', the prospect of having this man appeared better than having no man at all. As Cynthia states, she 'didn't want to be without the boyfriend', and this relationship represented her 'last chance' of getting a man. Despite women's advances socially, their value often remains at least partly dependent upon their ability to attract and hold male attention, and women who fail to do so are readily positioned as abject – as the sad spinster, unwanted woman, and representation of failed femininity (Reynolds & Wetherell, 2003). As Jill Reynolds and Margaret Wetherell observed in their study of the accounts of single women, 'Women in long-term relationships do not tend to be asked (in a concerned tone of voice), for example, 'how did you end up married?' (2003, p. 490). Single women are expected to account for their 'condition' in a way that married women are not. Women's identities are regulated and policed by a set of assumptions – both 'compulsory heterosexuality' (Rich, 1980) and mandatory marriage (or at least partnership), which position lesbian and single women as denigrated 'others'. In order to secure her relationship and a positive identity, Cynthia said she squelched parts of herself, in a process that ultimately resulted in depression.

Drawing on her interviews with depressed women, Dana Jack (1991) developed an understanding of depression rooted in women's relationships. As a result of their subordinate social position, and through socialization and identification with their mothers, girls and women are pushed to prioritize affiliation and define themselves through relationships. In contrast, '[m]en usually have more economic freedom to come and go, as well as the prerogative of selecting younger partners when they enter middle age' (Jack, 1991, p. 41). Thus, women are faced with the social imperative to 'attract and hold' a mate, but within a social context that leaves them less secure about their attachments than men. Born out of women's desire to secure relationships, women direct their energies to becoming pleasing, caring, and helping. They learn to strive to be what is socially most desired and valued, an identity typified by adherence to traditional gender roles, referred to by Jack as the 'good' woman.

> These women try to accomplish their goals – to keep their husbands and thereby secure the attachment – through fulfilling the role of the traditional 'good wife.' Because they measure their effectiveness from the perspective of others (being there for others, nurturing others, pleasing others), they listen to others' demands and requirements more than to their own feelings and needs. When this occurs without mutuality or reciprocity, they experience a loss of self – they feel disconnected, unsupported, and alienated from themselves.
>
> (Jack, 1991, p. 39)

As women attempt to fit into the role of the 'good' woman, the gap between their outward and inward experiences of themselves widens, as does their increasing anguish over inauthenticity. Guided by 'an image provided by someone else – the husband, parental teachings, the culture' (Jack, 1991, p. 32), women undertake massive self-negation in order to avoid conflict and possible abandonment. Just as Cynthia described above, women learn to ignore the voice of their true selves. In an effort to seek intimacy, and guided by an ethic of other-centredness, women lose their authentic selves in a process of 'silencing the self' which Jack identifies as depression.

Jack's work has been instrumental in bringing a gendered lens to understandings of women's depression. Her work highlights how the pressures on women to live up to the 'good' woman ideal are integral to women's depression, and has contributed significantly to the de-pathologization of women's distress. However, in adopting a relational model, a rather narrow understanding of how women are influenced by cultural expectations of femininity is proposed. For instance, internalized beliefs about the 'good' woman role are central to Jack's understanding of women's depression. While Jack is critical of patriarchy and the perpetuation of oppressive gender roles for women, this model stops short of appreciating the extent to which society and culture shape individuals' experiences. As a consequence of this somewhat limited epistemological scope, attention is ultimately drawn to the individual woman who internalizes gender role 'beliefs' thereby putting herself at risk for depression. For instance, drawing on Gilligan's (1982) theory of moral development, Jack asserts that 'a woman is particularly vulnerable if she equates caring for others with self-sacrifice' (1991, p. 110). Thus, this model risks constructing depressed women as 'cultural dopes' (Stoppard, 2000) who blindly conform to social expectations for women. Jack appears to struggle with this notion herself, when she asks, 'Why are these beliefs so resistant to change? Why can't a woman simply see that they are destructive to her and embrace new, less restrictive ones?' (Jack, 1991, p. 119). She answers her own questions by turning to the internalization of gender roles through identification with the mother and the ambiguous qualities of moral thought that make it hard for women to assess the validity of the stereotypes they have internalized. Her own response appears to address why it is so difficult for women to resist gender stereotypes, but then leaves open the corollary question, 'How is it that some women *do* resist the entrapments of the "good" woman?' When women's (in)ability to resist cultural imperatives is explained in terms of identification with one's mother and moral reasoning, the model comes dangerously close to reifying both mother-blaming and underdeveloped morality as sources of women's depression. Therefore, models that can extend Jack's analysis while providing a deeper appreciation of the ways in which the social, cultural, and political contexts of women's lives are entwined in their individual experience are required.

More recently, Janet Stoppard (1997, 1998, 1999, 2000) has adopted a discursive approach to understanding the ways in which the 'good' woman identity is central to women's depression. From a discursive perspective, the 'good' woman ideal is not considered a static and prescriptive 'role'. It is not considered a 'belief set' that women either comply with or reject 'in their heads'. Rather, this ideal is constructed, maintained, and reified in social interaction, through language. When we understand women and women's experiences, we do so through language shot through with hegemonic constructions of idealized femininity which assume women's caring, nurturing, relational nature. Adherence or resistance to these gendered prescriptions do not transpire only in women's heads, but through discourse and in their social interactions. Further, Stoppard (1997, 1998, 1999, 2000) highlights the ways in which materiality and discourse are inextricably linked in the creation of women's depression. By shifting attention from women's *thoughts* to the material realities and the hegemonic discourses that construct women's *lives*, a broader view of women's distress emerges. With a material-discursive lens then, I will return to an examination of the ways in which women talk about depression and, in turn, the ways in which these accounts are structured and constrained by both materiality and dominant discourses of femininity.

WOMEN'S EVERYDAY LIVES: MARRIAGE, MOTHERHOOD, AND MARTYRDOM

Thus far, I have elaborated on two central themes in women's accounts of depression: the traumatic and chronic experiences of violence and poverty, and women's struggles in heterosexual relationships. These experiences are notably gendered, born out of patriarchal social systems that construct men as dominant and women as subservient to men's needs. Women bear the major brunt of interpersonal violence (WHO, 2000a), are economically oppressed (Belle & Doucet, 2003; UNDP, 1995), and are largely held responsible for the work of maintaining relationships (Jack, 1991). Accordingly, each of these issues has been elaborated as a central feature of women's depression (Belle & Doucet, 2003; Culter & Nolen-Hoeksema, 1991; Jack, 1991; Marecek, 2006). In the following section, I will elaborate on another recurrent theme, one rarely considered in understandings of women's depression: women's everyday lives (Stoppard, 2000). That is, it is not only the 'major life events' that are woven throughout women's accounts of depression, but also the mundane. Shared across almost all accounts were stories of the daily struggles of women's lives – caring for children and dependent adults, working in paid employment, and the work of maintaining households. For instance, Meredith's story of depression begins with her description of her life as a young mother in the 1960s, sitting in the kitchen after supper, feeding her baby and overseeing her older children's chores.

> I should jump ahead about ten years to when I hit the bottom. That was a real bottom and that was when I had <four children> [...] I had **four** little boys between 1960 and 1968. And at this point my husband was a house builder and he was, he is a very hands-on person who found it hard to delegate, he had to be there and do it all himself? And so he was never home, he was never there and [...] I found that ve::ry hard to deal with and would try to talk to him about that and he was just so:: intent on being this successful busi- nessman that he couldn't hear me. He couldn't hear what I said at all. .hh And I remember, and I was going through that around the time of that fourth child was born and I remember when I came home from the hospital with this fourth baby. Beautiful little boy and I was sitting in the kitchen and giving him his bottle and I had the other boys cleaning up the kitchen one night. ... the baby would have been three or four weeks old, something like that. Here's the seven and eight year olds over there washing dishes and and the the the four year old, yeah he was three and he would have been three and a half, he was doing his little thing whatever that was and I can remember sitting there and saying to myself, ((smacks her lips)) ((sighs)) 'this is what it's going to be like for the next twenty years'. And <my heart> sank to the bottom of my shoes. I just thought, this was, this was, I don't want this. This is not what I want for my life. [...] And not- no emotional support from my husband and ... that's when another depression set in and I, over the next two or three years I became clinically depressed and I really needed treatment. I should have had treatment. And that was very, that was a **rea::lly**, really difficult time.

>   (Meredith)

Meredith's story of depression is one of the everyday experiences of many women's lives – feeding babies, caring for children, doing dishes, and making meals. Viewed from the outside, the scene described might be considered a beautiful representation of domestic life – a still life Norman Rockwell of a mother feeding her 'beautiful little boy' and observing her children's contribution to the household chores. However, what might be viewed as idyllic by outside observers was experienced by Meredith as 'hit(ting) the bottom' of despair. She describes being isolated and profoundly unhappy, but feeling 'trapped' and unable to see a way out. Further, her distress was unheard and unacknowledged. Although she described trying to talk to her husband about her feelings, she said, 'he couldn't hear me. He couldn't hear what I said at all'. She described herself as so profoundly depressed that she needed treatment, but when asked what 'treatment' should have involved, she responded 'I probably should have, should have been out of the house for . . . you know maybe a week at a time. [...] I should have been staying at my mother's cottage or going to visit a friend somewhere and having somebody to take care of the children'. Although she refers to her experience in clinical terms ('clinical depression', 'treatment') her understanding remains rooted in the realities of her daily life as a mother. For Meredith, treatment would not have meant medication or therapy, but childcare and relief from the demands of her life as a wife and mother.

Bea, another woman in her sixties at the time of the interview, also recalled being depressed as a young woman managing multiple caregiving roles.

> Like alright now this is, this is a day example when I worked at the day care. And I was fostering [children] at the same time. I'd have to be to work at 9:30 in the morning until 5:30. So in the morning before I went to work I'd get all the beds made, I'd get laundry done, I'd almost do a day's work before I'd go to work. Then I worked at the day care for you know, all day until 5:30 and you're busy at a day care. Then I'd come home and cook dinner for my husband and our daughter and I don't know how many foster children. Then at night I'd make their lunches for them. And it just, it never stopped. See?
>
> (Bea)

Although dramatic changes in women's social roles have taken place since the 1950s and 60s, women's accounts of depression today remain inextricably linked with stories of hurried and harried lives stretched between their responsibilities as mothers, wives, employees, community members, daughters, and daughters-in-law. Bearing remarkable similarity to the accounts of older women, the following excerpts are from interviews with younger women who described their recent experiences of depression in the context of combining their work in the home with full-time employment.[1]

I get up in the morning, I get my daughter ready, we are off to work. My lunch hours are spent running around the malls to pay bills or to pick up this or whatever. I get home, I cook supper, I do homework and then there is the bath. Then there is quality time of playing and she [daughter] is off to bed. Then I'm in the bedroom ironing ... and the next thing you have to go to bed because I have to get up early again the next morning and start all over again ... and now my husband, his aunt, she has got Parkinson's and she is suffering from depression herself, so she is having a hard time coping, so I am paying her bills and I am doing her laundry and I am doing his father's laundry.

(Jane)

I was expected to carry on at the same level of intensity [at work] that I had before I had the baby hh and I couldn't do it. You just simply physically can't do sixty hours a week when you got a little six month old baby at home. [...] So you know back into the same kind of work pressures and then having this little baby and, and [...] wanting to have the house clean or wanting to take care of the baby or wanting to- .hh you can't give up those things easily so the people around you can't even help you. As much as they **want** to if if he [husband] did something he wouldn't do it right anyway so I'd have to **re**do it.
ML: OK. So you felt the support there but weren't able to access it.
Oh it was definitely there I just cou- I just couldn't make use of it. It was definitely- it was there, it was you know, every day '<what can I do, what can I do to he::lp?<' I said 'It's OK it really is, everything is fine, it'll all be fine it's OK'
ML: If you had asked him for help though what would that have meant for you to say I need help?
... ... Well- I that would have meant not, that would have meant giving up something.

(Heather)

These women, like many of the other women I have interviewed, told stories of their daily lives consumed by domestic practices and governed by the needs of others. Their lives appear organized in relation to *discourses of femininity* – what it means to be a 'good' woman and enacted through *practices of femininity* (Stoppard, 2000). These practices are the actions through which women regulate and discipline themselves in order to align themselves within the limits of proper femininity. They are markers of women's worth and, as illustrated in Heather's account, difficult to relinquish. For younger women, practices of femininity often revolve around efforts to produce an attractive female form (dieting, exercising, wearing fashionable clothes and make-up, and increasingly, having plastic surgery). For women who are wives, mothers, and care-givers, an additional set of practices apply in the form of an endless cycle of women's work. As articulated in the two excerpts above, such practices of femininity include caring for children, cooking meals, helping children with homework, giving baths, ironing clothes, cleaning, making beds, attending to the sick, doing laundry, and having 'quality time' with children. These activities are never-ending, amorphous, and elastic – one is never sure if they have been adequately completed (Stoppard, 2000). A meal is prepared, but should it have been made from scratch? Should children be enrolled in multiple extra-curricular activities, or will over-scheduling be harmful to the child? What exactly are the standards that would signify that a woman is 'good' enough? Trying to live up to an unattainable standard can lead a woman to feel helpless and perpetually inadequate. Moreover, practices of femininity tax women's bodies and resources, but remain an expected part of their everyday lives (Stoppard, 2000).

Women and care-giving: mothers and monsters

Nowhere are the practices of femininity more powerful and invisible than in the matters of childbirth and childcare. While typically regarded as 'natural' for women, and therefore irrefutable, women's care-giving role is clearly a product of its patriarchal and capitalist context 'that privileges the work done in the public and "productive" market and renders invisible the work women do in the home' (Evans, 1998, pp. 47–8). Women's ability to give birth and breastfeed have been taken in patriarchal society as the basis of their 'natural' inclination to care for children (Wearing, 1990). Accordingly, hegemonic constructions of femininity construct women as naturally endowed with the propensity to care for and nurture others (i.e., the 'maternal instinct'). Therefore, discourses of femininity 'both dovetail with and support family and social arrangements in which women perform most of the work caring, and at the same time place the needs of others ahead of their own' (Stoppard, 2000, p. 18). Within this construction, women's work in the home is both taken-for-granted as intrinsically motivated by care and concern, and therefore in no need of remuneration. Indeed, it is the selflessness and sacrifice associated with women's caring that are revered (O'Grady, 2005). 'The dichotomy-producing tendencies in Western thought also encourage the notion that one works for love *or* money, not both

(Folbre & Nelson, 2000). Such dichotomous thinking encourages the idea that commodifying care dries up real love, or worse, makes the sacred profane' (England, Budig, & Folbre, 2002, p. 457). Thus, women are assumed to adopt caring responsibilities happily and unproblematically out of a natural inclination toward this 'labour of love', in a social arrangement that largely benefits others (O'Grady, 2005; Stoppard, 1998, 2000).

Although women have always borne children, the practices now so clearly identified with the roles of 'wife' and 'mother' are relatively recent phenomena (Collins, 2000; Hays, 1996; O'Reilly, 2004a; Rich, 1986; Stoppard, 2000; Wearing, 1984). For instance, public concern for the well-being of children emerged alongside of the industrial revolution and the rising need for healthy and productive workers in factories (Stoppard, 2000). Being in the home, mothers were identified as best able to oversee children's development, a role that expanded in urgency and scope with the rise of the mental hygiene movement (Stoppard, 2000). The social reorganization that took place after World War II also served to entrench the Western image of the 'happy homemaker' (O'Reilly, 2004b). During the war, women were needed in the workplace to fill the jobs left by men who went to battle. However, when the war ended and the troops returned home, women were forced to give up their employment and return to the domestic sphere. This dramatic shift was propelled by a refined definition of what constitutes a 'good' mother – the ever-nurturing 'stay-at-home mother'. Further, this ideology developed a new level of moral urgency with the emergence of Bowlby's attachment theory (Hays, 1996; O'Reilly, 2004b; Varcoe & Hartrick Doane, 2007). Women's participation in work outside the home became equated with 'maternal deprivation' and regarded as profoundly damaging to the child. Thus, to be a 'good' mother was to be a stay-at-home mother: one whose sole focus is on the needs of the child.

Although the ideology of sacrificial motherhood may appear to have had its heyday in the 1950s and 1960s with the rampant popularization of images of the 'June Cleaver'[2] mother, some feminist scholars have argued that mothers today face even greater challenges in their motherwork. As Andrea O'Reilly (2004b) explains, the current approach of 'intensive mothering' in the West emerged in the 1970s and is qualitatively different from the mothering practices of thirty and forty years ago.

> Today, the ideology of good motherhood demands more than mere physical proximity of mother–child: contemporary mothers are expected to spend, to use the discourse of the experts, 'quality time' with their children. Mothers are told to play with their children, read to them, and take classes with them. As the children in the 1950s and 1960s would jump rope or play hide-and-seek with the neighbourhood children or their siblings, today's children dance, swim, and 'cut and paste' with their mothers in one of many 'moms

and tots' programs. . . . Today, though they have fewer children and more labour-saving devices – from microwaves to takeout food – mothers spend more time, energy, and I may add money, on their children than their mothers did in the 1960s. And the majority of mothers today, unlike forty years ago, practice intensive mothering while engaged in full-time employment. Mothering today, as in the post-war era, is 'expert driven.' However, mothering today is also, under the ideology of intensive mothering, more child-centred than the 'children should be seen but not heard' style of mothering that characterized the post-war period.

(O'Reilly, 2004b, p. 8)

O'Reilly (2004b) theorizes the recent movement toward 'intensive mothering' as a response to the changing demographics of motherhood. In particular, this ideology emerged in tandem with women's increasing social and economic independence. As such, it can be understood as a form of backlash, demanding more and more of mothers who find themselves with less and less time. She explains,

It seems that just as women were making inroads and feeling confident, a new discourse of motherhood emerged which made two things inevitable: that women would forever feel inadequate as mothers, and that work and motherhood would be forever seen as in conflict and incompatible. I believe that the guilt and shame women experience in failing to live up to what is, in fact, an impossible ideal is neither accidental nor inconsequential. Rather, it is deliberately manufactured and monitored. Just as the self-hate produced by the beauty myth undercuts and undermines women's sense of achievement in education or a career, the current discourse of intensive mothering gives rise to self-doubt or, more specifically, guilt that immobilizes women and robs them of their confidence as both workers and mothers.

(O'Reilly, 2004b, p. 10)

While it may be difficult enough or near impossible for women of privileged social status to conform to the motherhood ideal, women who are poor, single, divorced, lesbian, or disabled are even further removed from this positioning, and are often regarded as less competent and suitable mothers (Gillespie, 2000; Morell, 2000; Phoenix & Wollett, 1991). Women who are poor are particularly oppressed by the ideology of intensive mothering. In order to support their families, mothers who are poor are often forced to work long hours in order to make ends meet, or depend on government assistance. Either way, they lack the resources required for intensive nurture work (e.g., child enrichment classes, activities). And, either way they are readily vilified – as the negligent mother, or the lazy 'welfare' mother

31

(Collins, 1994, 2000). Reflecting on her Canadian context (although certainly applicable elsewhere) and the intensification of a conservative politic, Boyd (2004) referred to the vilification of mothers who struggle to provide for their families as a kind of 'national sport'. Whereas governmental services are presumably intended to support those in need, these services are most often framed in a pejorative and punitive light. For instance, terms such as 'welfare dependency' have 'made receiving welfare a personal pathology, something that became harder to "escape" the longer it went on, while such descriptions as "long-termer" and "recidivism" virtually equate using welfare with a criminal offence' (O'Connor, 2001, p. 254; cited in Belle & Doucet, 2003, p. 107). Moreover, as Baines, Evans, and Neysmith (1998) have argued,

> Images of 'welfare moms', 'crack babies', 'child abusers' and 'intergenerational poverty' dominate the media and fuel a conservative ideology and a 'get tough' approach that justifies attacks on the welfare state. Child welfare services are focussed on women's failure to care rather than the provision of services that enhance the capacity of families to care.
>
> (Baines et al., 1998, p. 14)

An inability to provide for one's children means not only moral condemnation in terms of identity, but also to risk the ultimate sanction – the removal of children from the home (Phoenix & Woollett, 1991). Thus, the social construction of what it means to be a 'good' mother and child welfare policies work hand-in-hand to disempower women living in the margins of society, while also pushing them towards self-surveillance and self-discipline. In the context of hegemonic constructions of the 'good' mother, the material realities of women's lives are ignored and erased. What comes into view instead is the measure of an individual woman's moral worth.

The ideology of motherhood has compounded implications for those women of colour who are poor and who already face racial stereotypes that situate them as deficient (Collins, 2000; hooks, 1982). Collins (2000) described how historically, the limited employment opportunities available to African-American men have made it impossible for their families to depend on male wages alone. Whether through being forced to work for White profit during slavery, or through the continuing history of economic oppression, African-American women have largely not been allowed the luxury of being stay-at-home mothers. As Collins (2000) states, 'Motherhood as a privatized, female "occupation" never predominated in Black civil society because no social class foundation could be had to support it' (p. 53). Indeed, the fact that African-American women worked outside the home was central to the infamous Moynihan report (1965) in which the economic, political, and social problems experienced by African-Americans was blamed on their 'dysfunctional' family structure (Morton, 1991). 'Or as critique Michele Wallace put it: '"The Moynihan Report said that the black man was not so much a victim of white institutional racism as he was of an abnormal family structure, its main feature being an employed black woman"' (1990, p. 12; cited in O'Reilly, 2004c, p. 189). While the report by senator Moynihan was immediately condemned, its message embodied the entrenched racism that continues to affect the perceptions and treatment of African-American mothers. For example, Cleeton (2003) recently showed how poor African-American women living in inner cities were transformed in public discourse from 'from single mothers who could not begin prenatal care before the second trimester because too few physicians will treat Medicaid patients, into sexually immoral, illegal-drug-using women who deliberately harmed their babies' (p. 41; cited in Varcoe & Hartrick Doane, 2007, p. 306). Aboriginal women in North America, Australia and New Zealand (particularly those living on Reservations) are often similarly depicted: as lazy, irresponsible, drug-using mothers. These stereotypes and portrayals abound despite the fact that these women routinely lack adequate housing, clean water, economic opportunities, and health care for themselves and their children. Thus, 'while motherhood may be construed as "natural" elsewhere, racism and classism configure these particular women as *naturally inadequate*' (Varcoe & Hartrick Doane, 2007, p. 306).

The implications of the ideology of intensive mothering are wide-reaching for women's lives and identities. It serves to erode the confidence, self-worth, and resources of working- and upper-class women and further vilifies mothers who are economically and socially marginalized. Indeed, even women who are *not* mothers are evaluated against the standards of this ideology. That is, motherhood is a naturalized discourse; it is taken-for-granted that women are drawn to care, and want to become mothers. Although less frequently now than in generations past, women who fail to realize their 'natural instincts' and have children remain subject to being denigrated as sad, selfish, childish, and morally suspect (Gillespie, 2000; Morell, 1994; Ulrich & Wetherell, 2000; Woollett, 1991). Indeed it has been suggested that the meaning of childlessness for women is the cultural equivalent of being a 'nonwoman' (McMahon, 1998). Children are seen to 'complete' women's lives, and women who do not have children are often viewed as lacking and unfulfilled (Morell, 1994). Given the assumption of 'motherhood as mandatory' (Woollett, 1991), women who do not have children are typically assumed to be *unable* to bear children and framed in terms of tragedy and suffering (Gillespie, 2003) – as sad, barren, and broken. Women who want to have children but are unable to are painted with labels such as infertile, sterile, and barren, which imply 'a failure not merely in reproductive terms but as women' (Woollett, 1991, p. 59).

Women who *choose* to be childless (or 'childfree', Gillespie, 2003) are often regarded as even more unnatural and pathological. In her research with women who self-identified as voluntarily childless, Rosemary Gillespie (2000) found that despite significant changes in the lives of women including their increased participation in the workforce, economic independence, and access to contraception and safe abortion, a pronatalist discourse continues to dominate. The women she interviewed described having their choice reacted to with disbelief, disregard, and as deviant. They were frequently treated as unfeminine, uncaring, selfish, or like children who had not yet passed into the normal adult female role. Infantilized or vilified, the identity of the childless woman is pervasively denigrated. While it is acceptable for women to work, it is not acceptable for them to forgo motherhood. Instead, women are expected to 'have it all', and be the 'superwoman' who can successfully juggle intensive mothering with a successful career. Thus, rather than seeing a decline in discourses of motherhood, Gillespie (2000) suggests that they 'may have simply changed, modernized and become more sophisticated in ways that accommodate social change' (p. 230).

Hegemonic constructions of femininity provide a narrow range of acceptable positionings for the adult woman. In order to fit its confines, she is to be a devoted mother. She is to have the resources, support, skills, and inclination to invest in intensive mothering, and she is to find pleasure, satisfaction, and fulfilment in her role. While it is certainly true that motherhood brings enormous joy to the lives of many women, the widespread expectations that women should have children and should *only* feel happiness and contentment in their roles as care-givers are problematic. Raising children often brings pleasure and fulfilment, but it also presents a host of material and discursive constraints in women's lives that are normally ignored and dismissed as legitimate sources of distress. The discourse of proper motherhood, coupled with its relentless practices often leaves women with little space in which to express exhaustion, frustration, or sadness. Instead, women often feel guilt and shame when they are unable to manage the never-ending cycle of domestic and care-giving work with unwavering affection and devotion (Jack, 1991; Mauthner, 2002; Nicholson, 1998; O'Grady, 2005; Stoppard, 2000). When women express sentiments or engage in behaviours that are not guided by an ethic of care, they risk social condemnation. Behaviours that do not coincide with the dictates of discourses of femininity are readily constructed as 'unnatural', and inevitably provoke moral judgement (Greaves, Varcoe, Poole, Morrow et al., 2002).

Problems arise for women then, when exclusive care and concern for others is not experienced happily and unproblematically. For instance, in investigations of women's accounts of depression following childbirth, women often report feelings of ambivalence, loss, frustration, sadness and exhaustion (Lewis & Nicholson, 1998; Mauthner, 2002; McMahon, 1995; Nicholson 1998; Ussher, 2006; Weaver & Ussher, 1997). At the same time,

34

women have also described their difficulties in voicing such experiences. For instance, Natasha Mauthner (2002) interviewed women who had experienced depression after childbirth and found that their accounts of depression revolved around a conflict between the perfect mother they wanted to be and the mother they felt themselves to be. Mauthner's analysis is punctuated by accounts of women who talked of trying to fit into the 'good' mother mould, denying and discounting their own needs and desires. Guided by an ethic of caring, women felt that their moral worth was at stake and they had no choice but to try to fit into cultural definitions of the 'good' woman and mother. 'Good' mothers were defined as being selfless and self-sacrificing, able to handle the challenges of motherhood in a calm, pleasant, and effective way. Failure to maintain this ideal was taken to indicate personal and moral inadequacy. As a result, women silenced their feelings of exhaustion, frustration, sadness, and anger.

Similarly, in their research with new mothers, Lewis and Nicholson (1998) noted that alternatives to the discourse of motherhood are not easily accessible, resulting in limited opportunities for women to reconstruct their experiences of themselves in ways that are meaningful and valued.

> Interviews suggested that there are few ways of talking about problematic experiences of motherhood which do not imply that women are poor mothers and deficient women. Women may need to deny the losses they experience in order to present themselves, to themselves and others, as adequate mothers, at the same time as they are aware that they have lost elements of their lives which were important to them . . . Without being conscious of this process of loss and change women may have few ways of explaining current problems and negative feelings of grief and loss. These feelings may be more readily incorporated into constructions of failed motherhood.
>
> (Lewis & Nicholson, 1998, pp. 187–8)

Repeated throughout women's narratives of depression are references to feeling overwhelmed by the demands and circumstances of their lives as mothers, while at the same time feeling as though they should be able to manage with unfailing patience, kindness, and caring concern. The concept of what it is to be a proper 'good' mother (kind, loving, serving, caring) appears dyed in the wool with which women weave their stories, shaping their very understandings of themselves and their experiences. When women are inevitably unable to live up to the idealized image of the perfect mother, they are likely to feel defeated and depressed. As Heather described, feelings of being unable to be a 'good' mother and 'good' wife marked the lowest point in her depression.

I remember saying to my husband when it was real bad I remember saying 'Honey maybe you should just divorce me or like put me in a hospital or like an institute or something and divorce me and then you can go and get married, find somebody nice who's going to be a better mother to [child] and a better wife for you because I clearly can't do it.' And I remember really believing that was the only solution.

(Heather)

As so poignantly expressed in Heather's account, women often blame themselves and are blamed when they are not able to live up to the standards of the 'good' mother.

Women and care-giving: women caring for dependent adults

Given that providing care is a practice at the heart of discourses of femininity, women are often expected not only to care for children, but also other family members requiring attention such as ill and dependent adults. Like participants who talked of the strain of motherhood, Barb talked explicitly about how the work of care-giving left her depleted and exhausted. Her description of depression is entwined in her account of caring for her mother who had a terminal illness and Alzheimer's disease.

My mother got very ill for three years and she ... ... you know, her apartment, closing it down, putting her in a special care home, .hh then you know, fighting to get her into a nursing home, and then she died. .hh [...] I just felt I was the only one. They do that to women in a family you know, it is like ha ha ha ha
ML: *You were the only one ...*
Well my brother walked away from it when she got ill and he never even came back when she die::d. He still, I don't know what his problem is [...] So um ... it was on my shoulders. My husband [who is a doctor] was not too suppo:rtive because he felt that he would be clashing with his colleagues. She lived here in [city], umm ... and my children sort of, well 'we will support you mom but we don't know how and please don't ask us to visit gramma.'
ML: *[OK, so you were really alone*
So it was that kind of], so I felt very alone, I lost a lot of weight, I didn't sleep, I cried a lot, didn't eat anything, felt at

times as if I was stretched so thin ... I was invisible. It was terrible, but I got myself into it and didn- it was so gra::dual that you don't realize that it's umm. And you don't know how to get out.

(Barb)

For Barb, depression was a consequence of the societal expectations placed on women to provide care. As a result of this shared understanding, it was taken-for-granted that she would take up the work of caring for her mother. As she said, 'they do that to women in a family you know'. Left on her own by family members and the health system, her body eroded under the weight of the responsibilities she shouldered, an embodied experience she eloquently described when she said, '[I] felt at times as if I was stretched so thin . . . I was invisible'. The work of care-giving can wear down women's emotional and physical energies, but remains taken-for-granted as an assumed outgrowth of women's 'natural' caring nature. Thus for women, care-giving represents a kind of 'invisible tax' which can slowly erode health and well-being. A tax applied 'so gradual(ly) that you don't realize . . . and you don't know how to get out'.

Barb's story is not unusual. Like Barb, the majority of informal health care providers around the world are women (National Alliance for Caregiving (NAC) & AARP, 2004; WHO 2001). Indeed, it has been argued that 'because women comprise more than 80% of "family" caregivers, it seems that family care has become a misnomer for *female* care' (Brewer, 2001, p. 218). Women not only provide more hours of unpaid care than men do, but they also provide more intense levels of care (NAC & AARP, 2004). Even in countries that provide 'universal health care', the burden of care continues to fall on women (Canadian Research Institute for the Advancement of Women, 2001). Increasingly, dependent adults are being transferred from hospitals and institutions into the 'community'. However, what is euphemistically referred to as 'home care' means a daily reality of lifting and cleaning bodies, giving medication, preparing food, doing laundry, changing bedding, arranging medical appointments, and, for many, being on call 24 hours a day, seven days a week. In the following excerpt, Barb provides a glimpse of what she experienced as her mother's care-giver.

Well she would call me. When she was in the special care home she called me a lot. I had talk mail, she would leave me these terrible messages like .hh one message was, 'I'm going to go out that side door and get myself lost in the woods'. And then she would cry on the phone and I would get this like three or four times a night. And my husband would get angrier and angrier but he never shows his anger. So it was like, 'Oh yeah, uh huh.' But it tears you apart, it really does ... and she tore me apart bi:::t by bi:::t by bit. And it was terrible. It was really bad. [...] I would get to the special care home and they would say, you know 'She has phoned for some apartments' ... and I thought 'No:::! she was assessed at the hospital'. You know, she wasn't sa:::fe with her own care, she had gotten to that point. Ummm then she would do things that- she had an ulcer on her leg and you knew it was self-inflicted. And she'd end up in the emergency room in the middle of the night and of course being the go(h)od duti(h)ful daug(h)hter that I was I went over there! And the emergency room is no fun, I mean every time she went it was a different do:ctor. We would go through this, 'Do you want a code on her [to revive]?' ((laughs)) You know, it was like, Uh! 'Yeah, umhumm- No! I don't want a code on her! Because she's signed a life directive and I **know** this'. And then she got Alzheimer's. She had severe osteoporosis, she had cancer of the bone. She was on a lot of medication. You arrange dental appointments for her and she won't come most of the time, she was like a chi::ld again. Alzheimer's is a terrible disease for the family, not too bad on the patients because they are not aware of it. But you know, and then just a lot of little things that just ... <piled on top of each other>.

(Barb)

Barb's account serves as a reminder that in contrast to the celebrated image of the serene womanly nurturer, providing care is often hard and stressful work. Further, providing care to dependent adults is work that women do alone. Like Barb, most care-givers experience isolation, receiving little support from friends and family (National Family Caregiver Association (NFCA) & National Alliance for Caregiving (NAC), 2002). Not surprisingly, informal health care providers suffer from increased risk of a range of health consequences, including depression, cardiac problems, lowered immune system functioning, lower levels of perceived health, and significantly higher rates of mortality (Kiecolt-Glaser, Dura, Speicher, Trask, & Glaser, 1991; Schulz & Beach, 1999). Indeed, it has been estimated that as many as two-thirds of care-givers experience depression after taking on care-giving responsibilities (National Family Caregivers Association/Fortis,

1998, cited in Bedini, 2002) and women care-givers are at particular risk. Compared to male care-givers, women care-givers report higher levels of depression, anxiety, unmet needs, and burden of care (Ussher & Sandoval, 2008). For women, caring often becomes all encompassing, tied to their identities as women, and leaving little or no time to oneself, preventing attention to one's own health and well-being (NFCA & NAC, 2002; Ussher & Sandoval, 2008). Moreover, there are the financial costs of caring, including the costs of medication, hospitalization, rehabilitation services, support care, as well as the repercussions from absenteeism from work, and the frequent reduction or abandonment of paid work. Compared to their male counterparts, employed women care-givers are more likely to miss time from work, alter their work schedules, consider quitting work, reduce work hours, and take early retirement (Levand, Herrick, & Sung, 2000).Given that women make more concessions in their paid employment than men, and are over-represented among the poor to begin with, it follows that women, and marginalized women in particular, are most likely to suffer economically when they become care-givers (NAC & AARP, 2004). Indeed, the devalued and unpaid work of care-giving, for children and elders alike, is central to the perpetuation of women's poverty (Arendell & Estes, 1994; Brewer, 2001; England et al., 2002).

> Women's poverty frequently reflects their biographies as caregivers, and it is not surprising that the women who are most likely to be poor are single mothers and elderly women living on their own. The undervaluing of women's work in the home and in the labour market results in inadequate incomes for a large proportion of single mothers who are without the financial support of a traditional male 'breadwinner'. The disadvantaged relationship between gender and employment accumulates over a lifetime to produce low pensions, and the poverty of many older women can be regarded as the economic legacy of their caregiving. Not all caregivers are poor, and not all poor women are caregivers. However, as Hilary Graham (1987; 223) commented more than a decade ago: 'Poverty and caregiving are, for many women, two sides of the same coin. Caregiving is what they do; poverty describes the economic circumstances in which they do it'.
>
> (Evans, 1998, p. 47)

Women are regarded as the 'natural' caregivers around the world. However, while daughters provide the bulk of elder-care in the West, in East Asian countries such as China, Japan, and Korea, it is daughters-in-law who typically provide care because of the traditional patrilocal family structure (Harvey & Yoshino, 2006; Levand et al., 2000; Zhan, 2004).

Despite dramatic social and economic change in the East, the Confucian ethic of filial piety, or *xiao* remains strong. According to this principle, elders are to be revered and cared for and their ways maintained (Zhan, 2004). While eldest sons are regarded as responsible for the care of their parents, practically, the work of care-giving is performed by sons' wives (Levand et al., 2000; Spitzer, Neufeld, Harrison, Hughes, & Stewart, 2003). This traditional family arrangement has been supported by governments who have historically failed to provide public services for elder-care. For example, before the 1960s, no public support systems were available in Japan for those providing elder care (Harvey & Yoshino, 2006). In China, the services that exist today have been described as limited, unreliable, and cost-prohibitive (Harvey & Yoshino, 2006; Holroyd, 2003; Izuhara, 2002). In South Korea, substantial efforts have been made in recent decades to preserve traditional values associated with elder-care through government-sponsored initiatives such as widely publicized national prizes for filial piety (Levand et al., 2000). Further, given the emphasis on family responsibility, harmony, and loyalty, there is profound social stigma associated with the procurement of external assistance (Harvey & Yoshino, 2006). Families are supposed to care for their own; to do otherwise is to bring shame not only to the individual woman for failing in her duty, but to the entire family (George, 1998). Thus, like their sisters in the West, when women in the East provide care, it is often with limited or no support.[3]

The isolation and strain faced by women who provide care is further intensified for many immigrant women separated from the extended kin units and social supports of their countries of origin. Language barriers, foreign service structures, and the economic disadvantage faced by so many further constrain their ability to care for their families and themselves (Spitzer et al., 2003). A common problem of those who migrate to Western countries, for instance, is that their professional credentials are denied and they are forced into low-paying service jobs that do not allow the financial compensation or the flexibility required for care work. Moreover, these women are often regarded by families as the keepers of the culture, responsible for ensuring the maintenance of traditional values against the threat of Western homogenization. Thus, immigrant women often experience an intensification of their care-giving demands, but in the context of diminished resources with which to perform this work (Spitzer et al., 2003). Therefore, the clear links that have been found between depression and care-giving are likely intensified for those immigrant women who face additional challenges in terms of isolation, stress, and poverty. Moreover, women who migrate to the West appear to be at increased risk of becoming depressed as they encounter the meanings and practices of Western culture. For instance, one study of Chinese immigrants in the United States found that women who were acculturated were two times more likely to become depressed than those who were not acculturated (Takeuchi, Chung, Lin, Shen et al., 1998).

This difference was not found for men, pointing to the importance of gender and gender norms in formulations of women's distress.

Clearly, when the work of care-giving is provided by women, it is often done in isolation and at great personal cost. For instance, Barb described how her health eroded under the constant demands of caring for her mother, and the frustrations of negotiating the health care system alone. She described being hospitalized with a severe viral infection in her lungs and becoming extremely depressed. In reflecting on this time in her life, she discussed how her body wore the signs of physical depletion and exhaustion. She said, 'My body had been eroded so badly that, you know, something has to give. I mean if your brain doesn't clue you in about it and you don't take notice, then your body fails you'. In this account, Barb points to the intersection of the limitless demands of her responsibilities and the finite resources of her body – to the intersection of discourses and practices of femininity. Consistent with Janet Stoppard's (2000) work on women's experiences of depression, Barb's account provides a poignant example of the 'ways in which women are caught between the socially constructed imperatives of cultural discourses of femininity and the limits imposed by material conditions, which include their physical embodiment. One consequence of a life lived at the intersection between what is culturally expected and what is materially feasible is the set of subjective and embodied experiences which are called depression' (Stoppard, 2000, p. 212).

While hospitals, institutions, and governments may consider it 'cost-effective' to have patients cared for 'in the community', this short-sighted policy perspective ignores the long-term implications of this arrangement for women's health. Ignored and silenced are the distress and depletion many women experience as a consequence of their care-giving labour. Indeed, the invisibility of women's distress in this arrangement appears to be the linchpin holding together a system that depends on women's caring compliance. Like Barb, care-givers often continue to push through despite the toll on their bodies and minds. However, the decision to continue with care is not merely a matter of individual reasoning or choice. Although this is suggested in Barb's account ('if your brain doesn't clue you in'), clearly much more was at stake. In the absence of family and health care support, like Barb, many may simply have little choice when it comes to the decision to provide care. Moreover, the social expectation that women should care out of a natural 'goodness' and inclination to nurture constrains women's actions in this regard.

What are the implications for identity for women who provide care despite the toll on their bodies and minds, and perhaps more importantly, for those who do not? While the first tend to be regarded as selfless and are revered, the latter are more readily positioned as selfish and are vilified. Accordingly, women who provide care for dependent adults often talk about duty and obligation, and women are more likely than men to report feeling they have no choice but to provide care (NAC & AARP, 2004). Again, this is not to suggest that genuine loving concern is not involved in women's decision to care. However, what *is* suggested is that any behaviour that is *inconsistent with* a sentiment of genuine loving concern presents a significant problem for care-givers, and for women care-givers in particular. While exhaustion, frustration, anger, resentment are all reasonable reactions to the unreasonable situation of providing continuous and intensive care, the ability to express and act on these experiences is limited by a culturally shared moral imperative that links women's goodness with their caring and self-sacrifice. When caring for the self and caring for others are at odds, the caring imperative takes precedence. Barb invokes this imperative when she describes caring for her mother up until the time of her death.

> But I must say though in all the time that I took care of mother, .hhh when she die::d I didn't feel guilty. You know because I knew I had tried my hardest for her.
> *ML: Yeah*
> Yeah, it was like the grief kind of ended when she died.
> *ML: Yes*
> Because I was the one that ... no pulse, we sat by her bedside, she was dying of pneumonia in the nursing home. And I sat there. I'm the one who said 'She is not breathing any more'. I am the one who ... put the sheet over face, called the nurse! You know. It is **ha:::rd** it's really hard.
> *ML: You were there for everything.*
> For **everything**, ewwwwww, yeah! It still upsets me at times but not like it did. I don't think about it at night any more.
> *ML: Yeah*
> It doesn't bother me in that if my brother came out of the woodwork somewhere ... that I would feel really upset that I didn't do everything I could have. That he could fault me for that.
>
> (Barb)

Here, Barb uses moral language ('guilty', 'fault') in describing how, although physically and emotionally devastated by the experience, she can take comfort in knowing that she did 'everything (she) could have'. From a discursive perspective, Barb's situation comes into view, not merely as the result of her 'beliefs' or 'moral reasoning', but as caught in the narrow confines of discourses of femininity. To have done anything less than 'everything' would have meant to pay a very real price in terms of identity. However, to have continued with care as she did meant a body and mind depleted in an embodied experience referred to as depression.

As long as prioritizing the care of others and self-sacrifice are socially prescribed as moral imperatives for women, the identity of the 'good' woman will remain a 'pedestal ringed with barbed wire' (Ussher, 1991, p. 294). While behaviour that is consistent with the 'good' woman identity is revered, women who step outside the boundaries of the pedestal (even if only to falter from exhaustion) pay a price in terms of loss of a valued identity and social legitimacy. Further, when women transgress the dictates of proper femininity they are also readily constructed as its 'photographic negative' (Kline, 1995) – the monster, the bitch, the whore. Representations of women vary across ethnic and racial groups; 'Native American girls are encouraged to see themselves as "Pocahontases" or "squaws"; Asian-American girls as "geisha girls" or "Suzy Wongs"; Hispanic girls as "Madonnas" or "hot-blooded whores"; and African-American girls as "mammies", "matriarchs" and "prostitutes"' (Collins, 1994, p. 57). Across these variations, however, is the fundamental splitting of women into the 'good' and the 'bad'. Held up to images that denigrate or cripple in their expectations of service, girls and women struggle to position themselves in positive and valued ways. Thus, rather than see women as silencing themselves (Jack, 1991), a discursive perspective shifts understanding to consider how women are silenced by hegemonic constructions of femininity that offer few legitimate opportunities for women to speak of their experiences. There are no dominant stories or language with which women can safely represent their distress, dissatisfaction, or desire to attend to their own needs and interests. Caught between the options of the Madonna or the monster, when women step outside the confines of the 'good' woman pedestal, they are left without footing to construct themselves and their experiences in valued ways. Instead, they are readily constructed as 'mad' or 'bad' (Ussher, 1991, 2006).

THE DISMISSAL OF WOMEN'S DISTRESS

When women talked about depression, they also described their difficulties in expressing their sadness and being heard. Repeated throughout the interviews were stories of thwarted efforts to seek understanding for their pain and despair. Faced with dominant constructions of femininity, if a woman has secured the makings of 'every girl's dream' – the house, the husband, and children – it is assumed that there is no cause for distress. For instance, Dianne spoke of being dismissed when she called a crisis line. The fact that she had a family appears to have eclipsed an empathic understanding of her distress.

43

I called the [crisis help] line. I don't want to criticize but they haven't been helpful in my case OK? Because they kind of said 'Well if you're not suicidal there's nothing we can do. What do you have to worry about or what do you complain about? You know, you're in, you live in a family, you have a husband, your children are doing OK.' That's the kind of answer I got and it didn't help.

(Dianne)

Joan talked about being married, a mother of two children, and a home-owner. She also talked about her intense desire to radically change her life so that she could pursue her passion for education. She explained how her desire to shift her life direction was dismissed by friends and family members. She said,

I got tired and I started to think there was something wrong with me. Because everyone kept saying you know 'Why why do you want to do this [go to university]. I don't understand why you want to do it. And isn't your life OK the way it is?'. Well no I guess it wasn't. I wanted something else. And um. So I continued to get more and more and more depressed to the point that I was crying all the time that I couldn't get out of bed. [...] And that was not where I had ever expected myself to end up. And I was always thinking about other things and wanting to read and learn and do things so I just felt like my life was over and ah everyone kept telling me **I should be satisfied and that was enough for me and you know I had a house to pay for and so on and so. And I didn't want the house anymore. [...] And it was funny because up until then I always thought a house was so important.** I thought a house was a home but I was starting to see that I hated my husband ((laughs)) you know. I think I was resenting my children in a lot of ways and rel- and then I'd fee- the old guilt would kick in that I was resenting my children because I didn't think I should resent my children and you know it just it was snowballing. And um ... I decided that ... the only way out would be to kill myself. That there was no other way out because nobody seemed to be hearing me. And I really, when I think about it now it was almost as if I had tried talking until I was blue in the face and no one heard me and I and I would try to explain this is why it's

important to me but you're just supposed to live your life and
get on the treadmill. You're not supposed to ask questions.
This is what you do:: is what everyone kept telling me, you
know, **this is your life** you don't you don't change mid-
stream. And this is how it is and I got so tired of the way
people were responding that I eventually just gave up and
thought they are right what the heck and went into this shell
and was very depressed. [...] I had always identified myself
for so many years as this wife and mo::ther so my
depression really hit rock bottom and then I made a decision
that I would kill myself.

(Joan)

Although Joan was seen to 'have it all' – a husband, children, and a home,
she felt dissatisfied and lost. Her attempts to express a desire for change
were met with resistance from family and friends who could not understand
her experience. Talking outside the dominant discourse, her distress went
unheard ('nobody seemed to be hearing me', 'I had tried talking until I was
blue in the face and no one heard me'). She saw and was offered no options
other than to remain on 'the pedestal' and be a wife and mother, but when
she experienced this positioning with anger, despair, and resentment, she
became even more critically depressed. As Joan's account so eloquently
portrays, the space around the pedestal can be an abyss. She said, 'I had
always identified myself for so many years as this wife and mo::ther so my
depression really hit rock bottom and then I made a decision that I would
kill myself'.

The dismissal of women's pain was not reserved for women who were
wives and mothers, but was also pervasive among younger women and
those who did not have children. For instance, Amanda, a young college
student, talked of being dismissed when she tried to talk to her father about
how she was feeling during a relationship break-up. She said, 'I've heard
my dad say that many times like you know. **At your age what problems
would you have.**' Not only was her distress silenced, but in some ways it was
actually celebrated. Along with other women interviewed, Amanda talked
of receiving a wealth of positive attention for having lost weight when
depressed.

I'd always wanted to be thinner like I always felt like I was
supposed to fit in a certain image and my mom's quite thin
and so is my sister. And um my mom ah she doesn't like
extra weight like she's very she could be very critical towards
me when it comes to weight. .hh But when the depression

set in and I um lost all that weight I lost like sixty pounds altogether and that took me down to about a hundred and fifteen pounds and for someone my height that's absolutely ridiculous. But I um I lost all this weight and people kept telling me 'Amanda you look so good' And everybody was telling me how **wonderful** I loo::ked and just during the while I was going through my depression.

(Amanda)

Weight loss (or gain) is a central 'symptom' of depression and Amanda's depression was severe. She recalled being so thin that she fainted on a regular basis. She recalled feeling 'raw', unable to eat or keep food down. However, what came into view for many was not her pain and incapacitation, but her body and her increased adherence to the thin beauty ideal. Emerging from these interviews, then, is the finding that what matters most is not how women *feel*, but how they *measure up* against the image of the feminine ideal. Women's experiences of exhaustion, depletion and erosion appear inconsequential next to the requirement that they should fit the mould of the ideal woman (Bordo, 1993; Malson, 1998). Women's suffering is often disregarded as incomprehensible, or simply invisible.

The participants in my study, who were all White, talked about having their expressions of distress unheard and dismissed. Additional layers of silencing may apply to the lives of women from cultural backgrounds in which the expression of distress is particularly prohibited. For instance, 'saving face', the ability to maintain valued public appearance for the sake of oneself and one's family is extremely important to most Asian groups (Kramer, Kwong, Lee, & Chung, 2002). In these communities, open displays of emotion are discouraged in order to prevent the exposure of weakness and to maintain social and familial harmony (Kramer et al., 2002). It has been argued that African-American women may also face additional pressures to 'keep it together' for the sake of their families and communities (Beauboeuf-Lafontant, 2007a, 2007b; Collins, 2000; hooks, 1982, 1993). The following excerpts are from interviews with Black women about experiences of depression and distress. They point to the repeated theme of the imperative of strength among Black women, and the ways in which this requirement stifles women's expressions of distress.

A strong Black woman is someone who *endures* a lot . . . A strong Black woman would be like, 'Oh, well, you know, that's what's given to me, and I'm going to endure. And *that's* what makes me strong.' (21, single, no children)

(Beauboeuf-Lafontant, 2007a, p. 37)

46

I think Black women are stronger [than Whites]. They've been, I mean, I'm talking about going back with generations so you were raised to be, you know, the strength of the home, the mother.

(Schreiber, Noerager Stern, & Wilson, 2000, p. 41)

I think it all relates back down to slavery when we had to be strong for our kids . . . we had to protect them, had to be strong for them. We couldn't show that we were . . . actually feeling inside and just basically had to hold the family together. And it's just been installed into the daughters . . . that *you* need to be strong, to hold your family together. You can't depend on no man . . . *You* need to be strong'.

(Edge & Rogers, 2005, p. 19)

As these women's own descriptions suggest, the image of the 'Strong Black Woman' has been traced back to slavery when women were forced to do the same work as men (hooks, 1982). While upper-class White women were regarded as frail, Black women were forced into hard physical labour and frequently subjected to systemic sexual and physical torture. To account for the disregard of Black women *as women*, they were reduced to 'masculinized sub-human creatures' (hooks, 1982, p. 71); as 'the mules of the world' (Neale Hurston, 1937). This representation justified and naturalized the oppression of Black women (Collins, 2000). In resisting this racist depiction, Black communities in contrast, celebrated their women's ability to withstand and endure. As the centre-point of communities, Black mothers, othermothers,[4] and community mothers have been charged with the task of raising the next generation of Black children in a process that both empowers and is empowering – a movement captured by the motto of the National Association of Colored Women (NCCW), 'lifting as we climb' (Edwards, 2004). In this way, Black women's motherwork has been a form of political activism and resistance against White oppression (Collins, 2000). Thus, 'the stereotypical image of the 'strong' Black woman . . . became the new badge of black female glory' (hooks, 1982, p. 6). 'Motherhood, as a consequence, is a site of power for black women' (O'Reilly, 2004c, p. 172).

The reframing of Black women's experience in terms of strength (rather than in the dehumanizing terms of slavery) is typically regarded as a positive and empowering step. However, Black feminist scholars have recently turned their attention to the costs and consequences of the 'Strong Black Woman' ideal on women's lives. For instance, bell hooks (1993) has argued that this glorified image provides a mask to hide women's suffering. Similarly, in her analysis of Black women's accounts of depression, Tamara Beauboef-Lafontant (2007a, 2007b) has argued that the discourse of the 'Strong Black Woman' normalizes and erases the distress that comes from living a life that is almost exclusively other-oriented. She has described how the expectation that Black women should be strong and care for their families and communities impedes their ability to care for themselves, express distress, or ask for help. She explained, 'the discourse of strength asserts that when struggle is so omnipresent and needs so profound, how can a woman – in good faith – focus on herself?' (Beauboef-Lafontant, 2007a, p. 42). To rupture the image of the 'Strong Black Woman' is to admit weakness, be 'selfish', and ultimately, to let down the community. As one woman in her study said,

> So, I'm supposed to figure it out, and *really* that's what I've been doing. I've been *forcing* myself to figure out how I'm doing what I'm doing. Because *people expect me to be this person*, you know, I'm not. If I was to, say, for instance, lose my apartment. Or if I was to lose my car. Or my lights went out. My people would freak out. Because that's not supposed to [happen]. I'm *too strong* for that. And, you know, I have this, all this *power* to make things different. And I'm not supposed to suffer like other people. (29, divorced mother)
>
> (Beauboef-Lafontant, 2007a, p. 40)

Further, Beauboef-Lafontant argued that this focus on strength and resilience can obscure women's views of injustice, and consequently, their abilities to react against them.

> Given that mustering through adversity was so critical to earning of the badge of a 'real' Black woman, many interviewees were hampered in their abilities to openly discuss injustice in their lives and take action to challenge those conditions that were unfair but deemed as inevitable.
>
> (Beauboef-Lafontant, 2007a, p. 40)

Therefore, the celebrated image of the 'Strong Black Woman' operates as a complex site in which 'dominant ideologies are simultaneously resisted and reproduced' (Collins, 2000, p. 86). She is an agent of resistance against racial oppression, while at the same time, she can be used and abused as a pawn of sexist oppression. Either way, she serves as a constant reminder to Black women to be strong, to swallow pain, and to keep going.

> Black women will not talk, will not show their depression . . . Because I think they feel that they always have to be together . . . A Black woman will not *let* someone know they're depressed. They will just go through the motions of life.
>
> (Beauboeuf-Lafontant, 2007b, p. 22)

I do think that Black people *get* depression, but I don't think that we're allowed to *have* depression. I think it's quite a matriarchal society and therefore *you've* got to cope. *You've* got to sort your family out, and so therefore *you are not allowed* to be depressed.

(Edge & Rogers, 2005, p. 19)

Since women's distress is so often un-speak-able, it is not only dismissed and silenced by others but it is often rendered incomprehensible to women themselves. For women who are striving toward the ideal of the 'Strong Black Women', feelings of distress and exhaustion may be normalized and ignored as legitimate concerns requiring attention (Beauboeuf-Lafontant, 2007a, 2007b). Similarly, some of the White women I interviewed in Canada suggested that they were confused by their depressive experiences given their apparently 'normal' lives. For instance, in the first excerpt below, Emily stated that she did not consider that she was depressed, given that her life appeared satisfying from the outside. In the second excerpt, Heather struggled to understand why she became depressed in the absence of serious problems such as trauma or abuse. Both these women expressed difficulties in understanding their depressive experiences, given the invisibility of their everyday work as women and the apparent compatibility of their lives with the image of the 'good life' so often presented.

ML: Would you consider yourself to have been depressed at that point?
At that point, definitely. I was depressed but ...
ML: Did you understand it in that way?
No! I didn't. Well maybe I, I, maybe it sort of tweaked in my brain. But I thought, you think to yourself, what do you have to be depressed about? Here you are, you've got a good career, you're making good money, you're respected in what you do, you have all kinds of friends, and the kids as I mentioned before the kids coming hanging around on Friday night, bringing their girlfriends or boyfriends to introduce them to me. You know, that type thing, you, you have got so much going for you, what do you have to be depressed about? And my mother! Also mentioned, said that to me one day, she said, 'Oh Emily, I don't know what you would have to be depressed about'.

(Emily)

But you know it would be so much easier if I had **something** to- and I remember thinking this too, if I could just blame something for this. If I could blame that I was **abused** or that I was some-, I- I can't I **really** clear- **I can't**. I really have nothing to blame.

ML: That would have been easier in a way or?

I don't know, maybe I don't know. See now that sounds rea:::lly bad. Like I'm thinking it would have been easier had I been abused. Not that way.

ML: No, no just to understand the depression.

Maybe, maybe it would have been easier to understand if I ... had, you know if I had a real definite reason for being depressed. Maybe things were just too:: good for me, I don't know.

ML: Well, it sounds like when you were really down you were thinking like why, why is this happening and you didn't have anything to point to and so that would have been confusing.

For sure yeah, absolutely, absolutely. Which made me look inward because I had no outward ... you know I wasn't being abused, I wasn't in a bad relationship like you know I didn't have any of that stuff. I had a very charmed life.

(Heather)

When a woman's life fits within the parameters of 'the good woman's good life', she may be left without ways of understanding feelings of distress and dissatisfaction. Thus, discourses of femininity can be seen to silence and subvert women's pain in multiple ways. First, discourses of femininity are centrally involved in how women are constructed by others and how they understand themselves. Their daily experiences are viewed through a shared, socially constructed lens of what it means to be a woman, and it is taken-for-granted that women will be contented and fulfilled in their prescribed roles. Second, discourses of femininity require the enactment of a circumscribed set of practices of femininity. Often ignored are the ways in which this endless labour taxes the limited energies of the physical body. Women's work is rendered invisible – outside of the scope of accounting as a legitimate source of distress. Further, the splitting of women into Madonna or whore, angel or monster, leaves women no room to express distress and dissatisfaction, and to make changes in their lives without also invoking moral judgement (Ussher, 2006).

When a woman tries to understand her depressive experiences, her everyday life often remains invisible as a possible source of her depletion and distress (Stoppard, 2000). Indeed, she may see 'no reason' for her experience at all, often leading to the conclusion that her depression must be chemical in origin. Bea, who understood her depressive experiences purely within a medical frame, spoke of her experiences as both incomprehensible (to herself and family members) and unwarranted. She described having been depressed decades ago when her children were small and having searched for a long time for a legitimate way to understand and alleviate it.

After I was married I remember taking the little boys to a park and sitting there and crying and crying and crying. And lots of times my husband would say, 'What are you crying for?'. But I wouldn't know why I was crying eh? And then I'd want to go for a lo::ng drive, a lo:: ng car drive just to get away from the house and as soon as we started nearing the house again I'd get this ((taps her chest)) like a tight feeling, probably just like a, almost like a panic attack because I had to go back. And um, so I probably was wanting to run, run run from it [and then I remember

ML: Run from your house?]

Yeah run from the house. I suppose because I was blaming everything, the the housework and I was tired and you know I had a:ll that ahead of me to do and I remember getting the children off to school. And going back to bed and sleeping till noon then having to get up and getting them something to eat and going back to bed. Just so ti:red, ti::red, ti:::red.

ML: Just scraping by.

Yeah and I used to say if somebody came to the door with a million dollars I'd have to say 'Look I'm sorry I'm', I just couldn't go anywhere with them. So I went to the doctor then. And that would be way back in sixty-five I guess. And he, I told him I said 'My blood must be low because I ca::n't get out of bed I'm so tired' And he said 'No it's your nerves' see and I said 'Oh no, it couldn't be my nerves.' Because I wasn't screaming or hollering or crying or anything just so:: ti:::red, couldn't get enough sleep so he put me on a medication, I'm sure it was phenobarbitone I think. And then I'd go to a doctor after that. And I'd say 'Ah oh I would get so a::ngry:: and just terrible, terrible rages, rages, rages and then I'd be OK'. And he said 'Just like Jekyll and Hyde' and I said 'Yes it would be.' So he said, 'Count five days before your period and start taking pills to help you through it'. .hhhh Well that didn't help, that didn't help but it. Was just I knew when these spells were coming on because I'd I'd feel the

51

heaviness in my chest you see and oh it was just an awful feeling and I used to say to my mother, ah ah, 'Mom there's something wro:::ng with me'. And she said 'Well there shouldn't be you've got a good husband, he works, you've got three healthy children, there shouldn't be anything wrong with you'. So I couldn't relate to anyone, ah, my feelings or anything.

(Bea)

Throughout her interview, Bea talked about her intense distress and her difficulties in understanding what was wrong with her. In this excerpt, she portrays her feelings of depression, panic and rage as bubbling up, but without an apparent source ('And lots of times my husband would say, "what are you crying for?" But I wouldn't know why I was crying eh?'). Bea's daily life, described earlier as consumed with care for her husband, children, foster children, as well as those she cared for as a day-care provider remained taken-for-granted and outside the scope of accounting. She describes being tired, angry, and distressed, and yet has no words with which she can express these feelings without being positioned as abject – the selfish monster mother ('and I used to say to my mother, ah ah, "Mom there's something wro:::ng with me." And she said "Well there shouldn't be you've got a good husband, he works, you've got three healthy children, there shouldn't be anything wrong with you."'). Caught between the options of the idealized 'good' woman identity (the beatific mother who is able to care and cope with patience and equanimity) and the bad (the selfish mother-monster who is impatient, aggressive, and angry), she is left silenced and misunderstood. She said, 'So I couldn't relate to anyone, ah, my feelings or anything'. Given the invisibility of the conditions of her life within a patriarchal society, understandings of her rage, tiredness, and panic are stripped of context and readily reconstructed within a medical frame as vestiges of her fecund female body – as symptoms of PMS.

In her account of her distress, Bea references 'Premenstrual Syndrome' ('PMS') and feeling 'just like Jekyll and Hyde'. The metaphor of the monstrous feminine appears repeatedly in investigations of women's experiences of distress, and of premenstrual change in particular (Chrisler & Caplan, 2002; Swann & Ussher, 1995; Ussher, 2006). In her extensive research on women's experiences of menstruation and PMS, Jane Ussher (2006) found repeated references to the Jekyll–Hyde character in women's accounts.

Dr Jekyll to Mr Hyde. Horrible, bitchy, vicious, violent and depressed.

I am like two people, my normal self and this impatient, uptight person.

It is like having a Jekyll and Hyde personality.

I'm just stressed and anxious – not a pleasant person to be around. Its like Dr Jekyll and Mr Hyde.

(Ussher, 2006, p. 47)

The construction of women's distress as a medical problem (e.g., PMS) serves to decontextualize their pain and eclipse the realities of women's everyday lives. However, it may also provide refuge for women who fall from the pedestal. For Bea, the bifurcation of her identity into true-self and monstrous-self serves to protect her from being vilified for feeling and expressing anger and distress. Like Dr Jekyll, she constructs her true self as placid, calm, and content. Like the interloper Mr Hyde, her anger is situated as the product of biochemical processes. Thus, it is not *her*, but her dangerous and unruly body that is at fault for her decidedly unfeminine and unmotherly rage (Ussher, 2003a, 2006). By drawing on the metaphor of the chemically induced monster, Bea (although not necessarily intentionally) protects her identity from being positioned as abject. She can maintain the identity of the 'good' mother, despite her feelings of depression, since these are constructed as 'spells' and as distinctly apart from her sense of self. However, this protection is at a cost. Constructed as monstrous, her body requires scrutiny and containment and her only option for responsible action is to submit to the expertise of the medical profession.

THE MEDICALIZATION OF WOMEN'S MISERY[5]

From the early beginnings of what is now known as the biomedical model and beyond, women's bodies have been scrutinized and pathologized (Foucault, 1980b; Ussher, 1991, 2006). Regarded as the source of women's madness, badness, or weakness, the female body has been constructed as in need of medical surveillance. Premenstrual syndrome (PMS), premenstrual dysphoric disorder (PMDD), and post-natal depression are but a few of the recent labels used to regulate and ultimately control the female body and the woman within (Ussher, 2003a, 2003b, 2006). Despite a lack of scientific evidence to support this contention, women are regularly constructed as moody, irrational, and out-of-control, particularly around times of change in women's bodies: menstruation, pregnancy and menopause (Chrisler & Caplan, 2002; Ussher, 2006). This idea is ubiquitous in Western culture, appearing in literature as well as popular jokes, television sitcoms, movies, and advertisements. Stories of women driven mad by corporeal fluctuations abound in media representations as well as in the court system where PMS and PMDD have been used to successfully defend women's madness and badness (for reviews of the historical, cultural, political, legal, and economic roots of the social construction of PMS, PMDD, and postpartum depression, see Chrisler & Caplan, 2002, and Ussher, 2006). The medicalization of women's distress, including depression, serves to direct a scrutinizing gaze on the minutiae of women's bodily functions, while occluding the larger realities of women's lives. This myopic view ultimately supports women's oppression by leaving patriarchy intact and blaming women's bodies for their distress. When women's distress is understood in terms of bodily malfunctions, all distress can become viewed in this way, and women are left without grounds for arguing for real change in their lives. As one woman noted,

> Um . . . ah, yeah, [partner] would blame everything on getting my periods. You know, it's . . . and so, you know, to me, it seems as if I was irrational all the time . . . He'd go, 'Now, how long till your periods?' and it'd be two weeks away. And he'd pick up on it like that. And everything would be blamed on that. So, in other words, he was saying to me, 'Well, I'm not going to take you seriously, because you're premenstrual.'
>
> (Ussher, Perz, & Mooney-Somers, 2007, p. 154)

Ultimately, a biomedical understanding has the effect of pathologizing women's unhappiness and obscuring from view the depressing conditions of their lives (Caplan, 1995; Chesler, 1972; Ussher, 1991, 2003a, 2006). Instead of allowing substantive changes in women's lives, it encourages them to self-monitor and self-regulate, for instance, with antidepressants. Medicating women's misery, without changing the conditions that so often produce it, ultimately has the effect of 'paving over pain', directing women to be modern-day versions of Stepford Wives who manage their lives in a calm, docile, pleasant manner (Ussher, 2006).

Therefore, in addition to discourses of femininity that offer women little room to manoeuvre in legitimate ways, the biomedical model provides another set of dominant cultural assumptions that compound the invisibility and illegitimacy of women's distress. Understandings of women's distress rooted in biomedical models erase the conditions of women's lives, pathologize their bodies, and subject them to regulation by the medical model (eg., drug therapy, ECT). Moreover, the very assumptions of biomedicine provide yet another layer of illegitimacy shrouding women's pain (Lafrance, 2007a, 2007b). Although depression has been situated within the domain of biomedicine as a 'disorder', it has not been afforded the same legitimacy as other 'medical conditions' (e.g., heart attack, cancer) and remains suspect. Repeated throughout women's narratives of depression were stories of having their pain dismissed and disregarded. While Bea situated her depression as a medical condition, she lamented not having this understanding honoured and shared by others.

> If you suffer from migraine headaches or say if you were diabetic you could say to a person 'Oh, I've got a terrible migraine again' or 'My diabetes is acting up.' But with depression just to say 'Oh I'm depressed,' that doesn't go with people. 'Oh come on, come on you promised, you're you're well, there's nothing wrong with you, you promised, you can go, you can go.' See?
> *ML: What do you think the difference is there?*
> With?
> *ML: Between people being able to say 'I've got a migraine or my diabetes or' and*
> Well, they accept that. But just to say, 'Well I'm depressed,' ah, they feel well ... 'Good kick in the butt. You **can** do it, get up and you you **can** go. There's nothing to prevent you from doing it. [...] You haven't got the flu, you haven't got the cold. What's preventing you?' So they **don't understand**.
>
> (Bea)

In this excerpt, Bea compares depression to the medical conditions of migraine, diabetes, flu, and cold. Where the latter are proposed as legitimate excuses for inactivity or dysfunction, the former is not. The discursive strategy of comparing oneself to others ('social comparison') has been explored as a way of constructing one's identity and experiences (Widdicombe & Wooffitt, 1990; Wood & Kroger, 2000). For instance, Wood and Rennie (1994) found social comparison at work in their research with women who had been raped by men they knew and dated. Drawing on the dominant construction of the 'Hollywood rape' (involving being attacked by a stranger, not using protection, ejaculation), participants struggled to identify their experience within this frame. In expressing their difficulty in securing legitimacy and understanding, participants drew comparisons between their experiences and the 'Hollywood rape'. In the same way, Bea compares depression with what are seen as more legitimate medical illnesses. In constructing an imagined dialogue between herself and an unsympathetic other, Bea contrasts the ease with which some sufferers garner understanding, and the inability of those with depression to do the same. Claims of distress ('Oh I'm depressed') are countered with a barrage of dismissive retorts ('Oh come on, come on you promised . . .'). Without tangible evidence that depression is outside one's control ('What's preventing you?'), the sufferer remains inseparable from the suffering and is readily positioned as responsible for her own dysfunction. In the following two excerpts, depression is again compared to medical conditions with the consistent effect of presenting depression as misunderstood, stigmatized, and dismissed.

> It's a hell of a thing to have. It's a really bad thing. I'd far sooner deal with any of my physical ailments than I would depression. Depression's hard.
> ML: What makes it so much harder?
> Well, I find it's so personal. Nobody can understand how bad you're feeling. And like you can go to a doctor, you got bad asthma, you can't breathe? They can understand that. They can see it, they can feel bad for you and they can really try to help you without feeling so::rry for you. When you're feeling depressed, people don't understand they figure you've just got the blues and you're not dealing with it.
>
> (Joanne)

> The male employees have the heart attacks. They've got this wound that they can bear and people send them flowers and you know come visit them in the hospital. Women have nervous breakdowns. Nobody talks about that, no:body sends you flowers, no:body comes to visit you, no:body even barely talk to you because they're too scared to because you might fly off the deep end. With men, [in a sympathetic tone] 'Hey that poor man has had a heart attack.'
>
> (Emily)

Across these excerpts, participants claim a biomedical understanding of their depressive experiences while at the same time situating depression as beyond the limits of what constitutes a proper medical condition. In examining the discursive structure of these accounts, it appears that the key for establishing legitimacy within a medical discourse is the degree to which sufferers have access to tangible evidence of the 'reality' of their distress and dysfunction. Joanne compares depression, a subjective 'personal' condition, to asthma which she states can be observed and therefore understood ('They can understand that. They can see it'). Similarly, Emily constructs depression as a stigmatized experience by comparing it to a heart attack which leaves the afflicted person with a 'wound' to 'bear'. Therefore, when the source of one's distress or dysfunction is directly observable, the sufferer's character is not questioned and is deemed worthy of sympathy and understanding. However, without objective evidence that one's condition is beyond one's control (e.g., blood test, X-ray), a sufferer's pain and identity remain suspect (Lafrance, 2007a, 2007b).

ASSUMPTIONS OF BIOMEDICINE: WHEN OBJECTIVE SCIENCE FAILS SUBJECTIVE EXPERIENCE

The medical model currently dominates public discourse of illness and health and the assumptions of this model shape the ways sufferers understand themselves and are understood. In an extensive deconstruction of the biomedical model, Gordon (1988) identified two central 'tenacious assumptions in Western medicine'. The first, naturalism, assumes fundamental distinctions between nature/spirit, body/mind, and objectivity/subjectivity, with the former of each pair privileged over the latter. Within the assumption of naturalism, matters of the body are considered more 'real' than matters of the mind, and the best way to know the true nature of reality is through objective means. Accordingly, disease is identified through observation of data offered directly by the body, rather than through the secondary and confounded means of subjective reports.

The second assumption, individualism, further assumes the primacy of the individual and individual freedom (Gordon, 1988). In order for humans to reflect objectively on nature (and themselves) they must be able to separate themselves from their subjective and cultural context. Individuals are viewed as independent from, and even imposed upon by, the societies in which they live. Disengagement from social and cultural determination is not only a goal of 'good science' but also a goal of Western life in the form of self-actualization (Kitzinger, 1992). Western individualism dictates that one should stand apart from the crowd, exert one's own will, and follow one's own path. The idealization of the self-contained, self-regulated individual ultimately serves to maintain the capitalist status quo, holding individuals responsible for their own plight, while also producing more productive citizens (Blum & Stracuzzi, 2004; Gardner, 2003; Rowe, Tilbery, Rapley, & O'Ferrall, 2003). The management of one's own health has become a requirement of the self-regulated individual. Therefore, health has become conceptualized as a commodity that one has (one *has* good health) and a project for the self to work on (Brown, 1999). Taken together, the assumptions of biomedicine have led to our present conceptualizations of health and illness whereby it appears 'that medicine has replaced the Church as society's moral arbiter: disease is the contemporary sin, and health the new religious salvation' (Findlay & Miller, 1994, p. 296). Accordingly, efforts to ensure and maintain one's health have become a moral imperative for the individual.

Thus, naturalism and individualism form a dominant and mutually supporting set of constructs that determine the nature of legitimate reality (materiality), the legitimate way of knowing this reality (objectivity), and the implications for those whose illness experiences fall outside the parameters of these assumptions (stigma and delegitimation). When an experience of pain or dysfunction is identified as having a clearly biological etiology, it is deemed legitimate and the sufferer is seen as legitimately sick (Kirmayer, 1988). People who are sick have the right to be excused from responsibilities and are not to be blamed for their illness. However, problems arise for those whose experiences of illness or distress fall outside biomedical criteria for legitimacy (i.e., those without the requisite 'signs' of organic pathology). Health problems not adequately accounted for by problems of the body are relegated to being problems of the mind, and readily dismissed as 'not real' (Good, Brodwin, Good, & Kleinman, 1992; Kleinman, 1992; Radley & Billig, 1996). Furthermore, the construction of body and mind as opposing poles of human experience raises moral questions concerning volition, intention, and agency, whereby problems of the body tend to be seen as involuntary or accidental whereas problems of the mind are readily constructed as voluntary or intentional (Kirmayer, 1988).

Reliance on objectivity to delineate the 'reality' of a person's pain has as one consequence the delegitimation of a host of forms of illness, pain, and distress which do not have a clearly identifiable physical etiology (Lafrance, 2007a, 2007b). Moreover, the authority of biomedicine to arbitrate 'truth' and its guise of scientific neutrality combine to ensure that it is the patient, not the biomedical model, that is blamed when subjective experience does not fit within the boundaries of medical legitimacy (Kirmayer, 1988; May, Doyle, & Chew-Graham, 1999). An untenable situation is thereby created in which sufferers of multiple forms of distress and pain are 'stranded from any means of legitimation' (Cohn, 1999, p. 195). Accordingly, chronic, psychological, and stress or lifestyle-related illnesses (e.g., anxiety, depression, chronic fatigue, chronic pain, fibromyalgia, migraine, etc.) occupy 'a morally ambiguous realm' of reality (Kirmayer, 1988, p. 62). Research on the subjective experiences of such conditions is dominated by the issue of sufferers' struggles for legitimacy (Cohn, 1999; Horton-Salway, 2001, 2002; Jackson, 1992; Kleinman, 1992; Kleinman, Brodwin, Good, & Good, 1992; Radley & Billig, 1996; Rogers, May & Oliver, 2001; Toombs, Barnard & Carson, 1995; Ware, 1992, 1993, 1999; Wellard, 1998). For example, in a study of individuals' experiences of depression in the context of primary care, Rogers et al. (2001) reported that there was 'evidence that people felt they had the wrong type of problem and that the right sort was essentially a physical one' (p. 324). One participant in their study said,

When I get there [referring to doctor's office], I get the feeling that there's nothing wrong with me. I wish I had got something physical to show. Sometimes, when we are in the car, I hope we crash. I really have hoped we crash and that I wouldn't die, but that something would happen that would give me a real reason for being off work and feeling the way I do.

(Rogers et al., 2001, p. 324)

Delegitimation was also a common theme in Ware's (1992) investigation of people's accounts of chronic fatigue. Often, participants complained about not being believed or taken seriously because they did not 'look sick' and were not visibly disabled. Echoing the patterns of speech identified in the present study, a participant in Ware's study stated,

Because I'm not in agony or carrying a broken leg, there's always that little doubt, 'Well how bad really *is* it?' I tell you – it's bad. It's bad. I'm sure if I had a rash, or was vomiting, or my arm dropped off, it would be a lot easier for people to be nice to me.

(Ware, 1992, p. 351)

Similarly, Jackson (1992) explored the central concern for patients with chronic pain: 'how "real' or 'unreal' their pain is seen to be' (Jackson, 1992, p. 138). Where 'real' pain is signified by a physical etiology, by default, 'unreal' pain is regarded as imaginary, mental, psychosomatic – an 'all-in-your-head' type of pain. In an attempt to defend the 'reality' of pain experienced, one patient at a chronic pain treatment centre stated,

I disagreed with their big philosophies . . . Dr. V said pain isn't physical – you can't set pain down, look at it. But I said, 'well I see pain as part of the workings of the body, like electricity. You can't see electricity, but you grab the end of a wire in a machine, and it'll hurt you.'

(Jackson, 1992, p. 138)

In these accounts, sufferers struggle to validate their experience in light of a dominant set of assumptions that readily situate their suffering as imaginary, self-inflicted, or the product of malingering. When subjective experience does not fit into the assumptions of 'objective science', it is readily dismissed, and the dismissal of people's pain only serves to compound their distress. As Kleinman (1995) states, the delegitimation of such forms of distress and dysfunction is 'illness-enhancing . . . [it] intensifies suffering. Indeed, it re-creates suffering in a wholly other mode: illegitimate suffering' (pp. 181–2).

When people experience depression, they often do so in a context of misunderstanding and scepticism, leaving them bereft of legitimate ways of understanding and expressing their experiences. For women, the silencing of their pain appears particularly pronounced. It is notable that women predominate among various forms of 'illegitimate suffering', including depression (Kessler et al., 1993), anxiety (Silverman & Carter, 2006), chronic fatigue syndrome (Ware & Kleinman, 1992), fibromyalgia (Meisler, 1999; Reiffenberger & Amundson, 1996), migraine (Meisler, 1999), and vertigo (Yardley, 1997b; Yardley & Beech, 1998). Thus, it is important to consider that women predominate among such marginalized forms of distress – or alternatively, that forms of distress common among women tend to be socially marginalized.

The marginalization of women's distress was evident in Emily's interview when she compared her experience of depression with that of her mother's migraines. With both forms of pain rooted in women's lives and outside the parameters of legitimate medical illness, both tend to be disregarded as illegitimate. On the heels of her contrast between men who have 'heart attacks' (legitimate suffering) and women who have 'nervous breakdowns' (illegitimate suffering) discussed above, Emily told a story of the inability of her mother to interrupt her domestic responsibilities despite her pain.

> The male employees have the heart attacks. They've got this wound that they can bear and people send them flowers and you know come visit them in the hospital. Women have nervous breakdowns. Nobody talks about that, no:body sends you flowers, no:body comes to visit you, no:body even barely talk to you because they're too scared to because you might fly off the deep end. With men, [in a sympathetic tone] 'Hey that poor man has had a heart attack.' So I think [doctor] is a little bit more compassionate for the females. I mean she's a, she's she's a very good doctor and she does look after her male patients that are out on stress leave and have **had** heart attacks but I think she's a little bit more sympathetic to the females. Because, haha notwithstanding it's 2001, our lot in life is still the same, in my opinion.
> *ML: Our lot in life is still the same, [what do you mean?]*
> As, as ahhh] well I remember my mother when I was growing up, six kids, brought up on a farm my father worked in the woods, so mom pretty much milked the cows, looked after **six** kids, she suffered from migraine headaches, I remember she, **now I know** she had really severe periods each month. She, she taught school for awhile. She out in the middle of

the back woods in summer and winter, it was not fun. And I remember he::r, we came home from school some days and she would be lying on the floor in what we called the parlour, with things up over the windows because she was having such a bad migraine. She was throwing up, she couldn't move and then be Jesus ... three-quarters of an hour later she'd **have** to be better because she'd **have** to get up, she'd **have** to see that the cows were milked at night, she'd **have** to make supper for these six kids and all this and that. So 'OK, dear you want to have a nervous breakdown, you go over stand in **that** corner and you've got approximately one hour do it and get it over with OK? Then we expect you to be back here in front of the stove doing your thing.' You know what I'm saying?

(Emily)

Emily equates the misunderstanding and silencing of her distress with that of her mother. Both women suffered in contexts in which their pain and the silencing of their pain were tied to their lives as women. Emily's account also points to the ways in which materiality and discourse intersect. Her mother was constrained by her social position as the primary care-giver in the home. This constraint operated both materially (left alone, she had to tend to the farm – the cows needed milking and the children needed feeding) and discursively ('we expect you to be back here in front of the stove doing your thing'). Further, Emily's account illustrates the delegiti-mation posed by the medical model. Without a 'wound to bear', women are denied respite and are left with little choice but to carry on. Taken as a whole, then, the present analysis highlights how women are silenced by two dominant and mutually supporting sets of discourses: discourses of femin-inity and discourses of biomedicine. A further illustration of the inter-section of these socially constructed ways of understanding is also evident in Evelyn's interview.

As I talk with other people about depression, I find other people have said that to me. That they find that there's no excuse because you're just depressed, so that's no reason to lay around with your feet up.

ML: *There's no excuse for not ...*

For not having dinner on the table, or the laundry done, or trucking kids around and going to parent/teacher interviews, and whatever because you're just depressed. You know what I mean, like you don't have a broken leg, you look fine, so. I also found that in my recovery phase very difficult to handle, um when people would say how great I looked. [...] So that added more pressure that well, maybe it's all in my head. (Laughs) I said to [psychiatrist] one day [...] I said 'I think maybe this whole thing's in my head'. And he's got such a great sense of humour [...] and he looked at me and he said 'Well, where do you think it is, in your big toe?' Like it was just so funny. And I had to laugh. But it makes- that just adds more pressure to you to get better quicker. When people say how great you look it ah on one aspect it's a great compliment but on the other hand it ah really adds more pressure. Because if I look so damn good how come I feel so crappy. And maybe it is all in my head maybe I'm ... I'm holding myself back like maybe there's something I'm not doing maybe I::'m not doing something to make myself well quicker. [...] Whereas if you have a broken le::g, well there it is. You know it heals on its own. And you can see how it's healing. But when it's depression nobody else can monitor it. So, you know it's just such a it's the most difficult thing to get over I **ever** experienced **in my life**.

(Evelyn)

While Evelyn identifies her experience within a medical frame as clinical depression, she states that this way of accounting remains on the fringes of legitimacy. The centrality of objective evidence for claiming legitimate patient status is again at work in this account. Without tangible evidence of the 'reality' of her dysfunction ('you don't have a broken leg, you look fine'), Evelyn presents her claims of distress as not credible. The objective evidence that she 'looked good' and her subjective experience of 'feeling bad' are presented as irreconcilable, leading her to the threatening conclusion that she is perhaps responsible for her own pain. She is therefore left with 'no excuse' for not being able to function as a woman – 'for not having dinner on the table, or the laundry done, or trucking kids around and going to parent/teacher interviews'. Instead, her dis-ability is readily constructed in moral tones as laziness and failed femininity ('lay around with your feet up'). Thus, discourses of femininity and biomedicine converge in this account, resulting in the invisibility of her daily life as a source of distress, and the marginalization of her distress within a biomedical frame. Evelyn is silenced on two fronts: unable to safely point to her life or to her body as a legitimate source of distress. In this way, her pain is readily dismissed and undermined as mere fabrication (all in her head) or as an excuse to shirk domestic responsibilities (a bad mother). She is left constructed as either mad or bad. Therefore, women who are depressed (or who suffer from other forms of marginalized distress) appear to be doubly victimized; once by their pain and once again by an interlocking set of discourses that deny their pain.

SILENCING THE SELF, MASKING THE PAIN

Bereft of legitimate ways of understanding and expressing depression, women often spoke of hiding it instead. Many spoke of wearing a 'mask' or going into a 'shell'. For instance, in excerpts referred to earlier, Susan said she 'withdrew into a shell', and Joan talked about how she 'went into this shell and was very depressed'. In reference to her depressive experiences, Amanda said 'I hide it <very well>. When I did tell them [parents] a year later they still, they didn't believe they couldn't believe me because I I had put on a very good face'. Kate noted that when she has shared her depressive experiences with people, they have responded,

> 'What do you mean you have depression', you know, 'you're always lau::ghing and jo::king' and it's like, well, you know you can do tha::t and still be dead inside. Like you can do tha::t and then go home and sit like a zombie in front of the TV. Like it's, you know, there's me at work and then there's me at home and they're ... different people.
>
> (Kate)

Similarly, Emily stated,

> Sometimes you're, you're forced into doing things like going to the nephew's wedding or going to the fiftieth anniversary party. .hh not saying I enjoyed myself but you went, you put in an appearance and outwardly I looked like I was enjoying myself because I was talking to everybody, I was sheep herding everybody, I was looking after everybody, in my own little way I was still doing that. So outwardly everybody was saying 'Oh, Jeez, isn't that Emily great. She's looking after everybody and it's so nice to see her, she looks so great, she's always got a smile on her face'. Which I did, I always had a smile on my face but ahh that's- I did. I got through it. I got through it. I just got through it.
>
> (Emily)

In these excerpts, Kate and Emily talk of being of two selves: the woman in pain inside, and the smiling complacent woman on the surface. In their research with depressed women, Deanna Gammell and Janet Stoppard (1999) also identified hiding behind a mask as a recurrent theme in participants' accounts. One participant, Sarah, described forcing herself to maintain her work in the home even though she felt incapacitated by depression. Sarah said, 'And I just felt I couldn't function [at work] even though at home I probably put on a mask and I functioned. I just did. You know, pretend that everything was okay'. Similarly, in exploring one woman's narrative of postpartum depression, Natasha Mauthner (2003) found that

> even though she wanted to confide her feelings, her sense of shame and fear of moral condemnation prevented her from reaching out. Instead Sonya told me, she put on a 'mask' and 'played the role' of the coping mother. 'I can act if you like,' she said, 'I can appear okay to the rest of the world even though I feel terrible inside.'
>
> (pp. 88–9)

By approaching women's accounts from a discursive perspective, the reasons behind women's 'sense of shame and fear of moral condemnation' come into view as the result of an interlocking set of discourses that require women to behave in circumscribed ways and then deny their pain when they do or vilify them when they do not. Wearing a mask, like silencing the self, can be regarded as a way of coping in a context of pervasive delegitimation. However, the work of adopting a mask is exhausting, and women often struggle to keep it in place (Gammell & Stoppard, 1999). Moreover, the need to retreat behind a mask and its accompanying feelings of isolation and being misunderstood only serve to compound sufferers' distress.

> The thing is Michelle it's scary because how many times . . . have we heard, or I've heard that a person has committed suicide and ... it was always 'Oh they were such a wonderful person, my land I didn't know she was having any troubles or anything'. Right? So a person can really mask, or ah ... like portray the, portray the sce- the the scene that is normal, that should be seen right? You wouldn't want people to see that you're crying all the time, you're depressed and you're lonely when you shouldn't be lonely, you've got people around you all the time, you've got a family, why should you be sad? You've got a nice home so you you you don't want to portray that.
>
> (Bea)

CONCLUSION

In this chapter, I explored women's narratives of depression, attending to the material and discursive production of their lives. Violence against women, poverty, women's struggles in heterosexual relationships, and their everyday lives were all identified as central to women's depression. Each of these is shaped and regulated by discourses that construct men as inherently dominant, instrumental, and women as subservient, relational. These hegemonic constructions both reflect and support political, social, and interpersonal systems that condone, uphold, and indeed at times celebrate violence against women, women's economic oppression, their need to maintain and define themselves in terms of relationships, and their taken-for-granted work in the home. The splitting of women into the 'good' woman or the bad (Madonna or whore, mother or monster) results in a situation whereby women who step outside the confines of discourses of femininity are readily vilified, marginalized, and silenced. Moreover, the dominant understanding of depression as a biomedical problem serves to further eclipse the material realities of women's oppression while subverting their expressions of distress as 'not real'. In the face of such pervasive delegitimation, women struggle to be heard.

However, all of this is not to suggest that women cannot and do not speak out; it is not to suggest that they are passive victims to the power of patriarchy and its bedfellow biomedicine. As Foucault explained, 'Where there is power there is resistance' (1980b, p. 95). Not all women become depressed, and women who become depressed heal. Therefore, while it is important to recognize the power of such discourses to shape women's subjectivities, it is equally important to explore how such discourses are negotiated and resisted. It is important to appreciate how women are *silenced*, but it is equally important to understand how they *talk back*. The remaining chapters will focus on women's resistance through an examination of their stories of recovery from depression, wellness, and self-care. Listening to women's stories of health and healing provide unique opportunities to learn how women are able to negotiate and resist hegemonic discourses and how they can position themselves in ways that are more emancipatory and health promoting.

Notes

1 The first excerpt is from a participant in research conducted by Janet Stoppard and me on women's experiences of depression (Lafrance & Stoppard, 2007). The second excerpt is from my interview with Heather, a participant in my study on recovery from depression.

2 June Cleaver was a fictional character in the popular American television programme, *Leave it to Beaver*, which aired from 1957 to 1963. Typifying the

archetype of femininity, this character was devoted to her family and domestic perfection.

3 There are very few investigations of rates of depression in the East, however a study of a nationally representative sample of adults in Japan found that, like women in the West, women in Japan were also more likely to be depressed than their male counterparts (Inaba, Thoits, Ueno, Gove et al., 2005). However, it should be noted that the direct comparison of rates of depression across cultures is mired in problems as the expression of distress is culture-specific (Jenkins et al., 1991; Marecek 2006). For instance, the affective and cognitive expression of distress that typifies 'depression' is specific to modern Western society (Marecek, 2006). In South and East Asia, distress is often expressed in terms of pain or discomfort in the body (Jenkins et al., 1991; Marecek 2006).

4 In African-American communities, 'othermothers' care for children born to other women (Collins, 2000; James, 1993). It has been suggested that the tradition of caring for other people's children grew out of an African heritage of communal living as well as being a consequence of slavery (Edwards, 2004). When children were orphaned by sale or death of their parents, othermothers stepped in and laboured to ensure the care of their communities (Collins, 2000).

5 This phrase is taken from Pilgrim and Bentall's (1999) article 'The medicalisation of misery: A critical realist analysis of the concept of depression'.

CHAPTER 3

RECOVERY FROM DEPRESSION

As explored in the previous chapter, discourses of femininity shape women's lives and subjectivities in ways that both produce and deny their distress. Women's talk of depression was described as being entwined in discourses of femininity and marked by expressions of shame, guilt, inadequacy, frustration and depletion. In contrast, their talk of recovery involved the rupture or resistance of these discourses whereby women found ways to talk of themselves and their depression in a different language – language that enabled them to find footing with which they could express and act on their despair in new ways. Two central patterns of accounting emerged in the interviews. In the first, participants reasserted the legitimacy of depression within a medical model. In these accounts, recovery was heralded by the provision of a medical diagnosis that defined their experience as 'real' and their selves as blameless victims.[1] This line of accounting works to deflect the pervasive blame and castigation associated with women's experiences of depression and in particular their struggles, or inability, to maintain practices of femininity. The provision of a diagnosis offers a woman a means to legitimize her distress as outside the parameters of personal responsibility and to effect change in her life toward health. Importantly, the sick role allows a rupture in discourses of femininity whereby a woman may be excused from her usual roles and responsibilities and attend to her own health needs.[2] However, this line of accounting also comes with costs and pitfalls and I will explore the limitations of this way of understanding throughout this chapter.

In the second, and sometimes overlapping pattern of accounting, participants talked of recovery as a personally transformative experience. They described recovery as a process through which they threw off their 'good' woman selves and began to pay closer attention to their own needs, desires, and well-being. Here, the gendered nature of women's depression comes to the fore, instead of being hidden behind the veil of medicalization. Therefore, whereas discourses of femininity can be seen to be ruptured in the first pattern, they are resisted in the second. Women talked about having been the 'good' woman in the past, but in repositioning this usually revered identity in negative ways (for example as superficial, excessive, or pathetic), speakers opened up space for resistance. Where practices of femininity were described as central to depression, rejection of these practices was situated as pivotal for recovery. Women talked about the critical need for self-care: 'standing up' for themselves, 'letting go' of caring, cooking, and cleaning, 'saying no' to others' demands, and instead attending to their own health and well-being. That is, participants talked of prioritizing their own needs, a heretical notion for the 'good' woman.

In summary, women tended to describe recovery as either a re-naming of their experiences in medical terms, or as a re-authoring of their identities within a narrative of personal transformation. While these patterns can be regarded as divergent lines of accounting, both rest on the critical importance of legitimation. Although in different ways, both patterns of accounting work to negotiate legitimacy for speakers' distress, identities, and practices – legitimacy centrally threatened by hegemonic discourses of femininity. The focus of this chapter is on the construction and effect of these two patterns of accounting. By exploring women's narratives of recovery, I hope to show how the women I interviewed negotiated and resisted regimes of knowledge in their struggles to be well.

NARRATIVES OF RECOVERY THROUGH MEDICAL REMEDY

Participants' accounts of recovery repeatedly began with stories of having found means through which they could legitimately express and act on their distress – stories of being heard rather than silenced. A central way in which women's pain was validated was through the provision of a medical diagnosis. While the medicalization of women's distress has been roundly critiqued in feminist work as pathologizing women's distress and ignoring the oppressive conditions of their lives (Caplan, 1995; Oakley, 1986; Ussher, 1991; also see Chapter 2), many women do identify with a medical understanding of depression. Rather than simply dismiss these women's accounts and experiences as misguided, I would argue that it is important to listen to them – to hear why and how a medical construction may be useful and meaningful. Adopting a discursive perspective, I explored the ways in which women talked of depression as a biomedical problem and how this construction was involved in their recovery narratives. A strikingly common feature of these accounts was reference to the importance of 'having a name' for their condition.

> It was a validation that I had never had before and I had a
> **na:me**. It was like, you know, it's a bad attitude, it's not. I'm

not ... you know maladjusted, I'm not ill socially or whatever. It's just I'm depressed. And that's cool. Like it was really neat to have a name for that.

(Kate)

But I was glad when he [doctor] said [...] 'It's clinical depression'. And I think I was glad that I finally knew that I **did** have something wrong with me. That it was, yeah I had a name for it. And not just ti::red and la::zy and ... disinterested.

(Bea)

I was reading this book [that listed the diagnostic criteria of depression] and it was describing what I was going through [...] and all of a sudden I said 'Jeez, that's what's wrong. I'm depressed. That's what it is.' Just to be able to put a name on it? Because there are times when I thought I was different from everybody [...] But what I found in that book, I found that when you have the symptoms I had, that the way I was feeling in my condition was normal. See? I wasn't going crazy.

(Dianne)

These excerpts are representative of the way in which diagnosis was discussed by many participants. The effects of these instances of talk are two-fold. First, by highlighting that there is 'a name' for their distress, in addition to the use of the pronoun 'it', depression is objectified and constructed as an independent entity. That is, by invoking a medical diagnosis to account for their experiences, their pain becomes 'real-ized'. Bea's use of the descriptor 'clinical' also serves to elevate the ontological status of her distress to a verifiable reality (something which might be observed in a medical context). Thus, by arguing that depression is an experience that does fit within the bounds of the biomedical model, participants' accounts work to validate their pain as real.

Second, situated as having a reality of its own, depression is discursively isolated from the character of the sufferer. In these accounts, personal flaw and biological flaw are presented as competing hypotheses, and with the verification of the reality of one (biological flaw verified through diagnosis), the other (personal flaw) must be false. As described in the previous chapter, women's accounts of depression often centred on their feelings of badness, wrongness, and personal inadequacy. Many spoke of feeling different than others, even as children, and it was made clear that this difference was wrong. When one is fundamentally flawed (as a 'bad' woman, for instance), there is no hope for change. There is no feeling better. However, being repositioned as *having* a problem, rather than *being* a problem, the speaker's identity is protected. For instance, in drawing on a diagnosis, Kate defends against being constructed as having a 'bad attitude', being 'maladjusted' or 'ill socially'. Bea defends against the accusation that she is 'ti::red and la::zy and . . . disinterested', and Dianne is repositioned from 'different' to 'normal'. Thus, by isolating their condition from their identities, speakers are absolved of personal responsibility for their own distress – a threat lingering across accounts of depression.[3] Indeed, a diagnosis can provide assurance that a woman's pain is not of her own doing – that it is not fabricated, malingering, or 'all in her head'. It is notable that while depression is officially classified as a 'mental disorder' (APA, 2000), when women drew on a medicalized understanding of depression, it was always constructed as a biological illness, not a mental illness. Thus, the version of 'illness' promoted in participants' accounts served to protect them as legitimately 'sick', rather than 'mad' or 'bad'. Indeed, as Dianne stated, a diagnosis assured her that she 'wasn't going crazy'. This medicalized formulation of depression also appears in Joanne's account.

> It was kind of a relief to have somebody say, 'Yes, you have something seriously wrong, you know, this is what it is.' [...] There's something really wrong with me that they have even a name for it [...] It's a sense of relief that there is something **there** that people know about that you know you're not the only person in the world that's had it and you really do have something. You're not just making this up, you know. And that's kind of good because people do have a tendency to sort of look at you and say, 'Well, you just want attention.' Well no, attention's nice, but no, that was not the plan here. If I wanted attention I could dance on the table, I don't have to try and kill myself.
>
> (Joanne)

Here, reference to diagnosis enables Joanne to speak of her distress as 'something serious'; something known to be real since it is shared by others and identified in a taxonomy ('they even have a name for it'). As with the other accounts, Joanne notes the importance of having 'a name' for her experience, constructing it as an independent entity. In talking about her distress as an objective reality, she wards against having her experience constructed as merely her own subjective (mis)interpretation, and her self positioned as histrionic or malingering. Further, she defends against the accusation that she fabricated depression 'for attention' by drawing an extreme contrast between the triviality of attention seeking (dancing on tables) and the extent of her despair (suicide). The use of this contrast has the effect of further establishing the reality and severity of her pain. This pattern of discursive defence is repeated in Cynthia's account where she described her relief in having been diagnosed as depressed.

> Something in me made me go to the doctor and I went into her office and she sat down and she said 'What's the matter?' And I said 'How do you know if you are depressed?' And she said 'OK I have got ten questions to ask you.' And I was nine out of ten. [...] So she said, you know, 'You're depressed! There's no way out of it.' [...] So anyway, 'fi:ne' I said 'OK what do I have to do?'
> *ML: How did you react to that?*
> I was so relieved. I was so relieved I thought thank God! There's something wrong with me! I'm not- there- it's got a na:me. Like it's not that I am just a terrible, awful person who is unattractive, like I guess I thought my only problem was I didn't have a man in my life? (laughs)
>
> (Cynthia)

As in previous excerpts, Cynthia's distress is objectified and isolated from her character through her talk of diagnosis. Verification of this position is built up through reference to diagnostic criteria and the use of numbers as an objective measure of her distress. Her comment, 'I was nine out of ten' constructs her depression as both measurable (and therefore worthy of scientific/medical examination) and extreme. Her construction is further buttressed through her use of reported speech. 'Reported speech' or 'active voicing' (constructing one's account so that it can be heard as the reported talk of another person) has been examined as a discursive strategy through which 'speakers can establish the objective reality of a phenomenon' (Hutchby & Wooffitt, 1998, p. 225). By drawing on the reported speech of a medical authority, the fact of Cynthia's diagnosis is presented as the only possible understanding, one for which there is 'no way out'. By building up her experience as an external and imposing thing ('it's got a name') she defends against the unstated but apparently ever-present suggestion that her distress was the result of personal inadequacy – the result of being a 'terrible, awful person who is unattractive' and unable to secure 'a man'. Therefore, reference to diagnosis enables her to defend against being constructed as a representation of failed femininity. It is her body (over which she has no direct control) not her self that is at fault. In this way, a medical construction of depression can protect women from the consequences of stepping off the pedestal of the 'good' woman. That is, it provides the promise of refuge against the delegitimation and silencing that come from the contravention of discourses of femininity.

Further, when one is positioned as sick, or afflicted, one is able to take up actions to remedy one's condition. For instance, Cynthia recounted reacting to her diagnosis with both relief and a readiness to act ("fi:ne' I said 'OK what do I have to do?"). As in Cynthia's case, the first line of action for many was taking antidepressant medication. For some, this 'cure' was experienced as worse than the affliction, resulting in multiple foreign, distressing, and painful side effects. The accounts of these women are in concert with recent critiques of antidepressant medication that have found these to be no more effective than placebo (at best) and associated with death and increased risk of suicide (at worst) (Currie, 2005; Fergusson, Doucette, Cranley Glass, Shapiro et al., 2005; Healy, 2003; Healy & Aldred, 2005; Liebert & Gavey, 2006). For these reasons and others, some of the women I spoke with rejected the medical model, positioning themselves as survivors of medicalization as much as of depression. For other participants, medication was described as almost miraculous and integral to recovery. In these accounts, recovery was described as an externally imposed event that left speakers feeling better about themselves and the world around them. Agency in recovery was attributed to the medication, and consequently the speakers were constructed as somewhat passive recipients of its effects. For instance, Cynthia likened recovery to having layers of sadness peeled off her, and Kate equated recovery to being given sight after a long darkness.

> You never realize how bad you are feeling until you start feeling good? And it was so funny because at the ... beginning, like the first of April, the first of May, the first of June, it was like an onion peeling and <every month> almost to the day something would <lift again>? You know like another layer would lift off and I started feeling better and better and better.
>
> (Cynthia)

> And it was like when I was eighteen I had my eyes tested and I thought my eyes were fine until I got glasses and I was like 'Oh I should be able to see that street sign that's just across the street'. Like I didn't rea:li:ze how bad it wa::s until I was better and then I looked back and thought like all of

these yea::rs you know that I was feeling the way that I was
feeling and there was no:: reason for it.

(Kate)

The adoption of a medical understanding of depression, however, does not
necessitate a purely passive stance on the part of patients. Although the
alleviation of depression was predominantly attributed to medication,
women also spoke repeatedly about the importance of taking care of
themselves in order to facilitate their recovery and prevent relapse – actions
otherwise beyond the reach of the 'good' woman. Therefore, the construction of depression as an independent and invasive entity (a disease or
disorder) allows speakers to construct themselves as responsibly 'fighting
back'. Drawing on a war metaphor, participants commonly spoke of
'fighting' depression, and being 'on guard' against recurrence.

.hh in terms of depression. I just have to al::ways be aware. I
just have to be very aware all the time. .hh umm.
ML: Aware of?
Aware of any danger in anybody who might or any situation
that might precipitate another depression. I have to be very
aware. I I just I'm on guard- >**not** on guard all the time<, but
you know I watch and I'm very aware
ML: Yeah
to to not allow that to happen again.

(Lynn)

depression is a chronic illness and I never really viewed it as
a chronic illness maybe before [...] I have learned **no::w::**
that it is a chronic illness. And as with all chronic illnesses
you a::lways have to be on the warpath or always on the
lookout for signs and symptoms.

(Evelyn)

A war metaphor is common to people's accounts of illness. For instance,
one frequently hears references to 'fighting' or 'going to battle' with cancer.
Consistent with a biomedical construction, a war metaphor constructs
depression as a destructive impostor, and the patient as an innocent victim
of attack. However, a medical construction of depression need not position
individuals as without agency. Drawing on a war metaphor, speakers are
able to deflect blame for their affliction while also retaining agency in their
retaliation. Notably, when women talked about 'fighting back' or being 'on

73

guard' against relapse, they talked about interrupting their usual practices of femininity and taking time for themselves.

> How do I fight? I have to think about it every day. I have to **do** something every day. I have to even if it's just reading a little um um thought or something I have to be aware, conscious. I have to- like right now I'm registered in um um workout program at the gym that's something else I'm doing not to get back to where I was. I'm trying to have something organized that I **have** to do to be fit, to eat better, to sleep well, all parts- to have time just to think, to do nothing too, some people call it meditate. I'm not sure if that's what I'm doing I'm just trying to stop sometimes.
>
> ML: *So it sounds like you're taking care of yourself.*
>
> Well I, I am. More than I was before and I allow myself some time.
>
> ML: *Would that, would those have been things that you would have done before?*
>
> No, no. I did them before but as I said it's not that I was doing them or not doing them it's the attitude I had. I had the feeling if I was spending money for myself on myself I was taking it away from the family or the other people in my family. Well now I try to convince myself that I deserve it. And I **have** to do it. It's not a choice. I have to do it for myself. I have to take care of myself. I'm at that point where I'm still trying to convince myself. But at the same time I'm doing something.
>
> (Dianne)

Drawing on a war metaphor enables Dianne to take up agency in her recovery and effect change in her life. Consistent across other women's accounts, the changes required for recovery involved a shifting of focus from exclusive care of others to the adoption of some care of the self. Thus, a medical construction of depression, in conjunction with a war metaphor allows a disruption in discourses of femininity that require women to prioritize the needs of others. Positioned as in battle with depression, Dianne is permitted to fight back – to bolster the troops in a sense through exercise, eating well, getting enough rest, and taking time out of her hectic day. Consistent with hegemonic constructions of femininity, it is clear in her account that if self-care is motivated by illness it may be permissible, but if motivated by self-interest, it is not. Dianne defends against the suggestion that her self-care is selfish when she dismisses this notion as misguided ('I had the feeling if I was spending money for myself on myself I was taking it away from the family or the other people in my family'). Further, her position is buttressed through the use of 'stake inoculation' where she discursively defends against having her account undermined as motivated by self-interest (Potter, 1996b; Wood & Kroger, 2000). By constructing self-care as something undesired but required ('I try to convince myself that I deserve it. And I **have** to do it. It's not a choice.') she defends against accusations of selfish motivations – against being positioned as a selfish woman. Indeed, by offering resistance to her own self-care ('I'm at that point where I'm still trying to convince myself'), Dianne positions herself as a woman whose natural inclination is to *not* look after herself – as an inherently 'good' woman who is required to act in selfish/bad ways. Therefore, this way of accounting allows a rupture in discourses of femininity whereby a woman may be excused from practices of femininity, and allowed respite and self-care.

Problems with medical constructions of women's depression

Clearly, the biomedical model offers some promise of discursive salvation for women suffering from depression. This way of accounting can serve to legitimize their pain as 'real' and protect them from being blamed for their own distress. Moreover, it can provide a fissure in discourses of femininity: a means through which women can take care of themselves without being vilified as selfish, bad women. Given the pervasive delegitimation surrounding women's experiences of depression (and the dominance of the biomedicine in Western society), it is little wonder that they so often draw on the power of the medical model to understand their distress. However, a medicalized construction is not without problems and multiple trouble spots emerged in participants' accounts. First, while a medical construction (in conjunction with a war metaphor) can allow a rupture in patriarchal regimes of knowledge, ultimately an idealized notion of femininity is upheld as the standard of women's moral worth. Positioned as ill, a woman may be temporarily excused from her usual roles and responsibilities, but these remain untroubled and undisturbed as rightfully hers. Worse, it is the woman's body and not the oppressive conditions of her life that come into view as pathological. The myth of the monstrous feminine is held in place when women's bodies are constructed as unruly, dangerous, and in need of control (Ussher, 2006). Being positioned in this way has serious implications for a woman's subjectivity and her very sense of self. For instance, Bea, who drew exclusively on a medical construction of her depression, said of antidepressants, 'I wouldn't go back to just one a day because it takes two to hold me'. Here, she constructs herself (and is likely constructed by others) as a monster in chains – it takes not one, but two doses of

75

medication to restrain the monster within. A consequence of being positioned as inherently unstable and dangerous is that one is left not only easily undermined and disregarded by others, but also unsure of oneself. As Cynthia stated, 'it's hard with depression because you're not sure, you're not sure if what you're feeling is normal at all. [...] it's hard to know what's normal and what's no:::t'. While a medicalized construction may offer some promise of legitimacy, ultimately, it serves to silence and subvert women's voices, positioning them as in need of surveillance and control under the masculine gaze of medical science.

Second, as explored in the previous chapter, discursive moves to situate depression in the realm of biomedicine are easily trumped. As Joanne stated in an excerpt above, instead of accepting depression as a legitimate disorder, 'people do have a tendency to sort of look at you and say, "Well, you just want attention"'. Similarly, although she was diagnosed as depressed and given a doctor's order to be off work, Emily recounted being dismissed and ridiculed by her employer when she presented a medicalized view of her distress.

> [I] went to see my male doctor and he put me off work for a week. And also I came back, I remember going back to the office and saying to my boss, 'I've got this medical excuse here, I'm off for a week.' And he, I remember my boss pointing out, 'Well what for?' And I said, 'Well, it says on here that it's stress leave' and do you know what he did, he said ((in a dismissive tone)) 'Yeah right!' And he kind of laughed. And I thought you frigger, frigger, frigger! You know and this was in the nineteen nineties! We're not talking the fifties. ((laughs)) This is the nineties and I resented that, I didn't say a word because again I, you know, I thought, why bother.
>
> (Emily)

While speakers may draw on diagnosis to construct depression as a legitimate illness, there is no guarantee that others will accept this formulation. Indeed participants pointed repeatedly to stories in which this construction was dismissed and thwarted by family, friends, and work colleagues. Therefore, the medical model remains a precarious ground on which to construct depression as a legitimate experience (Lafrance, 2007a). Although it can be argued that all language use is flexible or 'precarious', I would also argue that some ways of speaking may be more easily taken up and established than others (Reynolds & Wetherell, 2003). Or, stated the other way, the adoption of some positions may be more contestable than others. Here, it is argued that a medical discourse depends on objective evidence of pathology, a resource unavailable to those suffering from depression (Lafrance, 2007a, 2007b). Failing to meet this standard of legitimacy positions speakers on uneasy footing, and the degree to which they can claim legitimate patient status within a medical discourse is limited. Confirmation of this argument emerges from the finding that with only one exception, all women who constructed depression as a biomedical problem also situated it as a contested and stigmatized experience. While women talked with relief about 'having a name' for their experience, they also talked about having this construction dismissed and thwarted by others, leaving them feeling misunderstood and marginalized (see Chapter 2). Karen's interview represented an exception, or 'negative case' to this pattern in the data (Wood & Kroger, 2000). She was the only woman who constructed her experience within a medical frame, but who did not also lament the marginalization of this construction. Interestingly, Karen was also the only participant to have previously believed that her distress was the result of fibromyalgia and environmental illness. I asked her to reflect on how she felt when her experience was redefined as depression.

ML: I wonder how you felt because all along you had been understanding the way you were feeling in terms of allergies and and reaction to your environment and
mhm
ML: and then when you had to shift that understanding to depression ...
[it was wonderful.
ML: what was that like] okay
because I thought I'm not in a bubble any more. I can go on a city **bus**. I can go to the **malls** um ... if there's a little bit of **mould** in carpet you know I mean everybody has a little bit of allergies of things that bother them but **before** I just felt like I wanted to stay ho::me in my own house. Where I had everything the way I wanted it. Um nobody could bother me there I could breathe freely I could do what I want. I wouldn't let my boys wear perfumes or aftershaves or there was no::thing scented in our house. And it was really a terrible feeling thinking is this the way I'm going to have to be the rest of my life. Plus a lot of people don't understand the allergies and the environmental illness. And I thought that that was what I had and I that I was, you know, >nobody understood me, nobody nobody liked me because I had that< so then when I realized I **didn't** have that but I had

depression knowing depression was **treatable. People understood it**. It was like **hey!** I'll take depression any day.

(Karen)

Whereas other participants drew comparisons between depression and a host of medical conditions (heart attack, broken bones, diabetes, etc.) with the effect of situating depression as a marginalized experience (see Chapter 2), here Karen presents it as understood and accepted. The difference lies in the condition to which depression is compared. When compared to more objectively located conditions, depression is marginalized. But when compared to fibromyalgia and environmental illness, conditions even farther on the fringes of medical legitimacy, depression is treated as valid and understood. This exception shows the relative legitimacy of various forms of pain and distress within the medical model. The more influence one is seen to have over one's condition, the less legitimate it is seen to be. When one has objective signs and symptoms of disease, indicating that the condition is 'real' and outside one's control, then one is granted legitimate patient status. However, without these requisite signs, the biomedical model becomes a precarious ground on which to construct one's experiences as legitimate. Therefore, while situating one's depression within the medical model was described as liberating, validating, and as opening up space for action toward recovery, it can also be seen as a particularly tentative and slippery construction (Lafrance, 2007a, 2007b).

A third trouble spot that emerged in participants' medicalized accounts of depression results from the fact that legitimacy within the medical model rests on the requirement that one's condition be the result of a dysfunction of the physical body, not one's life or personality. Indeed, protection from personal blame for one's own distress within the medical model hinges on this very requirement. A focus on the body eclipses consideration of one's self or life, leaving sufferers without a way of understanding the whole of their subjective experience. For instance, Kate situated depression as an inherited attribute, like having 'brown eyes' or 'brown hair'. However, unlike inherited physical features, depression is entwined with her subjective experiences of her life, and she struggled with the questions 'What part of my experience is a product of who I am, and what part is the product of depression?'

But it just, it's something, it's something that I have accepted, like it's I have brown, well normally naturally brown hair. You know I have brown hair, I have brown eyes, I'm heavy set and I have depression. Like it's just, it's something that I have a really difficult time separating from the rest of me. And that gets problematic sometimes.

ML: How does that get problematic?

.hh Because I wonder sometimes, my world view tends to be a little pessimistic. I don't have a lot of faith in humanity, I don't have a lot of faith in in how we're we're living on this planet. Um, I don't have a lot of faith in the future of the human race and ... I'm not a very trusting person in terms of opening up to people and sometimes I wonder, you know is that the way, is that because that's how I am naturally as a person? Or is that because my thinking has been influenced you know for so many years by this condition that I didn't even know that I have. [...] it just it gets very complicated and confusing because I wanna- I I don't want ... the depression to be the main thing that shaped who I am. And sometimes I wonder like how fa::r ... how much of an influence it's had on me and and who I am, and how I think, and how I relate to people, and and that sort of that whole thing.

(Kate)

While Kate, like many other participants, worked to resolve this problem by integrating medical and life-based understandings in a kind of 'diathesis-stress' framework, three women, Karen, Cythia, and Bea, constructed depression as a purely medical problem. The narrow parameters of this construction do not allow for a consideration of the ways in which the conditions of their lives may have contributed to their distress. Indeed, any such considerations appeared to threaten the validity of their distress as real and their identities as blameless. For instance, during my interviews with Cynthia and Bea, I raised the question of the role of their personal involvement in the recovery process. In both of these instances, this suggestion appeared to challenge the legitimacy of depression as a 'real' biological condition and their assertions that medication was the key to their recovery.

ML: Do you see yourself differently as a person? [A person after recovery, a person, or do you think of your- your-yourself differently?

.hhh ahhhhhhh] Well I kind of, I feel better about myself now. I think that's come with maturity. [...] Like I can, I can get a thought in my head, well you know that woman is better looking than me.

ML: Yeah

and I can think, 'Well Cynthia, you know, c'est la vie.'

ML: Yeah

Whereas twenty years ago I would go home and cry about it.

ML: Yeah

I have been in the fetal position crying about stuff.

ML: Yeah

You know. I **never** do that anymore so. Hhhh

ML: How do you reconcile that? Because it sounds as though you have had a lot of changes in terms of those perceptions about being good enough and then also the medication. So how do you put those together in terms of your experience of recovery?

.hh I, yeah I don't think, like I talked about maturity but I don't think I would be where I was today mentally without the Fluoxetine.

ML: Uh huh

I need the medication. I really do. And when you, when I saw your little ad I thought well now does she mean me ... because I mean, if I went off my medication I think in three weeks I'd be depressed.

ML: Uh huh

Maybe not as mu:::ch. But if- but it's nothing, I mean if I have a chemical imbalance it's just like ... well maybe cholesterol, I was going to say my cholesterol level because I could- I could control that with with die::t. But I guess it's just the same as I control my chemical imbalance up here with with medication. .hh But I was so relieved when the doctor said 'You're depressed' because I thought 'Oh that's what it's and it's not my fault.' [...] Because I thought everything was my fault before and [...] I still have a very hard time forgiving myself. You know. And whether that's a symptom of depression or whether that is just ... what people are like, I don't know. Can, can people have low self-esteem and not have depression? ... I don't know, that I don't know. I guess, huh I don't know, maybe you can have low self-esteem ... but- I wish we could put- what I wish we could do is like stick a thermometer in your ear and check your serotonin level.

ML: Yeah

((laughs)) You know what I mean? I wish a person could do that. So they could look at a number of people and say 'OK

this person has this symptom and their serotonin, you know you are down a quart or something?'
ML: Yeah
Then we'd kno::w. But I don't know how we'll, how we
ML: We would know who was [really depressed kind of thing or?
Yeah! Or we'd know if, we'd know] what depression was more I think. Or we'd know if, **yes**, I'm sure- I mean I know self-es- low self-esteem is **related** to depression but is it necessary in order to have depression, or is depression- is **a::ll** depression is, is serotonin level?

(Cynthia)

In this excerpt, Cynthia struggled to understand her subjective experience of herself in the context of a medicalized understanding of depression. Indeed, the suggestion that personal factors may have played a role in her depressive and recovery experiences appear to threaten her construction of depression as a legitimate problem of the body's mechanics and such suggestions are dismissed and deflected in her account. For instance, her statement that she feels better about herself now than twenty years ago is explained away as maturity, situated as an inevitable evolution. In my questioning, I asked Cynthia to reconcile her experiences of personal change with a neurochemical understanding of recovery. Presented with these apparently irreconcilable ways of understanding ('my body' or 'my life'), she reasserted that recovery was purely the result of medication ('**I need** the medication. I really do') and backed away from the implication of personal involvement in recovery almost to the point of relinquishing her status as recovered ('if I went off my medication I think in three weeks I'd be depressed'). Thus, my questions appear to pose a threat to her status as a legitimate patient, her construction of depression as an objective reality, and her use of medication as a legitimate intervention. Cynthia buttresses her claim that depression is a biomedical condition by comparing it to high cholesterol, an objective physical condition. However, this comparison appears unsatisfactory in its potential suggestion of agency ('I was going to say my cholesterol level [...] I could control that with with die::t'). This comparison is hedged ('well maybe') and then abandoned. She redirects her account to how liberated she felt when diagnosed with clinical depression, a claim she is understandably loath to give up ('but I was so relieved when the doctor said "you're depressed" because I thought "Oh that's what it's and it's not my fault"'). By constructing medical-based and life-based narratives as incompatible polarities, she then wrestles with how these can be reconciled. ('Can, can people have low self-esteem and not have depression?'; 'is it necessary in order to have depression, or is depression- is **a::ll** depression is, is serotonin level?'). Struggling within the narrow parameters of a biomedical discourse, she wishes for the ultimate objective solution, a serotonin thermometer capable of isolating these confounding variables once and for all. Having an objective device for measuring her condition would finally bring personal absolution and legitimacy for herself and her pain. Her longing for a diagnostic test of depression speaks again to the failure of depression to meet the standard of objectivity, and its precarious footing in the medical frame. Further, her account highlights how a medical perspective leaves sufferers with only a partial understanding of their experience. In her talk, Cynthia attempts to reconcile how she feels about herself ('I still have a very hard time forgiving myself') within a medical conceptualization of her distress ('is **a::ll** depression is, is serotonin level?'). In essence, she is left having to situate her depression in her body or in her life, neither alone providing an apparently satisfactory answer.

In my interview with Bea, the suggestion of personal involvement in recovery appears to pose similar challenges to the construction of her pain as 'real', her self as blameless, and her use of medication as legitimate.

> *ML: Are there any other things, other than the medication or any other factors that you think were helpful in terms of your recovery?*
>
> Well I suppose another thing dear, like there's not as much stress in my life now.
>
> *ML: Oh*
>
> Because the children are all grown up and they're gone. And um, financial, there's no well I mean there's always financial problems but not like when you're raising children. So I guess maybe it's at a stage of life too that the children are gone and and the money is::, it's not as tight as it was years ago. And ah a lot of things now that I don't get stressed out ov- like I did when you're, when you're raising a family and everything, it's stressful. [...]
>
> *ML: Do you see those, that ... your life ha- ... that you're- the easing up on the stress as a result of your retirement contributed to your recovery or was it a by-product?*
>
> No, no dear I'd say it was the Prozac. I would really, really give all the thanks to the Prozac. I would yeah.
>
> (Bea)

Like Karen and Cynthia, Bea's account of recovery is framed exclusively in terms of medication ('it was the Prozac. I would really, really give all the thanks to the Prozac'). By attributing some acknowledgement to the effect of changes in her life, she appears to risk weakening her claim thereby opening herself to personal responsibility and blame for her own distress. Instead, she upholds a uniquely medicalized account, leaving the stressful realities of financial strain and childcare outside the parameters of accounting – an issue that emerged later in her interview when she talks about being depressed, and having had three children by the time she was eighteen years old.

> Because I- and I used to- that was a ba::d. Oh::! That was te::rrible. Because, I was like a trapped animal. I couldn't get out. And I really couldn't
> *ML: You couldn't get out*
> because, well no I, I couldn't get out honey because where would you go with three kids? You certainly wouldn't take them to the store. I didn't drive ... and even if I did, I, I wouldn't take three little boys to the store because they'd drive you crazy right? They would be tearing all over the place. And when you have three little children like that, not too many of your friends ask you out for a cup of tea. Because they don't want those kids com(h)ing in, see. So I mean I was like a <trapped animal>.
> *ML: Yeah*
> Really
> *ML: Do you see that, that situation as being a contributing factor to the depression at the time?*
> Well I think I did suffer depression honey. Because and again I say, if I was on Prozac way back then, I, like I say to my little my boys now, they're men, I'd say, 'I know I would have been a <much better mother.> Because I would have put you in your snowsuits, we could have gone for walks, we could have gone out and made snowmen, ((crying)) I could have made cookies with you.' You see? ... I could have enjoyed them. But they were just work. Laundry and laundry and bedding and it was just, it was just work work work work work no enjoyment hey?
>
> (Bea)

In this excerpt, Bea recalls living like a 'trapped animal' as a young mother of three. However, when this line of accounting is brought to bear on the cause of her depression it appears to challenge the legitimacy of her distress as 'real' (biological) depression. For instance, she responds to my suggestion that her situation may have contributed to her distress by reasserting that she 'did suffer depression'. Further, she states that if she had been medicated when she was a young woman she would have been able to enjoy her children rather than see them as a source of never-ending work. In this frame, hegemonic discourses of femininity are upheld as she recollects with distress the lost opportunities to have been a 'better mother': going for walks, playing in the snow, and baking cookies. While a strictly medicalized understanding can work to legitimize pain as real and patients as blameless, it does so by eclipsing any consideration of how the conditions of a woman's life may have been 'depressing'. Ultimately medicalization serves to reinforce discourses of femininity that lie at the very heart of the problem of the delegitimation of women's distress. At the same time, Bea's account reminds us that when women are encouraged to forgo a medical explanation of depression, they are also being asked to relinquish a powerful means of legitimizing themselves and their distress, however limited this may be.

As described in Chapter 2, hegemonic discourses of femininity and biomedicine combine to marginalize women's distress and identities. In contrast, women's accounts of recovery point to the pivotal importance of having their pain and identities validated. One central way in which this validation was accomplished was through women's talk of depression as a diagnosable illness, thereby reasserting the legitimacy of depression within the medical model. While the argument was made that this construction is precarious and problematic, it can serve to validate women's pain and protect their identities from being positioned as mad, bad, and monstrous. A medicalized understanding frames depression as a 'thing', a consequence of one's biological, not personal, constitution. Personality or identity is thereby protected, positioned outside the scope of this accounting (e.g., depression, like a broken leg, could happen to anyone). Accordingly, references to identity were absent from medicalized accounts of depression and recovery, other than to position oneself as a fighter or a sentry on guard against recurrence. In contrast, identity was the focus of the second dominant pattern that emerged in the interviews. In this second pattern, participants talked about having transformed themselves through their experiences of recovery. Therefore, while talk of identity was absent from the first pattern of accounting, it was central to the second. And, while the first pattern of accounting allows a rupture in discourses of femininity (the sick role provides room for women to care for themselves), this second pattern involves more explicit resistance to discourses of femininity. Here, participants equated recovering from depression with renouncing their 'good' woman selves and beginning to prioritize their own needs and desires.

NARRATIVES OF PERSONAL TRANSFORMATION: RECOVERY AS RESISTANCE OF THE 'GOOD' WOMAN IDENTITY

Repeated throughout many participants' accounts was the construction of recovery as a journey of personal transformation. For instance, in describing her experience of recovery, Alexandra stated, 'it was just so cathartic, like I could just, it felt like I was e:volving right out of something else into something else'. Similarly, Susan commented, '[my psychiatrist] said "you changed, you came around three hundred and sixty degrees" and I did. I'm not the person. I'm not the person I was five years ago'. Dianne talked of beginning to recover when she started expressing her needs and 'letting my <true> <self> out'. And for Amanda, recovery from depression involved breaking free from the false front she had tried to maintain for others, and the emergence of her true self.

> Well basically the change came when I first came out when I thought I was a lesbian. I um in high school when I lived with my parents that whole image that I was supposed to portray because of my dad .hh ah back then I was very passive. Um compliant? Ah, tried to be happy. I was very happy like always had a smile on my face because that's the way it was supposed to be. I um ... I had friends back then and I never really had true friends. Like it was- I I look back now it was kind of a fake environment. Like I don't, .hh I wasn't who I wanted to be? Like I was this made-up image that you know all these characteristics that people wanted me to be and put that all- put it all- put it all that together and that was me. ((laughs)) So when I left home and when I started to like realize how I felt like that I felt like I was a lesbian. I I'm that was a turning point in my life [...] but today I- the difference with that is that I'm finally. Like I think there was a shell underneath like I when I felt like I had broken free like I felt like I was just there were pieces falling off you know, like I finally, like there was this shell that was breaking free and then like I stepped out. You know like ((laughs)) like this is who, this is who I am now? And I I think I've always been this way but I'm so glad that I like I'm so much more content with my life now. Like I feel like I finally found me.
>
> (Amanda)

Here, Amanda tells the story of her personal transformation in recovery. The image presented is of a woman trying unsuccessfully to fit into a mould and, through recovery, finally breaking free of this artificial entrapment and discovering her true self. This account is constructed discursively through two critical narrative features: (1) the characterization of her former identity as unreasonable and unsustainable; and (2) a discursive disengagement with this former self. She described her previous self as a patchwork of social expectations, playing out the person she was 'supposed to be': 'passive', 'compliant', and 'happy'. She then disengages from this construction of self by drawing an extreme contrast between her former (fake) self and new-found (authentic) self. Recovery is characterized as the process by which she came to 'break free' of her hollow 'shell', uncovering the person she has 'always been'. What is perhaps most notable about Amanda's account is how she is able to reposition her former self in negative ways. The constellation of descriptors, 'passive', 'compliant', 'happy', 'always had a smile on my face', typifies the 'good' woman, an identity normally revered. Here, though, Amanda repositions this ideal as fake and superficial, and consequently her resistance to this identity becomes warranted.

As in Amanda's account, when participants talked of depression, they frequently talked of themselves as 'good' girls or 'good' women. In fact, participants described their former selves in strikingly similar ways – as the 'good girl' (Joanne, Meredith, Alexandra), 'the good daughter' (Emily), 'the good dutiful daughter' (Barb), 'good mother' (Joan, Meredith), 'good wife' (Emily), and 'the obedient wife, little girl' (Joan). In the following excerpts, participants describe themselves in the time leading up to and during their depression.

> I was always expected to ... have really good marks ... be a very good girl ... do everything you're told. [...] I did all the cooking, all the cleaning, bought all the groceries, paid all the bills [...] I suppose that might have had a fair bit to do with getting depressed later on. I never learned how to be anything except what I was suppo:sed to be.
> ML: How were you supposed to be?
> I don't know, perfect and quiet ((laughs)) and quiet. Apparently I was supposed to be happier and more friendly.
>
> (Joanne)

> Yeah, I looked after him [husband] and his family for almost thirty years at that point. I did. It was expected of me. I was the good daughter, not the real good wife, but I was always here, you know, everything, the house was always good all

this and that. I never asked for a thing. <Never asked for a thing>, nothing! I never did.

(Emily)

I threw myself into the good mother mode and tried to be this good mom and .hh ...
ML: What does that mean?=
=Yeah well for me the good mother mode was having the really good birthday parties and loving my kids and doing everything that I could for my children and neglecting myself not and you know now in retrospect I realize I was neglecting myself not doing things I needed to do for my own self-growth ... ah not spending any money on myself always looking after my children going without all the ti::me.

(Joan)

I always wanted to be the I always tried to be the good girl all through my life. I tried to do everything to please my grandparents because I thought Oh! they took me and adopted me and raised me. If it wasn't for them I would have no life so I tried to do everything I could to please them and in essence I ended up not pleasing myself.

(Alexandra)

Descriptions of these past identities were remarkably similar. All of the above excerpts involve identifiers composed of the descriptor 'good' coupled with a feminine identity ('daughter', 'girl', 'wife', 'mother'). Notably absent across the transcripts were non-gendered identity references (e.g., good person or good worker). In referring to this 'good' woman identity, participants drew on a particular set of characteristics and practices. The 'good' woman is pleasing, obedient, and quiet; she serves her family by cooking, cleaning, and caring, and is happy and fulfilled by doing so. She puts the needs of others ahead of her own, neglects herself, and never asks for anything in return. In fact, *not* caring for herself emerged as a fundamental aspect of the 'good' woman identity (Lafrance & Stoppard, 2006).

Participants' constructions of their former 'good' woman selves were also marked by the use of extreme case formulation. Extreme case formulation is the use of an evaluative dimension at its extreme limit (e.g., using words such as 'always', 'never', 'everyone', or 'no one'; Wood & Kroger, 2000). This discursive device can be used with the effect of justifying claims (Pomerantz, 1986) and highlighting the 'rightness (or wrongness) of a state of affairs or action' (Hutchby & Wooffitt, 1998, p. 211). In describing their previous identities, participants repeatedly used words such as 'always', 'everything', and 'never' to describe the unrelenting nature of their practices. These words are likely appropriate descriptors of the extent of their labour and the social expectations placed on them. At the same time, this way of accounting accomplishes certain discursive effects. Extreme case formulation helps to portray 'the precipitating circumstances as necessitating action' (Pomerantz, 1986, p. 228). By highlighting the unyielding demands of the 'good' woman, speakers justify their resistance to this identity and the practices that accompany it. This discursive presentation is in contrast to other versions of the 'good' woman, where this ideal can be presented as attainable to those women who try hard enough, care enough, or, as promoted in advertising, purchase the right products.

Furthermore, the 'good' woman identity was portrayed in participants' accounts as an externally dictated and artificial mould which, despite their efforts, they could not fit into. That is, the 'good' woman self was contrasted implicitly with the humanist notion of true or authentic self (Kitzinger, 1992). In the preceding series of excerpts, Joanne talked of 'learning' to be who she was 'supposed to be' (as opposed to simply being who she truly is). Similarly, Alexandra 'tried' to be the 'good' girl to the detriment of her own well-being, and Joan 'threw (herself) into the good mother mode and tried to be this good mom'. In other interviews, Amanda talked of being in a 'shell', playing out an 'image', and trying to fit into a 'mould,' and Meredith talked of having tried to fit into the 'good girl frame,' into which 'you ne::ver quite fit'. Thus, in these accounts, the 'good' woman identity is constructed as a fake and constricting encasement binding their authentic selves. Together with the effect of extreme case formulation, this way of talking works to problematize the 'good' woman self, thereby justifying resistance to this identity in recovery from being depressed (Lafrance & Stoppard, 2006).

While descriptions of past selves remained consistent across accounts, the referents for these identities varied somewhat. Most referred to their past selves as 'good' women or 'good' girls. However, two other labels also emerged: the 'perfectionist/control freak', and the 'victim/doormat'. As with the 'good' woman identity, each of these sets of labels also work to reframe hegemonic discourses of femininity as harmful entrapments. Again, by repositioning the selfless 'good' woman ideal in negative ways, resistance to this identity becomes warranted.

The perfectionist/control freak

In talking about what they were like when depressed, Evelyn, Barb, Emily, and Heather all referred to themselves as 'perfectionists' or 'control freaks'. These terms were used interchangeably in the construction of the identity of a woman who was overly concerned with the domestic practices of cooking, cleaning, and caring. Thus, descriptions of the 'control freak' or 'perfectionist' identity were consistent with those of the 'good' woman. However, while other women talked about trying to adjust to others' expectations (e.g., fitting into a mould), participants who referred to themselves as control freaks or perfectionists talked about their own unrealistic expectations of themselves. For these women, the story of their transformation in recovery was in terms of 'letting go' of their individually held standards of practice.

> And ah it's a major change in lifestyle I found that. Major. I've had to change my lifestyle.
> *ML: How so?*
> In my I don't know if you call it my personality? Um. I am ... someone who is ah ... I don't know if I go out looking for stress? Umm ... I don't know what you call it. Perfectionist? Maybe? Or whatever? Ah ah I like things I like my house cleaned, vacuumed every day, or I like things done well. You know what I mean? So I've had to let go:: of all of that stuff. If it don't get done today? Phew. Done tomorrow.
>
> (Evelyn)

> Oh boys I'm going to sound like a control freak, I wouldn't be in charge. I have to be in charge of everything. No matter **what** goes on <I have to be in charge of it>, or I thought I had to be in charge of it. [...] You have a party, you have fourteen guests in **your** home, I'm one of those fourteen guests, I will have to look after every one of the other guests, make sure everybody's got enough to eat, drink, that somebody is talking to them, that that's just me I'm just like a little sheep herder you know.
> *ML: Mmmm*
> That I have to, that I feel responsible for everybody. For everything. I don't know **why** but I do. [...] I have noticed changes but I've had to force myself to do it. I have had to force myself.
>
> (Emily)

In constructing herself as a 'perfectionist' or a 'control freak', a woman accomplishes two discursive effects (although again, not necessarily intentionally). First, she is positioned as inherently consumed with the practices of the 'good' woman. Evelyn stated that being a 'perfectionist' was part of her 'personality', and Emily referred to herself as a 'sheep herder' who by nature feels responsible for 'everybody' and 'everything'. In her constant striving for perfection, the control freak is, in essence, the 'good' woman par excellence. In this way, her identity is constructed as too much of a good thing, an extreme case formulation of her own identity. Constructing herself in this way leads to the second effect of justifying the 'letting go' of her excessive demands and expectations – the perfectionist *has* to let go of her unrealistic standards or face physical and emotional exhaustion. This formulation is also evident in Heather's interview, where she described recovery as the process through which she came to identify herself as a 'control freak' and subsequently learned to 'let go' of her personal expectations of domestic perfection.

> My make-up was good, my hair was good, my my house was tidy, I ah my car was clean, just all of that really superficial stuff so that if anybody looked at me everything would look just fine. [...] **I used to wash my baseboards**. Have you ever washed baseboards?
> *ML: No*
> I haven't done it ever since but I can remember at that time, because I remember the apartment I was living in, actually being down on my hands and knees scrubbing the baseboards.
> *ML: Yeah*
> Who does that? Nobody does that. You know, so it was, it was just one of those things that I would have done that would have been important to me at the time.
> *ML: OK*
> And then the process in getting better. One of the really big parts of that was realizing you don't need to have clean baseboards. That there are other things in life that are more important than that.
>
> (Heather)

In this excerpt, Heather portrays an image of herself, literally 'down on (her) hands and knees', a slave to her compulsion to keep a clean house. In presenting her practices as well outside the norm ('Who does that? Nobody does that.') she positions herself as a 'freak', thereby accounting for the need to abandon her unrealistic expectations. Later in the interview, she said, 'So I realized that I couldn't wash my baseboards so I said "You know what? They get dust on them, screw it." .hh and I, because because it was do or die'. Ultimately, Heather described being able to let go of her pursuit of being 'a better mother' and 'a better wife' only when it became a matter of life or death. Therefore, drawing on the identity of the control freak has the dual effect of legitimizing the speaker's identity (as 'good' woman to a fault) and justifying the abandonment of the excessive practices required of this identity. By highlighting the discursive effects of Heather's talk, I am not suggesting that speakers purposefully (or manipulatively) present themselves and their experiences in certain ways. I am not suggesting that Heather is making up a story to put herself in a good light. Rather, my interest is in the ways available for women to construct their depressive and recovery experiences, and the discursive implications of these ways of accounting. In particular, I am interested in how threats to the legitimacy of women's distress and their identities appear ever-present, and in the ways in which women manage to negotiate these pervasive threats in their talk of recovery and well-being.

The victim/doormat

A second variant of the 'good' woman identity present in participants' accounts of recovery was the identity of the victim. The victim identity was characterized by two central features. First, she is primarily occupied with caring for others to the detriment of her own well-being. Participants described their past victim selves as pleasing, passive, and centrally concerned with relationships, which are also characteristics of the 'good' woman. Like the 'good' woman, the victim is quiet, obedient, and selfless. Second, the victim is characterized by a failure to resist transgressions. In fact, many participants talked of 'allowing', 'letting' or even 'enabling' various disrespectful or abusive acts, often in order to be 'pleasing' or to preserve significant relationships. For instance, Susan described herself as 'wimpy' and a 'pushover'. She said, 'I was a giver and I got taken over and over and over and over agai::n'. Similarly, Alexandra remarked, 'I was a doormat. Everybody walked all over me. Um I couldn't say no. I couldn't stand up for myself because I was so afraid somebody wouldn't like me'. The term 'doormat' was frequently used to reference the victim identity. In keeping with the victim identity, a doormat is literally defined as something that lies at people's feet and gets walked on. In describing her personal transformation in recovery, Deborah stated:

> when I said to my husband this is what you were doing [referring to my research project on recovery from depression] he he suggested that maybe I **hadn't** recovered to the extent to the kind of person I was before. And that's okay::::. Ah I like the kind of person <I've recovered to>. She's a little different than the one **before,** but I like her!

91

ML: mhm

Um ... the one before tended to be a doormat a fair bit. And there's a role for a doormat you know you get the dirt off your feet before you get in the house. But doormats get worn out too. .hhh um ... and they serve a function. And that's okay. **But** um I like what I've recovered to.

(Deborah)

In throwing off the victim identity, Deborah repositions herself in a way that enables her to resist being selfless, servile, and becoming 'worn out'. Many women talked of throwing off their doormat or victim selves by no longer allowing themselves to be negatively affected by others. For instance, Alexandra, who described herself as having been a doormat, discussed her tendency when depressed to 'put up' with mistreatment from others. In contrast, through recovery, she learned to no longer allow this to happen. To illustrate this change, she gave an example of having been enrolled in a class with a professor who was verbally abusive. She declared that she was no longer a doormat and stated, 'I thought I am paying **him** to stand up there and teach me this subject and I am not going to let him talk to me in a condescending patronizing manner!'. She went on to describe the process of lodging a formal complaint to address the situation. As in Alexandra's account, repositioning oneself as rejecting a victim/doormat identity supports women's efforts to stand up for themselves and resist oppression.

Adopting the identity of a control freak/perfectionist, or victim/doormat allows women to throw off their 'good' women selves and take action to defend their health and well-being. However, these identities are individualistic formulations that leave the social and political realities of a woman's life outside the scope of accounting, and consequently uninterrupted. For instance, in adopting a 'perfectionist' identity, the speaker accepts blame for her standards of practice, instead of critiquing social constructions of femininity that uphold crippling standards for women. Similarly, the victim identity enables resistance to this positioning in recovery, but it focuses on the abused rather than the abuser, and easily turns into blaming victims for not having resisted in the past (i.e., for having 'allowed' the abuse to occur). While these identities are drawn on to justify resistance in recovery, in essence, they construct a misplaced resistance whereby women are positioned as resisting themselves rather than the underlying social construction of femininity.

The feminist

In lieu of the control freak/perfectionist or victim/doormat identity, I would argue that the adoption of a feminist identity is preferable as it rightly locates the trouble in patriarchal systems of power/knowledge. However, with a few exceptions, this identity was largely absent from the interviews. Kate identified herself as 'aggressively feminist', but treated this identity as largely inconsequential to her understanding of depression and recovery and she drew heavily on a medicalized construction. In contrast, Joan described recovery as a process through which she became a feminist. A narrative of personal transformation was at the core of her account, and she described recovery from depression as the process through which she grew from the 'obedient wife, little girl' to the 'feminist'. Indeed, Joan stated that she considered herself not to have recovered from depression as much as she had 'recovered from patriarchy'.

> being able to identify myself as feminist that's exactly what it was. Yep yep. That's it. Mhm yep. That was the recovery. And I think that's why I know that I won't ever get there again because now I believe that I'm right ((laughs)).
> *ML: Yeah*
> and it's hh the rest of the world that needs some work. Right? Instead of- so now if I get down it's like, ((in a dismissive tone)) 'tishh! This isn't me. It's not my,' you know. And that's a big start for me because in depression it was always me. Like somebody could really mistreat me and I could go back home and figure out, 'oh if only I::, I:: should have said this and that wouldn't have happened. If I had said this.' I could bla::me myself even if I was completely innocent I could blame myself. [...] And I think ... feminism and being self-reflective are what are what pulled me out of the depression.
>
> (Joan)

Taking up a feminist identity protects Joan from self-blame and squarely locates the source of her problems in a misogynist society. A feminist identity not only enables, but *requires* resistance of patriarchal systems of power. During her interview, Joan spoke directly about rejecting the labels of 'wife' and 'mother'. She described learning to 'say no' to others' demands on her time and energies, and 'letting go' of the pressure to be 'this good mom', 'this super character'. Indeed, she positioned these changes in her life as 'being on strike'. Drawing on political language in this way, the unrelenting domestic practices of her former 'good' woman self come into view as exploitative and her rejection of these practices is legitimized as political resistance. In the following excerpt, Joan describes her journey in coming to redefine herself as a feminist.

We'd been on a journey together she [daughter] and I and
[husband] and [son] as I::'ve been coming to make sense of
who I am and being a feminist, and calling myself a feminist,
and us, you know, ripping apart our lives and always making
sure that we're not just going along with something [...] And
we and now we play we play with people like when somebody comes in I don't say 'My house is a me::ss', cause it's
not my house. You know and you know we would jokingly
say '[husband] didn't get the housework done this week' and
like you know just to see people's reactions and stuff but
when I was back in university I didn't know where our
vacuum cleaner was. Like my family did all of that because I
was on a mission and I was busy doing things and I felt hey I
did it for thirteen years you people might have to do it for the
next thirteen you know ((laughs)) That's how it's gonna be.
And so they jokingly- we got a new vacuum cleaner and one
day I got it out and I was doing something and I I ((gesturing
as though fighting with a vacuum cleaner)) said 'How does
this work?' And they howled because they thought how
many households do you suppose that the father, the
daughter, and the son have to show the **mo::**ther how to
operate the vacuum cleaner like they thought it was really
hilarious and so I've completely changed who I am.

(Joan)

In this account, Joan described recovery as a long and difficult process
through which she, and the rest of her family ripped apart their lives and
reconstructed new ones based on feminist principles. By shifting the rules of
engagement from one of maternal service to one of equality, Joan was able
to renegotiate her role in the family. From this new vantage point, Joan's
needs become both speakable and important, and she was able to restruc-
ture the family arrangement so that she could go back to school. Joan quit
her job, the family sold their home, and her husband and children took up
the bulk of the housework. While this reordering of the family might
otherwise be positioned as selfish for a woman (or indeed unthinkable),
here it is framed as justice ('I did it [housework] for thirteen years you
people might have to do it for the next thirteen'). Joan's resistance is
justified as equality, and at the same time it is positioned as well outside the
norm. Through her story of the vacuum cleaner, Joan both highlights and
resists women's taken-for-granted work in the home and positions her
resistance as radical and defiantly unapologetic.

As evidenced in Joan's interview, the adoption of a feminist identity enables women to speak of their distress, relinquish the limiting identity options for women and their accompanying practices of femininity, and disrupt patriarchal systems of power. However, with few exceptions, this identity was not taken up by the women I interviewed. This finding is not unique to this study, and recent research suggests that although increasing numbers of women endorse feminist principles, relatively few are willing to identify themselves as feminists (see, for instance, Liss, Hoffner, & Crawford, 2000; Rhodebeck, 1996; Snelling, 1999). In a Canadian study of how women talk about feminism and feminists, Julie Quinn and Lorraine Radtke (2006) interviewed female graduate and senior undergraduate students. When participants were asked if they would consider themselves feminists, the following types of answers were given:

I think, no, I don't particularly, like I don't . . . particularly go around saying, you know, I'm a feminist. (Isabel, age 37)

I would say yes I do, although I don't usually call myself that in front of other people because usually it has some negative connotations. (Betty, age 30)

Um, I think it depends on who I'm talking to or comparing myself to. I think that for the hard core feminists, I think it might be an insult to call myself a feminist because I wouldn't um, I I'm more for equality. (Wilma, age 26)

No, now the funny part is I probably am. But, where I come from there is a very BIG problem with that word. Feminism is a four letter word where I come from. (Kathleen, age 31)
(Quinn & Radtke, 2006, p. 190)

Studies conducted in England, Northern Ireland, and Canada have repeatedly found that while both men and women might endorse equality in their accounts, they also tend to reject a feminist identity (Edley & Wetherell, 2001; Percy & Kremer, 1995; Quinn & Radtke, 2006). Indeed, endorsements of gender equality are often prefaced with the well-worn disclaimer, 'I'm not a feminist but . . .', a phrase that highlights the negative implications of this identity. The reaction of right-wing conservatism to the rise of feminism has been to position the movement as a threat to traditional 'family values' and dismiss feminists as unattractive, unfeminine, and unreasonable (Percy & Kremer, 1995). These discursive moves serve to uphold the hegemony of patriarchy by undermining its critics as abject (Edley & Wetherell, 2001). Thus, the identity of the feminist remains a dangerous positioning, readily vilified as extremist (Quinn & Radtke, 2006) or monstrous (Edley & Wetherell, 2001). While a feminist identity may be regarded as ideal for positioning women in empowering ways, it remains shrouded with negative connotations in mainstream discourse and may consequently be an untenable position for many to take up (Quinn & Radtke, 2006). At the same time, it must not be forgotten that while participants tended not to take up the identity of the feminist, they did interrupt and resist discourses of femininity in their talk of becoming well. For instance, there was remarkable consistency in participants' use of a narrative of personal transformation in recovery. In drawing on this device, recovery was constructed as a process through which, in various ways, women came to resist and reject discourses of femininity in striving to be well. While this resistance was often individualized and depoliticized (e.g., in referencing oneself as a control freak or a perfectionist), these women's resistance to discourses of femininity can be regarded as steps in a promising direction.

Practices of recovery/practices of resistance

Thus far, I have explored the ways in which women talked about their identities before and during the time they were depressed. While referred to in different ways, these identities can all be typified as consistent with discourses of femininity. By repositioning the 'good' woman in negative ways, this otherwise revered identity can be resisted, and speakers' identities preserved. Further, resisting the 'good' woman identity opens up new possibilities for action. Consistent with the accounts of those who described recovery in medical terms (in conjunction with a war metaphor), recovery was described as a process that required increased attention to one's own needs and well-being.[4] Central to participants' recovery narratives were references to the importance of 'self care' – 'standing up' for oneself, 'letting go' of domestic practices, and 'saying no' to unjust demands and transgressions. These actions represent a wide set of practices antithetical to the 'good' woman identity, and so, once again, resistance to discourses of femininity appear at the heart of women's stories of recovery from depression. In the following sections, I explore the ways in which participants talked about relinquishing practices of femininity by focusing on the central metaphors of 'standing up', 'letting go' and 'saying no'.

Standing metaphor

In talking about their recovery from depression, participants made references to being able to 'stand on my own two feet' (Evelyn, Amanda, Lynn), 'getting back on my feet' (Emily), having 'stood up for myself' (Susan), being able to 'stand up to my family' (Alexandra), 'getting my feet back on the ground' (Heather), and having 'finally got my feet under me' (Lynn). In contrast, in talking about being depressed, they talked of having been oppressed and held down, dependent and propped up, or controlled from above like a puppet. For instance, Amanda talked about having always needed a 'person to lean on'. She stated that after the break-up of a significant relationship, she came to the realization that she could not rely on others but had to support herself. She said:

> I didn't have anybody. Like everyone was gone I just felt like I had no one else to lean on anymore. That's when I realized that I had to pick up the pieces. Like I had to you know get myself back up no matter how much I fell I had to pick myself back up because no one else was going to be there to do it for me.
>
> (Amanda)

Similarly, in describing her new-found sense of self-sufficiency, Lynn stated:

> It's okay for me to want. Want friends, want relationships, my family, want anything, but not okay to need it because if I need, that gives the other person the chance to pull my strings and I don't want somebody pulling my strings. ... I want to pull my own.
>
> (Lynn)

By drawing on the metaphor of standing, participants construct their new-found identities as independent and autonomous, governed by their own needs and desires (Yardley, 1997b). This metaphor typifies the Western ideal of individualism, whereby each person is fundamentally responsible for her (or his) own success and liberation (Kitzinger, 1992). Further, this metaphor is in stark contrast to the traditionally dependent feminine role. 'Standing up' for oneself is the opposite of being dependent on relationships and 'allowing' transgressions, features central to both participants' characterizations of the 'good' woman and the victim identities. Thus, the use of a 'standing' metaphor represents a form of discursive resistance to these identities. The following quote was used previously to explore the victim identity. This text is repeated here to illustrate the contrast between the speaker's constructions of her depressed (doormat) self and her recovered (independent) self, and how a standing metaphor is used to construct the transition between the two identities.

> I'm able to stand up to my family and say 'This is me, this is who I am, it's not my problem if you don't like it.'

ML: Mmm

I could never do that before. I am very very um I am very straightforward about this is what I want this is what I'll tolerate. This is what I won't tolerate. I set boundaries. I set conditions, and I look after myself.

ML: Were you like that before?

NO. I was a doormat. Everybody walked all over me. Um I couldn't say no. I couldn't stand up for myself because I was so afraid somebody wouldn't like me. And now it's like 'I don't really care ((laughs)) that's your problem not my problem.'

(Alexandra)

Resistance is an inherent part of the metaphor of standing – it means to exert one's own will against an opposing gravitational force that operates to pull one down. Indeed, 'standing up' for oneself is regarded as a commendable feat precisely because it involves resistance and the assertion of one's rights. This point can be further illustrated by examining an exception to the way in which this metaphor was typically used. Whereas most women talked of having previously been passive, compliant, and dependent, they described recovery as a process through which they started standing up for themselves. In contrast, Kate talked of never having been a doormat, but always having stood up for herself. Considering this, she is unable to account for why some people around her withdrew when she began to recover from being depressed. She said:

the experience of- that I had like with everybody sort of withdrawing and and just really being resistant to me getting better. It was ve::ry, it was very strange. Like it just you know because I didn't really see that I ... the changes that I was seeing happening seemed to be more internal [...] I mean I didn't become this pushy::: and I was always like really I mean I've been, I've been on my own since I was fifteen so I've always taken care of myse::lf, independent, because if I didn't do it there was nobody else was going to do it for me. So I was never a doormat, I was never like this wishy washy, 'whatever you want to do or you know just push me around because that's-' like I've always been someone who stood up for myself. **Ferociously** independent, you know **aggre::ssively** feminist, didn't put up with **any** kind of shit with any- you know from anybody so **that** didn't really change all that much except I just got more comfortable in

98

my own skin. I had a better understanding of what made
me tick.

(Kate)

According to Kate's account, people's negative reactions would have made sense had her resistance been new. However, she constructs herself as having always stood up for herself – as always having resisted discourses of femininity. She equates standing up for herself with being '**Ferociously** independent', '**aggre::ssively** feminist', and not putting up with '**any** kind of shit' – which she positions as antithetical to the pleasing, sweet, vulnerable, 'good' woman. Thus, 'standing up' for oneself is used in contrast to the idealized notion of femininity and through this metaphor, participants reposition themselves in more empowering and assertive ways. Although this account represents an exception to the pattern of use of the metaphor of standing, it fits with the analysis and highlights the function of this metaphor as a form of discursive resistance to the 'good' woman identity.

Saying no and letting go

In talking about their personal transformations in recovery, participants also referred to the importance of relinquishing domestic and caring practices by 'saying no' and 'letting go'. These phrases were always raised in the context of the practices of the 'good' woman and so once again represent discursive resistance to this identity. However, this is not to suggest that practices of femininity such as care-giving were abandoned altogether, or were constructed as uniformly constraining and oppressive. For some, helping others and being of service were central to their recovery narratives and many women described finding profound meaning in this work. For instance, Barb, Emily, and Helen talked at length about how they found strength and value through their volunteer work with people in need. Care-giving in itself is not problematic, and very often, it can be life-affirming. Moreover, while women's care work is often taken-for-granted and under-valued, it is oversimplistic to regard it as solely a site of gender oppression. Indeed, care-giving can serve *as a form* of social and political resistance. For instance, in communities where families have been denied the right to raise and care for their own children, mothering becomes a site of resistance against racial oppression. At the time of slavery in the United States, Black children were whipped, sold, and even killed by their owners with no recourse by their parents (Collins, 1994). Up until very recently, Aboriginal children in Canada and Australia were taken from their homes, and adopted into non-aboriginal families or placed in residential schools, institutions now infamous for widespread abuse (Fiske, 1993; Varcoe & Doane, 2007). Removed from their families and communities, generations of

99

children have grown up without the rights and benefit of their own heritage – their language, culture, traditions, and stories. In such situations, 'getting to keep one's children and raise them accordingly fosters empowerment' (Collins, 1994, p. 54). Thus, the homeplace for African-Americans has been described as having a 'radical political dimension' (hooks, 1990); a place where mothers educate their children and foster their social and political awareness, as well as their capacities for resisting oppression (Collins, 2000; Wane, 2004). In reference to African-American mothers, but equally applicable to other mothers who face oppression, O'Reilly (2004c) wrote:

> In a racist culture that deems black children inferior, unworthy, and unlovable, maternal love of black children is an act of resistance; in loving her children the mother instills in them a loved sense of self and high self-esteem, enabling them to defy and subvert racist discourses that naturalize racial inferiority and commodify blacks as other and object.
>
> (p. 179)

Therefore, motherhood and community care-giving can be regarded as sites of power and political activism (Collins, 1994, 2000; Edwards, 2004; hooks, 1984) and the personal reward and empowerment that can emerge from caring is clear. What is equally clear though, is that caring is not always rewarding and empowering. Women often perform care work at high personal costs. When done in the context of women's taken-for-granted self-sacrifice, it can deplete a woman's energy and undermine her sense of self and worth. When the women I spoke with talked about recovery from depression, very often they described a need to resist ('let go' and 'say no' to) the pervasive and interconnected assumptions that women should attend exclusively to the needs of others, and that they are selfish and bad if they do otherwise. Participants described unbinding from these assumptions as liberating and healing. In particular, participants described 'letting go' of the need to please, 'saying no' to undesired demands and requests, and loosening their hold on the taken-for-granted work of cooking, cleaning, and caring.

> How am I different? Well I dropped some of the ... things that I thought were required of me. I don't have that feeling about them any more.
> ML: What do you mean?
> My husband makes his own breakfast. I cut his grapefruit up at night because he is absolutely helpless that way and they would drop otherwise ((laughs)) I mean you can't stop doing

everything for them at once. But if I don't get up for breakfast with him, I don't feel guilty about it.

ML: OK

My house is not always the cleanest. I finally got a cleaning lady who comes for two hours a week and she does all the things I don't like doing! And I don't feel guilty about it [...] Oh lots of things, telling my son no. [...] Doing everything everybody wants me to do, I don't anymore .hh and I am not afraid to tell them why.

(Barb)

Here, Barb talks of how in recovery from being depressed, she 'dropped some of the things (she) thought were required of' her, most notably, meal preparation, house cleaning, and care-giving (her reference to saying no to her son refers to his repeated requests for her to baby-sit his daughter). By framing these practices as the product of her own unrealistic expectations ('I thought were required of me'), she justifies letting them go. In this way, an individualistic account serves to enable her to relinquish practices of femininity, but does not account for how she came to engage in them in the first place. It is interesting that each statement of resistance ('I dropped some of the things'; 'I don't get up for breakfast with him'; 'I finally got a cleaning lady'; 'Doing everything everybody wants me to do, I don't any-more') is coupled with a statement of defence ('I don't have that feeling about them anymore'; 'I don't feel guilty about it'; 'And I don't feel guilty about it'; 'I am not afraid to tell them why'). Feeling guilty implies having done wrong and deserving blame and punishment. By raising and rejecting feelings of guilt and fear, she defends against an unstated challenge of blame for having desisted from her 'good' woman practices. In repeatedly defending her recovery practices, Barb's account suggests that these were both essential to her recovery, and threatening to her identity as a woman. That is, 'letting go' and 'saying no' come into view as both practices of resistance, and behaviours that threaten her identity, because, in her repeated defence of them, she treats them that way.

Like Barb, Emily's account of recovery is also constructed as resistance to the 'good' woman identity. For instance, in describing her personal transformation in recovery, Emily stated:

So **yes**, I can certainly see the difference in me and it's made me a hell of a lot stronger person. I'm still a nice caring person ... but I learned to say no, uh huh! I learned to say no. I'm not Susie Homemaker, your socks are probably going to be **real** dirty once you leave here. But things that I felt that were important things are no longer as important. **Yes**. I'm not a slop you know and I still look pretty good when you dress me up.

(Emily)

In this account, Emily states that through the process of recovering she has become a 'hell of a lot stronger person' who can now 'say no'. This characterization is explicitly situated as a resistance to the 'good' woman identity when she states, 'I'm not Susie Homemaker' and defiantly pronounces that her floors are not perfectly clean. As with Barb's account above, statements of resistance are again coupled with statements of defence. Emily's claim that she now 'says no' is prefaced by first qualifying that she is 'still a nice caring person'. Furthermore, her statement that she 'learned' to 'say no' has the effect of presenting her as a person whose natural tendency is to comply and please. Thus, saying no is positioned as a function of circumstances, not her nature. Because she defends against this unstated accusation, the identity of one who is not 'nice' and 'caring' (and certainly not a 'good' woman) appears to accompany the practices of 'saying no' and 'letting go' (Lafrance & Stoppard, 2006). In rejecting practices of femininity, she also risks abandoning her position as a properly feminine woman. Emily's account brings into focus the negative implications for identity for women who resist the 'good' woman identity – being positioned as uncaring, unkind, and unfeminine. By raising and deflecting these potential accusations, Emily's account works to both assert her resistance of discourses of femininity and protect her identity as a woman who is strong, but still caring; no longer a dutiful housewife, but still attractive and feminine. Thus, the recovery practices of 'letting go' and 'saying no' come into view as practices of resistance: practices that can be at once health promoting and threatening to a women's sense of self.

Self-care

When women talked about recovery, they also highlighted the importance of finding space, time, and energy to take care of themselves. Relinquishing practices of femininity allows women to redirect their time and energies away from an exclusive focus on others toward the self. Indeed, self-care and 'letting go' or 'saying no' are two sides of the same coin. In order for a woman to be able to invest in herself, she must relinquish other resource-consuming activities. As Helen O'Grady (2005) has argued, 'caring for others has been at the expense of women's own needs, desires and goals' (p. 1). Indeed, it is all too common for women to acknowledge that they do not even know what they are interested in or what would bring them pleasure. Having been so focused on others for so long, their sense of relationship with themselves becomes neglected or lost (O'Grady, 2005). Being able to connect with the self in a compassionate way becomes crucial then, in women's attempts to 'recover' and be well (O'Grady, 2005).

The finding that self-care is an important piece of women's recovery from depression also emerged in other research conducted in England, Canada, and Australia (Fullagar, 2008; Ridge & Ziebland, 2006; Schreiber, 1996a; Vidler, 2005). For instance, Damien Ridge and Sue Ziebland found that through the process of recovery from depression, some participants came to re-evaluate their priorities and take better care of themselves. As one participant in their study said,

> If I want to go and walk in the hills on the weekend when I'm off, I will go and do it, whereas before there was always other people I had to consider. And it's not that I waltz out now and leave them all [her four children and husband]. I make sure that everything is all right.
>
> (Ridge & Ziebland, 2006, p. 1047)

Similarly, Helen Vidler (2005, 2006) interviewed women at various stages of recovery from depression and found that increased self-care and decreased self-sacrifice were described as important contributors to recovery. In fact, she argued that the ability to care for oneself differentiated those women whose scores on a self-report inventory indicated that they were depressed from those who scored in a range indicating recovery. She explained:

> Women in Group A (no longer depressed) reported realising retrospectively that putting themselves and their needs first, or balancing their needs with the welfare of others, was connected to an alleviation of depression. Most of the women in Group A were aware of having shifted their focus from prioritising others' needs, to concentrating on themselves so that there was more of a balance. Three of the women, all from the 'no longer depressed' group, believed that 'sacrificing the self' was the way women were socialised to be. Whilst some women in Group B (depressed at interview) were aware that they were focussing on others and neglecting themselves, they also felt it was impossible to change that way of behaving and put their own needs first. One woman in Group B was able to say quite clearly that she had been behaving in this 'self-sacrificing' way for so long that it seemed too difficult to change her behaviour. Several of the women mentioned how they felt compelled to act this way and that if they did not – they would see themselves, or believed others would see them, as a bad or selfish person.
>
> (Vidler, 2005, p. 298)

In summarizing her findings, Vidler draws attention to how self-care for women is important for their well-being, but difficult to put into practice. While some women managed to put self-care in place, others struggled or were unable. The previous excerpt from the study conducted by Ridge and Ziebland (2006) also hints at the difficulty for women to take care of themselves. The speaker asserts that she now attends to her own needs and desires ('If I want to go and walk in the hills . . . I will go and do it'), but at the same time she defends against the suggestion that she does so at the expense of anyone else. She positions her actions, and subsequently her character, in opposition to that of a flippant, self-centred woman who might simply 'waltz out . . . and leave them all'. In contrast, she asserts that she remains a 'good' mother and wife who takes care of her family before considering her own desires. She makes a point of saying that before going for her walks, she 'make(s) sure that everything is all right'.

The results of these studies and close attention to the details of participants' talk indicate that self-care is a practice that is not easily taken up. Rather, for many women it represents a dangerous and threatening practice. Indeed, 'standing up for oneself', 'letting go', 'saying no', and self-care are threatening practices *because* they are forms of resistance, positioning speakers outside the parameters of the 'good' woman identity. As Evelyn states below, in order to focus on her health, she had to ease up on her work in the home and begin to attend to her own needs. Although she makes this assertion, her account is hedged and qualified indicating the 'trouble' with women's declarations of participation in self-care.

> I've had to lea::rn that, so what [in reference to no longer keeping a perfectly clean house]? I'm still working on that and that gets to be:: that's something I'm still:: have to work on. But I'm gettin' there. Now I kind of enjoy having a dirty hou(h)se every once in a while but I've had to learn that those stress factors are ah things that I don't need to carry. And I've learned to let go of a lot of junk, a lot of that stuff. [...] I've done that through books. And just mental- I do a lot of meditation just sitting blank and I have a lot of relaxation tapes. And ah take time out just to listen just to sit and listen to my tapes. Do a **lo::t** of um relaxation tapes. And just not necessarily relaxation tapes but just instrumental tapes just where I sit. Goof off. And I don't miss that time. I always thought I didn't have the time to do that. But you know it hasn't made a bit of difference. Well I may have a little more dog hair hanging around my hou(h)se but it really hasn't made a::ll that much difference in the big thing. And I always

try to have a bath at night to soak. Not just the quick bath jump in and clea- you know get out, like you would. Like I always thought I didn't have time to take that time to sit. So I've had to really, there has been a lifestyle change, you know. Me is is number- should be with all of us looking after ourself as we say in nursing who takes care of the caregiver? But I haven't quite got that good yet. To really
ML: So you are practicing to take of yourself
Trying to, yeah.

(Evelyn)

In discussing how she has changed through recovery from depression, Evelyn states that she no longer gives priority to cleaning but instead invests in her own self-care. However, her account is hedged and qualified, indicating 'trouble spots' in the legitimacy of these claims. For instance, Evelyn begins by stating that she 'had' to 'learn' to let go of keeping a perfectly clean house and is 'still working on that'. Relinquishing her work in the home is thus presented as an unnatural activity for her, one that goes against her nature. Laughter punctuates both comments about having a dirty house, enabling her to state this troublesome claim while also undermining the negative implications for identity that accompany it. Through this use of humour and her equation of housecleaning with 'junk', her account works to legitimize her actions of letting go of housework. Letting go of housework and taking up self-care go hand-in-hand, and as seen in other accounts, Evelyn's treatment of self-care is also marked by defence and justification. For instance, her reference to taking time to just sit is immediately positioned as shirking her responsibilities ('Where I sit. Goof off'). By temporarily equating self-care with being irresponsible, her account then works to defend against this threatening understanding. She assures me that the time she takes is completely inconsequential and does not affect her ability to carry out her responsibilities. However, she then tempers this claim. She concedes that her house may not be as clean, but positions this as a relatively unimportant concern. She repeatedly chastises herself for having believed that she didn't have time to spare for self-care, with the effect of defending against this position as erroneous and misguided.

It is noteworthy that Evelyn begins to stake a strong claim about self-care ('Me is number-') but does not complete the sentence with the expected ending 'one'. Instead, she redirects the focus of self-care away from herself and toward a construction of self-care as a shared moral obligation ('Me is number- should be with all of us'). Thus, to claim that she prioritizes her own needs appears to threaten the 'goodness' of her moral character. The saying 'who takes care of the caregiver?' is raised to justify self-care but it appears unequal to the challenge of absolving her character. She goes on to situate self-care as 'good' but then states that she is not 'that good yet'. Discursively, these ways of talking have the effect of legitimizing her self-care practices while still positioning her as a woman whose natural inclination is to care for others before herself. Therefore, to acknowledge self-care threatens to position the speaker as a 'bad' and 'selfish' woman who willingly, or even eagerly, rejected her responsibilities in the home. Because accounts have the repeated effect of defending and legitimizing speakers' practices of self-care, these come into view as both liberating and threatening practices for women to take up. Thus, it appears that women who resist hegemonic constructions of femininity are faced with a discursive double-bind whereby self-care is central to their well-being, but threatening to their identities as women.

CONCLUSION

As described in Chapter 2, hegemonic discourses of femininity define a limited and arguably self-destructive set of practices for women that are at the heart of their accounts of depression: being pleasing, deferent, self-sacrificing, and taking care of others at the expense of the self. In contrast, accounts of recovery revolve around the rupture or resistance of these discourses. Central to participants' recovery narratives was their talk of increased self-care: relinquishing or excusing themselves from practices of femininity, and taking time to invest in their own health and well-being. However, this shift in priorities, and recovery itself, were not described as simple or easy affairs. Many talked of recovery as an arduous and ongoing struggle. In describing recovery Evelyn said, 'I would say a lot of push. I have felt um what did I used to call . . . it was like pushing a five ton elephant upstairs'. Lynn also described recovery as a difficult process. She said, 'it's **hard** work. Recovery is very hard work. It's not something you can work at today and set aside for two or three weeks while you do whatever else you want to do in your life. It takes hard work'. Similarly, Barb said:

> it was hard, oh my Lord it was hard.
> *ML: What was hard? What were the hard parts?*
> Getting up and doing anything. Doing your housework, making a meal, taking a shower.
> *ML: OK*
> Ummm putting your mind on other things. You learn little tricks as you, as you, as you recover to ... say to yourself, 'No I am not going to beat myself up about that, stop thinking

about that, go think about something else.' In the middle of
the night when I would wake up and I couldn't go back to
sleep because my mind would go. I would say 'Fine, pick up
a book and read, take your mind off of it.'

(Barb)

The struggle to recover involves not only pushing through the phenomenological weight of depression, but also the struggle for women to
legitimize, take up, and maintain activities that promote their health and
well-being. Given the pervasive and powerful discourses of femininity that
construct women in limited ways, many women talked about attending to
their own health and well-being only after they had become seriously
debilitated by depression and were ultimately forced to change their lives.
Thus, women's accounts of recovery repeatedly pointed to both the critical
need *and* the difficulty for women to legitimize and engage in self-care.
When women talked about self-care (understood broadly as relinquishing
exclusive focus on caring and domestic practices and attending to the self),
their accounts served to defend and legitimize these practices. These
patterns in the text led me to want to further explore women's accounts of
health, well-being, and self-care. Why and how is it that health practices
appear so difficult for women to take up? How do women defend and
legitimize their health practices? Are there ways in which women take up
self-care other than to be compelled by depression and depletion? In the
next chapter, I will explore the connections between women's accounts of
self-care and their overall health and well-being. I will also provide a deeper
examination of the material and discursive constraints and facilitators of
women's self-care practices. I will then elaborate on the findings of my
research with women who *do* self-identify as taking care of themselves in
their everyday lives. By examining the subtleties and intricacies of these
women's accounts, my aim is to explore and identify ways for women to
negotiate and resist hegemonic discourses, and reposition themselves in
ways that are more emancipatory and health promoting.

Notes

1 Interestingly, the degree to which participants drew on a medical understanding
of their depressive experiences did not necessarily correspond to the type of
intervention they received. Of the 19 participants in the recovery study, 11
participants did not construct a medicalized account of their distress. Instead,
these participants talked of depression primarily in terms of negative life events
and personality. Eight of these women had taken antidepressant medication,
among whom two had been admitted to hospital and one had been treated with
electroconvulsive therapy. Therefore, while almost all participants had direct
exposure to medical interventions, fewer than half of them constructed their
experience within a medical frame.

2 I am not suggesting that women are 'making up' or 'making excuses for' their distress and incapacitation. Rather, I am interested in how women's distress is so pervasively denied and dismissed, and how they resist this silencing in their accounts of recovery. Indeed, I would argue that the very fact that I feel the need to assert this claim again and again speaks to the pervasive delegitimation associated with women's depression – the apparently always lingering doubt and skepticism that depressed women face in their struggles to be heard.

3 Again, this is not to suggest conscious intentionality on the part of speakers.

4 Here, participants mobilize a 'needs' discourse in justifying their attempts to attend to their own health and well-being. However, a language of needs can be problematic as it prioritizes individualistic imperatives. As such, a needs discourse can be mobilized with very harmful effects. For instance, the discourse of the male sexual drive also hinges on a discourse of individual needs and can be used as a means of justifying unsafe sex practices, or men forcing women into sex. (Thanks to Nicola Gavey, personal communication 2008, for making this important point.)

CHAPTER 4

STRUGGLING TO SELF-CARE

The material and discursive context of women's
health practices

Whereas women's accounts of depression were entwined with discourses of femininity, recovery narratives centred on the rupture or resistance of these discourses. In their talk of recovering health and well-being, women spoke of the pivotal importance of relinquishing their exclusive focus on the needs of others and beginning to attend to their own needs and desires. Participants described beginning to take time for themselves to rest, exercise, read, volunteer, and play either alone or with family and friends. These accounts are in concert with mainstream health-promotion initiatives aimed at encouraging individuals to nurture their own health and well-being. Indeed, the message that women should 'take care of themselves' has proliferated in the past few decades and the promotion of self-care and leisure by health professionals and in the media is widespread. Physicians tell patients to exercise, eat well, and take time to rest. Mental health professionals repeatedly encourage clients to attend to their own needs. Articles in women's magazines suggest ways for women to get better sleep or more exercise. Such advice may be well-informed and well-intentioned as self-care activities such as leisure, relaxation, and exercise are associated with a host of physical and mental health benefits (Hansson, Hillerås, & Forsell, 2005; Health Canada, 2002; WHO, 2003a). For instance, regular exercise has been found to substantially reduce the risk of cardiovascular disease (Oguma & Shinoda-Tagawa, 2004; WHO, 2003b), cancer (Lee, 2003), diabetes (Hu, Sigal, Rich-Edwards, Colditz et al., 1999; WHO, 2003b), cognitive impairments (Wueve, Kang, Manson, Breteler et al., 2004), and depression (Allgöwer, Wardle, & Steptoe, 2001; Jenkins, 2003; Pondé & Santana, 2000). The benefits of taking regular time for relaxation are also wide-reaching, including reducing symptoms of depression (Broota & Dhir, 1990). In addition, such self-care and leisure activities offer opportunities for women to relieve stress, nurture their interests and relationships, foster a stronger sense of self, and develop support and a sense of belonging in their communities (Pondé & Santana, 2000; Wearing, 1990; Woodward, Green, & Hebron, 1989).

However, despite widespread public and professional knowledge of the health benefits of self-care, women often fail to engage in these behaviours.

For instance, women report less participation in leisure than men (Henderson, Bialeschki, Shaw, & Fresinger, 1989; Shaw, 1994; Woodward et al., 1989), and women with children report the lowest levels of leisure participation (Pondé & Santana, 2000; Shaw, Bonen, & McCabe, 1991; Thrane, 2000; Woodward et al., 1989).[1] Across the lifespan, and in every social class, women are less physically active than men (Armstrong, Bauman, & Davies, 2000; Crespo, Ainsworth, Keteyian, Heath, & Smit, 1999; Statistics Canada, 2006), and most women are inadequately active for health benefits (Brown, Brown, Miller, & Hansen, 2001; Henderson & Winn, 1996). Although research indicates that women are aware of the benefits of leisure and self-care and want to engage in such activities (Brown et al., 2001; Lewis & Ridge, 2005), very often they do not, leaving them feeling even more ineffectual and guilty when their best intentions are not realized (Drew & Paradice, 1996). Moreover, health care professionals compound women's distress and marginalization when they conceptualize a woman's struggle to self-care as a 'lack of compliance'. In this frame, the context of a woman's life is obscured. Brought into focus instead is a woman who is defiant or deficient – possessing a lack of knowledge, motivation, willpower, assertiveness, time-management skills, rational cognitions, or worse, a woman who is masochistic or personality disordered.

What mainstream health promotion initiatives so often fail to consider is that health care behaviours are not simply a matter of choice (Drew & Paradice, 1996). As Shelly said when I asked how she came to take care of herself in recovery, 'It wasn't like I, you know just decided kind of thing because I couldn't you know. If I could've I would've done it a long time ago.' Clearly, the practice of self-care is not as simple and straightforward as so many health promotion campaigns would suggest; women who struggle to attend to their own needs and well-being face a multitude of material and discursive constraints. If efforts to support women's health and wellness are to be effective, they must not only resonate with women but also fit into the landscape of their everyday lives. As Kickbusch (1989) suggests,

> If we accept that self-care is basically about the actions people perform to improve their health and well-being within a context of everyday life, in which health is rarely the main frame of reference, then . . . we must relate the actions to the meanings people attach to them, the norms they are subject to and the power of decision making available.
>
> (Kickbusch, 1989, p. 127)

This chapter will focus on the ways in which women talk about care for the self, defined broadly as the antithesis of women's taken-for-granted self-sacrifice. Following Kickbusch's suggestion, I will examine both the power of decision making available to women in their pursuit of self-care, as well as the meanings they ascribe to this practice. That is, I will explore the material conditions and the discursive practices that constrain or enable women's power to resist practices of femininity (including 'standing up' for oneself, 'letting go', and 'saying no' to an exclusive focus on others) and attend to their own needs, desires, and interests. I will also describe the multiple ways in which participants deployed the discourse of self-care to fend off, reduce, or otherwise deflect expectations and demands that they, as wives, mothers, daughters, friends, and neighbours, be on call to serve others, subordinating their own needs and desires. This resistance often entailed finding new ways to talk to themselves as well as to others, reforming their own internalized self-expectations of their 'good' woman subjectivity.

In this analysis, I approach the discourse of self-care with both openness and suspicion: openness because women's healing narratives so often point to its importance, and suspicion because of the ready overlap between the concepts of self-care and self-discipline. As Foucault (1977) argued, power rarely operates through force, but through knowledges that individuals take up and implement on themselves. Power is produced and reproduced through the internalization of regimes of knowledge – through self-discipline. Power operates by convincing subjects that they want to be certain types of people – 'good' women (thin, beautiful, caring), 'good' patients (compliant), 'good' citizens (productive). Through the internalization of regimes of knowledge, people govern themselves in ways that feel authentic while at the same time maintaining the hegemony of these regimes. Thus, when people self-care, they implement and produce certain knowledges. Rather than an expression of individual will then, self-care can be regarded as a form of 'panopticism in a benign disguise' (Frank, 1998, p. 331).

The self-care discourse is a product of the Western context from which it recently emerged. It is hybridized with other dominant discourses and thus can serve to orient individuals in multiple and sometimes contradictory ways. Rooted in a medical discourse, self-care is equated with patient compliance. In this way, self-care is an imperative of the 'good' patient and healthy individual. Indeed the language of 'health' and 'well-being' is saturated with a biomedical discourse. Thus, the hegemony of the medical model is produced when individuals self-care in accordance with doctors' orders and the rules of the medical establishment (cf. Foucault, 1975). In contrast, the discourse of self-care is also rooted in feminist discourse. Within a feminist frame, women are encouraged to be empowered to resist the medicalization of their bodies and to care for themselves in their own ways (for instance, consider the significance of the multiple edition text, *Our Bodies, Ourselves* [Boston Women's Health Book Collective, 2005]). Further steeped in contradiction, while self-care can be mobilized with

111

the effect of empowering women in their relationships with their bodies, a self-care discourse can also serve as a handmaiden of patriarchal oppression. For instance, patriarchy can be seen to be produced when women self-care through diet or beautification with the goal of increasing their value for male consumption.

The discourse of self-care also has deep roots in liberal individualism, encouraging each to 'look out for number one'. This Western construction reifies our understandings of ourselves as bounded individuals and necessarily invites the opposition of the self and other. Within this frame, care for the self and care for others are constructed as a zero-sum game where time to care for one is necessarily at the expense of the other. Thus, the value of relationality, collectivity, and community are not afforded by this construction. Further, the individualist notion of self-care turns attention away from the social and political realities of people's lives, leaving individuals held solely responsible for their own health, success, and prosperity. In this view, the implications of wide-scale social problems are ignored, including poverty, violence and abuse, poor and exploitative working conditions, inadequate child and health care, and environmental degradation. Moreover, the promotion of an expansion of self-care initiatives threatens the need for existing social services and can serve to justify the dismantling of publicly funded services (Kickbush, 1989).

Coupled with its roots in a capitalist discourse, an individualist construction of self-care takes on yet another set of contradictions. Since the valued individual is the productive individual, and health is essential to productivity, then maintaining one's own health through self-discipline (self-care) becomes a moral imperative of the individual (Findlay & Miller, 1994; Kickbush, 1989). At the same time, however, the spirit of capitalism and its accompanying Protestant work ethic lead to the situation in which productivity becomes the measure of an individual's worth. This pressure for productivity invites suspicion and derision for those who take time away from work. Thus, guilt may be aroused in workers when they do take up self-care as much as when they do not.

In short, the meanings and implications of the Western discourse of self-care are multiple, contradictory, and shifting. It can serve to produce and maintain the hegemony of various dominant discourses (e.g., the discourses of biomedicine, individualism, capitalism), and at the same time can be used in resistance of these discourses (e.g., within a feminist discourse). While Foucault focused on the ways in which power/knowledge is produced by individuals, he also suggested that the practices people engage in can be understood as both practices of self-discipline *and* practices of freedom. Without defining it directly, Foucault used the phrase 'care of the self' as an anchoring concept in his last book, *The care of the self* (1986). In an attempt to decipher what Foucault meant by this phrase, Arthur Frank (1998) traced the different ways in which this concept was treated in his work. Frank described Foucault's articulation of four different types of technologies of the self, the fourth of which

> permit[s] individuals to effect by their own means, or with the help of others, a certain number of operations on their own bodies and souls, thoughts, conduct, and way of being, so as to transform themselves in order to attain a certain state of happiness, purity, wisdom, perfection, or immortality.
> (Foucault, 1997a, pp. 224–5; cited in Frank, 1998, p. 335)

Frank suggests that for Foucault, 'care for the self' implied *both* disciplinary practice and an ethical practice of self-transformation. It is both a mechanism of control and a means of resistance and liberation. For instance, a woman's participation in physical exercise can be understood as both the production of patriarchal power *and* a means of resisting limiting discourses of femininity. The aims of this chapter are to explore women's accounts of care for the self, and to trace the assumptions and implications of different ways of accounting. That is, through a detailed examination of the ways in which women talk about self-care, I aim to deconstruct the power/knowledge produced by their telling. Of course, the ways in which discourse is constructed are dependent upon the location of speakers. This analysis is rooted in its Canadian context, and in particular in the context of the accounts of White Western women. And yet, this analysis is not necessarily unique to Canada as it centres on the far-reaching issues of women's distress, discourses of femininity and discourses of care. At the same time, however, the notion of self-care would be differently constructed, or indeed absent in other contexts, for instance, in more collectivist societies such as Hindu-India where understandings of the self are not separated from the social context (Miller, 1994, 1997, 2002). Considered in the places of its production then, I approached the interviews with a view to exploring the ways in which these women talked about caring for themselves.

TERMINOLOGICAL TROUBLES – REVISITED

Throughout this analysis, I use the term self-care to refer broadly to attention to one's own needs, health and well-being. That is, self-care is approached as the antithesis of women's taken-for-granted self-sacrifice. While the term does not fully encompass these meanings (and like all health-related discourse, tends instead toward a medicalized understanding), I have adopted it in part for the lack of a better one. In fact, the apparent lack of a better term is interesting in itself. Other researchers have alluded to the difficulty of fixing a useful and recognizable term to the idea of women's attending to their own selves (Green, Hebron, & Woodward,

1987, 1990; Henderson, 1991, 1996; Henderson & Bialeschki, 1991). For instance, engaging in enjoyable, healthy, and self-nurturing activities is often referred to as 'leisure'. However, while this term may be useful for understanding men's experiences, it has been found that the traditional idea of leisure as free time does not apply to women's lives (Green, Hebron, & Woodward, 1990; Henderson, 1991, 1996; Henderson & Bialeschki, 1991; Wearing, 1990). As Henderson (1991) explained,

> Traditional conceptions of leisure time and activity have been based on largely male models of the work/leisure dichotomy and on the assumption of freedom and lack of obligation . . . when female respondents are asked to apply these definitions of leisure, the respondents often respond that they have no leisure.
>
> (p. 368)

Further, women have been found to have difficulty discussing leisure because it is a 'vague and amorphous concept' that is 'difficult to articulate' (Green et al., 1987; Henderson, 1994; Henderson & Bialeschki, 1991). The difficulty in naming this concept may be particularly telling. Whereas Betty Friedan talked about women's dissatisfaction and demoralization in orienting around the roles of 'wife' and 'mother' as the 'problem with no name' (1963), I wonder if self-care, or the consideration of a woman's own needs and desires, is equally 'a solution with no name'? (Although surely only one solution among many.) If this is true, then the absence of language to refer to women's self-interest serves to silence and subvert any such inclination. 'After all, the power to name one's experience and to have that naming acknowledged by others as legitimate is considered the sine qua non of empowerment' (Vertinsky, 1998, p. 100). Therefore, the development of discourses that support women's self-care and self-interest becomes an important part of feminist projects toward women's empowerment. One aim of this chapter then, is to shed light on women's stories of self-care with a view to elucidating and elaborating on women's participation in practices that might promote recovery from depression, and nurture their health and well-being. I explore the material and discursive constraints and facilitators to women's self-care as well as the ways in which these are negotiated in their talk.

CONSTRAINTS TO WOMEN'S SELF-CARE: A MATERIAL-DISCURSIVE ANALYSIS

When women are asked to talk about taking care of themselves, they often report that they simply do not have the time (Drew & Paradice, 1996; Henderson & Bialeschski, 1991; Miller & Brown, 2005). As one single mother in a study of women's leisure participation said, 'If they would invent a thirty-six hour day I might get some [leisure] in' (Henderson & Bialeschski, 1991, p. 60). For many women, time is stretched between the demands of paid work, caring work, household labour, and community responsibilities. As a result, women, and mothers in particular, often do not have the time required for investing in leisure activities or their own health. Indeed, this finding was central to women's accounts of depression, and it also emerged in my interviews with women about self-care. For instance, Jan, a participant in a study I conducted on self-care, reflected on her life as wife, a mother of two, a full-time therapist, and part-time graduate student. For her, self-care was simply not possible at this time in her life, given the multitude of demands she faced.

> There was no self-care whatsoever, because it was time that was just, going to work [...] and then I'd come home, put them [children] to bed, read them stories, usually baths, things like that to keep, ah, going with that. The::n, we'd have supper together and then I would start my studying. And I would be studying, kind of late into the morning, have a couple of hours sleep, and then get up for work, get the kids ready, for school and that kind of stuff.
>
> (Jan)

Although both men and women report that lack of time is a chronic problem, it appears that women suffer most from a lack of discretionary time, and this has negative consequences for women's self-care (Henderson, 1991; Thomsson, 1999; Thrane, 2000; Wearing, 1990). For instance, employed men have been found to have more time for leisure than both employed and non-employed women (Shaw, 1991). Based on their analysis of time diaries of a nationally representative sample of Americans, Mattingly and Bianchi (2003) found that on average, men had a half an hour more free time per day than women. They concluded that if this difference exists in a consistent way, then men would enjoy 164 more hours of free time than women a year, the equivalent to more than four weeks of vacation.

Not only have differences been found in the quantity of men and women's leisure, but also the quality. When women do get time for themselves, this time is often fragmented and interrupted by the demands of childcare and other unpaid work in the home (Bittman & Wajcman, 2000; Mattingly & Bianchi, 2003). In contrast, men enjoy significantly more 'pure' leisure, free from the demands of others (Bittman & Wajcman, 2000; Mattingly & Bianchi, 2003). Thus, women's leisure is significantly 'less leisurely' than men's (Deem, 1988), and as a result, is likely less enjoyable, restorative, and beneficial.

115

The gender discrepancy in free time is largely accounted for by domestic and care-giving responsibilities organized within a heterosexual matrix, with the presence of both a spouse and children in the home reducing women's free time more than men's (Brown et al., 2001; Currie, 2004; Mattingly & Bianchi, 2003; Sayer, 2005; Thrane, 2000). While single and married men enjoy about the same amount of free time, married women have nearly an hour less per day than their single peers, even when other demographic variables are controlled for (Mattingly & Bianchi, 2003). Thus, despite advances brought forth by feminist initiatives, women in heterosexual relationships still do the lion's share of work in the home (Baxter, 2005; Dean, 1992; Lupton, 2000; Sayer, 2005; Shirley & Wallace, 2004). 'In other words, increased participation by women in the paid work forces has exerted very little effect on the gendered division of labours within the household' (WHO, 2000a, p. 60). In a study of time diary data collected across ten countries (Australia, Canada, Denmark, Finland, Italy, Netherlands, Norway, Sweden, the UK, and the US), Bittman and Wajcman (2000) found that women's average share of unpaid labour was 76 per cent, ranging from '70% in gender-equality conscious Sweden to 88% in "familistically" oriented Italy' (p. 174). Therefore, the unequal division of unpaid labour between men and women appears to remain a consistent finding across the West.

In addition to differing in amount, the domestic work typically performed by men and women also differ in kind. While men tend to do work that is time-limited and more readily completed at a time of their choosing (e.g., mowing the lawn, house repair), the work that women tend to do (e.g., attending to a crying child, preparing the next meal, doing laundry) is 'constant, repetitive and unrelenting' (Mattingly & Bianchi, 2003, p. 1002). Whereas fathers often offer supplemental care, mothers remain the primary care-giver (Henderson & Allen, 1991; Nentwich, 2008). Indeed, to be a mother *means* providing continuous care, being on call 24 hours a day. Thus, the social arrangements of husband and wife, mother and father, allow more freedom and flexibility for men, and as a result, more time for leisure and self-care. The difference between men's and women's ability to find time for themselves was described by an Australian woman who participated in a study of women's recreation. Comparing her own leisure to that of her husband, she said,

[H]e gets his own time, I mean he goes for a surf or he'll play golf, and it's different for him, he just sort of walks out of the house. He doesn't have to prepare anybody. You know what I mean? They [husbands] just walk out. 'Good-bye, I'm going' (laughs). He doesn't have to feed the children or shop for food or cook it.

(Currie, 2004, pp. 231–2)

Given the social construction of (heterosexual) femininity which orients women around the needs of others, for many women there is no 'non-obligated time' and consequently, there is no time for the self (Henderson, 1996; Henderson & Bialeschki, 1991; Wearing, 1990). This construction results not only in the material consequence of women's time poverty (Bittman & Wajcman, 2000), but also in the negative implications of what it *means* for women to take time for themselves. Investigations of women's leisure participation have repeatedly found that women are often reluctant to engage in self-nurturing activities, even when they have the material resources that would allow them to do so (Harrington, Dawson, & Bolla, 1992; Henderson & Allen, 1991; Henderson & Bialeschki, 1991; Miller & Brown, 2005). That is, even when women report that they *do* have some discretionary time, they *feel* as though they shouldn't spend this precious resource on themselves. Women's reluctance to take time for themselves has emerged in research on both women's experiences of mothering and the constraints on women's leisure. Ruth Paradice has conducted research in the area of women's experiences of mothering and Susan Drew has studied the reasons why women do not participate in physical activity. Noticing the overlap in the ways in which their participants talked about time, these two researchers merged their analyses and concluded the following.

> Strikingly, the participants' talk about time revealed the belief that they could not legitimately take time for their personal interests and pursuits. In women's accounts time was talked about as if it were a scarce commodity which they did not own. Women's time appeared to belong not to themselves but to all the other people in their lives who were dependent on them and was discussed as if it were a kind of currency which could be 'given' to tending the needs of others and could be 'spent' on activities such as work, house-work and childcare. These ways of using time were considered legitimate and appropriate. However women did not feel the same about 'spending' time on themselves, even though they frequently reported feeling desperate to have the opportunity to become involved in activities that were purely for themselves. This conceptualization of time is reflected in Bordo's comment 'that women learn to feed others not the self and to construe any other desires for self-nurturance and self-feeding as greedy and excessive. Thus, women are required to develop a totally other-oriented emotional economy' (Bordo, 1989, p. 18).
>
> (Drew & Paradice, 1996, pp. 563–4)

While particularly pronounced among women who are wives and mothers, the sense that one should care for others and not focus on the self appears pervasive. For instance, the following is an excerpt from an interview with

117

Amanda, a 21-year-old woman who was single and without children or dependents. In this excerpt, Amanda reflects on her experience of over-coming depression, and the accompanying changes in her sense of self.

> ((sighs)) How I've changed is that I think this is for the better but I sometimes feel insecure about this because I feel like it's not always a good thing ... I'm not hhh I'm not, I shouldn't say **se**lfish but I I call it selfish because I think it's kind of like, I think that's something that's built into me when I was young that thinking of yourself is selfish [...] .hhh but now, I'm so much more um ... like I care for others, the people that are important in my life, I am still a very loyal person faithful person. I would never do anything to people that I truly love. Um I would never intentionally hurt anybody. .hh But when it comes down to it like I I al- I think about wha- wha- what I want? Like I always stop and think about .hh you know how do you feel about this and I reflect a lot more on that now?
>
> (Amanda)

In this excerpt, Amanda describes how she has changed through recovering from depression. Her account begins with a sigh, announcing the treatment of a difficult topic. She notes that she now attends to her own wants and needs, but her account is hedged and qualified. Self-interest is presented as both positive and negative; while attention to her own needs is healthy, 'thinking of yourself is selfish' and her account works to address this threat to her identity. Her statement that she now attends to what she wants is predicated on a list of disclaimers that she is still nice and caring. She stumbles on her statement 'I I al- I think about wha- wha- what I want [. . .] and I reflect a lot more now?' and presents this more as an apologetic question than an assertion of self-care. Thus, even for single women without dependents, prioritizing one's own needs and desires can be a risky business.

Feminist scholars of leisure have drawn on Gilligan's (1982) pioneering work on women's moral reasoning to explain their reluctance to care for themselves (Harrington et al., 1992; Henderson & Allen, 1991; Henderson & Bialeschki, 1991; Miller & Brown, 2005). Gilligan (1982) proposed that women are guided by an 'ethic of care', socialized to prioritize relationships and attend to the needs of others. Defined in the context of their relationships, women judge themselves and are judged by their care and concern for others. She noted that in reasoning through ethical dilemmas, women spoke in a 'distinct moral language'.

This is the language of selfishness and responsibility, which defines the moral problem as one of obligation to exercise care and avoid hurt. The inflicting of hurt is considered selfish and immoral in its reflection of unconcern, while the expression of care is seen as the fulfilment of moral responsibility.

(Gilligan, 1982, p. 73)

Gilligan described how women's accounts often positioned 'selfishness' and 'responsibility' as opposing constructs. When faced with the choice to care for self (selfishness) or care for others (responsibility), the 'right decision' is clear. Thus selflessness and self-sacrifice represent essentially moral behaviour for women, and the transgression of this norm is considered immoral by default.

Therefore, when women transgress discourses of femininity and take up self-care, they do so at great risk to their very sense of self (O'Grady, 2005). In order for a woman to attend to her own needs, she must 'defend herself against a morality that supports the very destruction of her authenticity through rendering her selfless, a selflessness that is labelled "good" and "normal" for women' (Jack, 1991, p. 182). With selflessness as the norm, any diversion becomes viewed as selfishness. And it appears that there is little worse than being a *selfish woman*. Fear of being selfish emerged repeatedly in my interviews with women about recovery and self-care, and has been found to be a central constraint on women's participation in recreation (Bedini & Guinan, 1996; Henderson & Allen, 1991; Thomsson, 1999). Indeed, in her research on women's participation in exercise, Heléne Thomsson (1999) concluded that 'the fear of selfishness constitute(s) one of the most powerful and pervasive obstacles to recreational behavior for . . . women' (p. 52). As illustrated in the following excerpts, when women do engage in self-care, their experiences are often shadowed by guilt, discomfort, and feelings of selfishness.

Sometimes I feel I'm being really selfish when I do something for myself . . . I can feel the way the day-care staff look at me when I drop the children there on my day off, so I can go swimming – even though I've explained to them that the swimming is like a kind of physiotherapy for me. (34-year old nurse with two young children)

(Thomsson, 1999, p. 48)

Leisure is doing whatever I really want to do, yet if too long, I feel guilty. Once you have a family you start to doubt your own, not your own feelings, but you might think that I really should be helping my son with his arithmetic, or if it's a decision whether I

119

get to do something or my daughter gets to go to Girl Scouts . . . if the leisure time is entirely selfish and it goes on for a long period of time where I feel like I'm neglecting my family then, you know guilt sets in. Two nights out in a row, you know, that's pretty bad! (Sales-person, married, mother of 3 school age children)

(Freysinger & Flannery, 1992, p. 312)

As the previous excerpts illustrate, discourses of femininity and the expectation that women should submerge their own health and interests often infuse women's understandings of their behaviour, and subsequently their experiences. In their talk, self-care is constructed with (im)moral language ('selfish', 'guilty', 'bad'), marked by judgements that colour the way women experience time to themselves. Furthermore, the practices of letting go of work in the home and taking up self-care are not only up to the individual woman, but they are negotiated in her interpersonal relationships. As the woman in the first excerpt said, she can 'feel' the disapproving gaze of the day-care workers, compounding her feelings of selfishness. Although she states that swimming is a form of medical intervention ('like a kind of physiotherapy for me'), this medicalized construction appears to fall flat. Thus, even if a woman asserts her right and need to self-care, those around her may dismiss and undermine her efforts. As a result of the pervasive delegitimation associated with women's self-care, women often hurry through their leisure activities, if they do them at all. As one woman described, 'I feel I have to take as little time as possible and hurry back again . . . an hour's class is pushing it on a Saturday morning' (Drew & Paradice, 1996, p. 564). Thus, women's leisure, when it occurs, often tends to be fragmented, rushed, and laden with guilt (Drew & Paradice, 1996; Miller & Brown, 2005) – hardly the restorative practice women described as so essential to their experiences of recovery from depression.

Relinquishing an exclusive focus on others and taking up self-nurturing activities are threatening not only because they risk positioning women as selfish and bad, but also because they may involve giving up a valued sense of power within a heterosexual matrix. Outside of domestic and caring work, women have been afforded limited access to power over others (Henderson & Allen, 1991). Thus, 'to relinquish the power that comes from caring for others, when it has been the one arena in which the exercise of control and power has been given legitimacy for women, presents a complex dilemma' (Henderson & Allen, 1991, p. 101). The double-bind that women face (self-care is healing but threatening to women's identities) is thus further compounded when we consider not only what women risk when they resist the 'good' woman identity, but what they give up. Caring and domesticity are women's domain, and, however undervalued, they remain sources of power and sites for positive identity construction (Henderson, Hodges, & Kivel, 2002). The following excerpt exemplifies how work in the home remains a seat for both women's power and their oppression. In this excerpt, Marta describes how she protects time for herself by 'letting go' of housework and other domestic work.

> I'm a control freak, if you haven't figured that out ((laughing)) which I'm trying to change and let go, and people will not take on responsibilities until I let them go. That was a big awareness, because one of the big issues I had with my first husband, was that he would not **help** around the house.
> *ML: OK*
> But **he** could not **help** as long as I was doing it. [...] I had to let things go [...] One of the things I've learned is that there's- there's a difference between my husband helping and my husband being co-responsible.
> *ML: Tell me about that.*
> Well, see, help means that I'm still responsible. And that, a- a- as a woman I like that, because that gave me the **control**. [...] If I- if- if it's **my** laundry, it's got to be done <my way.> [...] it's my laundry, it was **my** house, **my** kids, **my** laundry, **my** groceries, **my** cooking, it was all mine.
>
> (Marta)

This excerpt from a participant in my study on self-care is consistent with the narrative of personal transformation drawn on in women's accounts of recovery from depression. In this excerpt, Marta described herself as a 'control freak', a woman obsessed with keeping a meticulously clean house. This positioning situates her as 'good' to a fault, thereby legitimizing her claim that she needed to 'let go' of doing all the work in the home. At the same time, however, her account illustrates how resisting the 'good' woman identity is a double-edged sword. She wanted to 'let go' of her standards of domestic perfection, but in doing so, she faced relinquishing a valued sense of control and power in the home. She said, 'as a woman', she 'liked [. . .] the control'. Although living for others may be physically and emotionally taxing, to do otherwise may be to pay too high a price in terms of loss of valued identity and power.

Therefore, the risk of being positioned as a selfish, 'bad' woman, and the prospect of abandoning one's seat of power converge to constrain women's ability to nurture their own health and well-being. Indeed, even when women are *required* to take better care of themselves for medical reasons, this can remain a threatening and difficult practice to take up. For instance, in their research with women who have been diagnosed and treated for cancer, Charlene Shannon and Susan Shaw (2005) found that participants talked of the importance of self-care. However, they also found that

> while the *desire* to spend time at leisure along with the *recognition* that leisure and time for self were important existed, a few women were less able to accompany this change in attitude with change in behaviour. These women indicated that they were still constrained by feelings of guilt associated with making leisure a priority over their household tasks, family, or work.
>
> (Shannon & Shaw, 2005, pp. 204–5)

As one participant in their study said,

> Leisure is more important. I don't do it, but it's more important. *I'm not clear . . . it's more important, but you don't do it?* Right.
> *I'm sorry, can you elaborate a bit. I don't understand.*
> I mean, I know it's more important. Like, what the . . . why are we doing . . . you know, why are we knocking ourselves out? You know what I mean? Like . . . we don't know what . . . tomorrow we might be dead. And what was the last thing you did? Well, let's see . . . today I cleaned my windows. Whoop di do. You know? Who cared when you died if your windows were clean. But that's what I'd probably do. You know? Probably I'd mow the lawn so my lawns wouldn't look bad. (Michelle, 54 year-old widowed homemaker and mother of grown children)
>
> (Shannon & Shaw, 2005, pp. 204–5)

As a consequence of the social construction of femininity, many women deny or give up their efforts to engage in leisure and self-care. Females are particularly likely to abandon their own interests when they become engaged in relationships and become girlfriends, wives, and mothers (Wearing, Wearing, & Kelly, 1994). For instance, Kelly, a 22-year-old university student who participated in the self-care study, was asked about impediments to her self-care. She responded:

> Well I spend a lot of time with my boyfriend as well.
> *ML: OK*
> We, um since we're apart in the summer we spend a lot of time together during the year. A::nd trying to get him to go out and exerci(h)se is just not going to happen so.
> *ML: ((laughing)) OK*

He's just, he's- he's as lazy as they come I guess. So, I- he's another factor like if he doesn't want to do it.

(Kelly)

Kelly is not alone in giving up her leisure in order to conform to the desires of her male companion. Indeed it is the norm for girls with steady boyfriends to forgo their own interests in order to spend time with them, often orienting around males' interests instead of their own (Herridge, Shaw, & Mannell, 2003). For instance, a study conducted in a rural Australian community found that '92% of boys played football and 80% of girls watched it on a Saturday. Only 28% of the girls reported playing any sports on a Saturday. Not one boy watched a girl's sport' (Dempsey, 1989, p. 32). The finding that girls tend to sacrifice their own interests for those of their boyfriends was also prominent in a study of the accounts of 'delinquent' girls in Canada (Reitsma-Street, 1998). One participant in this study said, 'I used to like sports and movies. But now I act differently. I changed my friends from girlfriends to a boyfriend who does drugs. We just hang around, with his boyfriends and their girls' (p. 95). Reitsma-Street (1998) described how the girls in her study aimed to attract and hold a boyfriend by caring for him and prioritizing his needs. Many of these girls described hoping to escape from the violence in their parents' homes by getting married and establishing homes of their own. In securing their relationships and prioritizing the needs of boyfriends, however, these girls not only reduced their leisure, but also their attendance at school, time for study, and preparation and training for employment. Moreover, these girls cited the importance of their boyfriends' needs and pleasure as primary reasons for not using safer-sex practices (Reitsma-Street, 1998). Thus, for these girls, the cost of sacrificing their own interests had far-reaching consequences including the violation of their health and safety.

For many girls, the denial of their own pleasure, play, and self-care intensifies with age and their increasing involvement in the heterosexual matrix. As girls enter adolescence, they become increasingly less likely than boys to pursue leisure interests such as physical recreation (James, 2000; Vertinsky, 1998). Upon marriage, women's participation in self-care and leisure activities further decreases by as much as half, with the lowest levels among women who are mothers (Shaw et al., 1991; Woodward et al., 1989).

Interestingly, research on women's self-care and leisure in the context of their relationships suggests that lesbian women may be better able to carve out time and space for themselves than heterosexual women (Bialeschki & Pearce, 1997; Ussher & Perz, 2008; Ussher et al., 2007). One study investigating the leisure participation of nine lesbian couples with dependent children found that these women tended to have particularly equitable distributions of household labour, and partners supported each other's independent leisure (Bialeschki & Pearce, 1997). The following excerpts illustrate the common way in which these participants described their leisure and self-care.

> She respects my leisure. If I want to do something else, it just never appears to be a problem when it happens. I find she encourages me to, things that I'm interested in, she'll encourage me into it. And so I feel like she respects my leisure.

> I think that we, considering the amount of stress and how fast we go, that we do a pretty good job of helping the other person get the rest or leisure that they need. And time to themselves or their exercise or whatever. It's considered an important thing.

> O, I think she actually gives me a whole lot of leeway on my leisure. She's very respectful . . . and there's just always that space there.
>
> (Bialeschki & Pearce, 1997, p. 125)

The authors concluded that

> The respect for a partner's need for her own leisure was surprising. Past research related to women's leisure has often indicated the need for the individual woman to have time for self. Seldom has a study indicated any support from a partner or family member.
>
> (Bialeschki & Pearce, 1997, pp. 125–6)

The authors proposed that these women were not limited to traditional gender roles and the accompanying gendered division of household labour. As a result, they were able to negotiate more equitable ways of being in their relationships – ways women in many heterosexual relationships may find harder to negotiate.

Differences between the ability of heterosexual and lesbian women to negotiate self-care have also emerged in research on premenstrual change (Ussher & Perz, 2008; Ussher et al., 2007). In this set of papers, the authors reported on their quantitative and qualitative investigation of 60 heterosexual and lesbian women who presented as experiencing PMS and 23 of their partners. The authors found that while heterosexual and lesbian women reported no differences in their experiences of premenstrual distress (e.g., feeling irritable, angry or depressed, sensitivity, dislike of the body, a need to be alone), the ways in which these feelings and experiences were understood, responded to, and negotiated in their interpersonal relationships differed significantly. In particular, male partners often responded to women's premenstrual experiences with a lack of understanding or responsiveness, rejection and dismissal. These women were frequently positioned, and positioned themselves as 'monstrous' when in the throes of premenstrual change. They also tended to operate in accordance with the traditional discourse of 'silent' femininity (Ussher & Perz, 2008) and the expectation that they should be calm, controlled, and self-sacrificing. Pressed thin by the physical and emotional changes that often accompany the premenstrual phase, however, these women described breaking their pattern of self-silence and consequently experiencing themselves as 'out of control', having a 'short fuse' or feeling like a 'pressure cooker'. Participants described experiencing these instances with distress, self-castigation, and heightened self-policing, resulting in a bracketing off of their unacceptable, unwomanly expressions of anger and frustration. The pathologization of premenstrual distress and the naming of PMS offers a way of understanding the split women experience between their 'normal', placid, kind, self and the 'premenstrual monster' – the 'Jekyll and Hyde' character (Perz & Ussher, 2006; Ussher, 2006). However, hegemonic discourses of femininity are fixed in place with this construction, maintaining the expectations of the 'good' woman and underscoring women's bodies as sites of madness and badness.

In contrast to the pathologizing and rejecting response of many male partners, lesbian partners were found to be more responsive and suppor-tive, recognizing both the validity of the premenstrual woman's distress, and the fact that her behavioural reactions may be intensified due to her embodied experience of sensitivity. Accordingly, women in lesbian rela-tionships did not tend to pathologize their experiences of premenstrual change as a medical illness or dysfunction, nor did they draw on the short fuse, pressure cooker or Jekyll and Hyde metaphors. Instead, premenstrual change tended to be constructed and responded to in a normalizing, accepting, and accommodating manner in which the premenstrual woman was allowed more understanding, space and time for self-care.

> It's about . . . someone just . . . recognising that you're actually feeling really out of sorts um, and, . . . taking some of the responsibility off you to actually manage it. It's more about, well, now you're feeling crap. And I know there's nothing that much that can fix that, except if . . . you don't have to worry about . . . where the food's coming from, or, you know, I mightn't even think about a bath, and then she'll say, 'How about you go and have a bath? And I'll run it for you,' and I'll be like, 'Oh that would be really nice!'
>
> (Ussher & Perz, 2008, p. 100)

The differences between the ways in which heterosexual and lesbian women's distress and self-care are understood, responded to, and negoti-ated interpersonally does not simply depend on sexual orientation, but rather on the patterns of relating between partners, including equity, reciprocity, mutual affection, and a recognition of needs (Ussher et al., 2007). There has been a suggestion in the literature that compared with heterosexual women, lesbian women may have particularly satisfying, egalitarian and empathic relationships (Connolly & Sicola, 2006; Dunne, 1999; Eldridge & Gilbert, 1990; Matthews, Tartaro & Hughes, 2003). However, as Ussher and Perz (2008) state,

> Many heterosexual women do have partners who provide a sup-portive context for their experience of premenstrual change and distress, which acts to facilitate self-care and reduce distress (Ussher et al., 2007). Indeed, supportive heterosexual relationships share the same qualities as supportive lesbian relationships – affection, containment of relational conflict and psychologically intimate communication between partners
>
> (pp. 105–6)

Thus, the ways in which women experience distress and respond with self-care are inextricably linked to their intersubjectivity (Ussher & Perz, 2008). Women's ability to nurture themselves is largely dependent upon their ability to express their needs, and have this expression responded to with acceptance and responsiveness. However, as is so often the case in hetero-sexual relationships, when women are constrained by traditional discourses of silent femininity which orient them around the needs of others, they often deny themselves and are denied opportunities to identify, express and meet their own needs and pleasures (Ussher, 2003a). While preserving a selfless orientation and abandoning self-care may serve to protect a woman's identity and sense of self, it often leaves her feeling unfulfilled at best, physically and emotionally depleted and exhausted at worst.

> [There] just isn't a lot of extra time to do anything I want to do, sandwiched in between what the kids need and the physical needs of the house and everybody else and what's left over . . . I don't think I have a lot of choice. I think things are pretty well laid out as to what is to be done and what's not to be done. One of my main gripes which is that I find that lacking. There isn't, uh . . . a a real me around.
>
> (Freysinger & Flannery, 1992, p. 313)

This excerpt from a woman's account of her experiences of her leisure, work, and family, again echoes the work by Dana Jack (1991), who argued that women are socialized to prioritize relationships. In the interest of preserving harmony in their relationships, women put the needs and desires of others first, thereby negating their own. Jack refers to this process as 'silencing the self' and equates it with depression. While this woman was not identified as depressed, her account is remarkably similar to the accounts of depressed women (Jack, 1991; Mauthner, 2002; Nicholson, 1998; Stoppard, 2000). When women talk about their lives, very often they express the physical and emotional exhaustion and an alienation from self that comes from living as a 'good' woman (O'Grady, 2005). Although self-silencing is destructive, women may feel they have few choices in a society that defines femininity and goodness with self-sacrifice. A woman's value remains in her ability to care; self-sacrifice is her virtue.

To summarize, the social construction of (heterosexual) femininity orients women around the needs of others, resulting not only in the material constraints on women's time, but also in terms of discursive constraint whereby women's self-care is equated with selfishness and immorality. A woman's freedom to attend to and nurture her own health, happiness and pleasure is dependent upon the nature of her interpersonal relationships, with more egalitarian, accepting and responsive relationships facilitating greater self-care. Further, a woman's freedom to self-care is dependent upon and regulated by the state, religious, and cultural practices of her local context that regulate her freedom of expression, movement, and choice, including reproductive freedom and access to contraception and abortion. The women I interviewed enjoyed the relative freedoms of a Western and largely secularized society, to move around, speak, make choices about reproduction, and interact with others, both male and female. Certainly, many of their counterparts do not enjoy such freedoms and instead face additional and entwined restrictions on their abilities to attend to their own needs, health, and pleasures.

In addition to the social and political constraints on women's freedom, women's ability to attend to their own needs is restricted by their access to material resources. It remains a consistent finding that women have lower income relative to men and that women are over-represented among the poor (United Nations Development Program [UNDP], 1995, 1997). Overall, women account for up to 70 per cent of the world's poor and women with children represent the largest group of people living in poverty (UNDP, 1995; WHO, 2000a). In industrialized countries, women who are single mothers, racial and ethnic minorities, elderly, and/or disabled are at highest risk for living in poverty (WHO, 2000a). For instance, Aboriginal women and women of colour are significantly more likely to be poor than white women (UNDP, 1997). Worldwide, a poor person is more likely to be a woman, African, a child or elderly person, landless, and a refugee or displaced person (UNDP, 1997). Thus marginalized women and women with care-giving responsibilities are at the highest risk for experiencing poverty.

Poverty can exact both direct and indirect effects on women's health through malnutrition, unsafe housing, and inadequate health care, as well as by limiting a woman's ability to attend to herself due to lack of resources such as money, time, energy, safety, and support. Indeed, it has been found that '[s]ocial class and economic factors are powerful indicators of leisure participation, with disadvantaged women (low income, unemployed, single parents, etc.) being more likely than other social groups to experience constraints to participation' (Brown et al., 2001, p. 134). Lack of transportation, the cost of equipment or supplies, membership fees, and the high cost of childcare have all been identified as barriers to women's leisure participation (Brown et al., 2001; Cody & Lee, 1999). For example, in a study of the leisure activities of women workers living in a poor neighbourhood in Brazil, discretionary money was identified as a central constraining factor. Those who were most likely to report leisure were single women with no children (Pondé & Santana, 2000).

In addition to economic disadvantage, women's health and their freedom to care for the self are also substantially affected and constrained by violence. Violence by men against women is a problem in all regions of the world; the lifetime prevalence of domestic violence has been estimated to be between 10 per cent and 50 per cent (WHO, 2000a, 2000b). Not surprisingly, experiencing physical, emotional, and sexual violation is associated with greater risk of a host of significant health problems including injury, chronic pain, gastrointestinal disorders, substance abuse, anxiety, depression, and suicide (Canadian Research Institute for the Advancement of Women [CRIAW], 2002; Mazure et al., 2002; WHO, 2000b).

Fear of violence constrains women's health and well-being even among those women who may not be directly exposed to violence in the home. For instance, 42 per cent of Canadian women compared with 10 per cent of men feel 'totally unsafe' walking in their own neighbourhoods after dark (Statistics Canada, 1995). Fear of being out alone after dark has been found to be a significant barrier to women's leisure participation in research conducted in the United States, Australia, England, and Canada (Henderson & Bialeschki, 1993; James & Embrey, 2001; Whyte & Shaw, 1994; Woodward et al., 1989). As a result of fear of violence, many women forgo solitary leisure, particularly after sundown which is a substantial period of the day in many countries, or they persist but with trepidation and anxiety (Woodward et al., 1989). Thus, in addition to the direct effects on women's health of economic marginalization and victimization, women living in such conditions are further burdened by substantial barriers to self-care.[2]

As the preceding analysis highlights, both material and discursive factors constrain women's health in general and their self-care practices in particular. Discourses of femininity and the concomitant expectation of selflessness weigh heavily in women's lives, leaving little room for women to legitimately conduct themselves in ways that might foster their own health and well-being. Given the pervasive and powerful constraints on women's health practices, the question remains: how *do* women manage to attend to and nurture their own desires, needs, and interests? Women who participated in the recovery study described taking up self-care, either as a form of medical management for depression, or as an outgrowth of their new identities brought about through their experiences of the depths of depression. Surely, other ways of understanding and experiencing self-care are available to women that do not require them to first burn out and become depressed and debilitated. In the remainder of this chapter, I will probe deeper into the accounts of women who *do* identify with the idea of nurturing themselves in their everyday lives (for a description of the self-care study, see Chapter 1). I will also explore how these accounts overlap and diverge from the accounts of the women in the recovery study, and from findings from other research in the area of women's self-care.

Findings are organized around two central patterns whereby participants negotiated hegemonic discourses of femininity in ways in which these discourses were either adopted/accommodated or resisted/transcended. I identified three main discursive devices for both patterns in the text and will describe each detail. In the first overarching pattern, idealized notions of femininity are uninterrupted or endorsed. Here, participants talked about adopting leisure and self-care through the mobilization of three ways of accounting: (1) situating self-care as a response to crisis; (2) the adoption of a 'tomboy' identity; and (3) arguing that self-care enables *better* care for others. In the second pattern, discourses of femininity are resisted through the use of another set of discursive devices: (1) a narrative of personal transformation; (2) the establishment of equity as a 'new normal'; and (3) the adoption of an eco-spiritual identity. While both overarching patterns ultimately have the effect of justifying action (taking care of the self), they operate by positioning women in different ways in relation to themselves and others. Following an applied discourse analytic orientation (Willig, 1999a), I will argue that the second pattern may be more useful for promoting more equitable gender relations and more sustainable constructions of self-care for women.

TALKING ABOUT SELF-CARE: ENDORSING AND ACCOMMODATING DISCOURSES OF FEMININITY

'It takes a meltdown to make you stop': self-care through crisis

Like so many participants in the recovery study, several women interviewed about self-care also stated that they took up this practice only after reaching a point of crisis in which they were forced to attend to their well-being. For instance, Daphne spoke of going through a painful 'personal growth journey' following the death of her infant child. In reference to this time in her life, Daphne said, 'I had to learn how to nurture myself. I had to learn [that ...] it was okay for me to have time for me'. For her, learning to take care of herself was essential to surviving the trauma of this loss. Faced with a dissolving marriage, Tanya also learned to take care of herself. She stated 'I had best focus on myself, because that's what's gonna be left. And if things hadn't worked out with my husband and I, and, ya know, our marriage had split up, what was left? **Me:::**'. Similarly, Pat described self-care as sparked by crisis. She noted that she was forced to give up work in the home and attend to her own health when she became debilitated by chronic fatigue syndrome. She described relinquishing her work in the home and attending to her body's needs when she was left with no other choice.

> But he [husband] was very helpful. [...] I'd eat supper, and basically I'd go off to bed, and he'd do like the dishes and the wash or whatever had to be done, because- and I guess that's some of the things that I thought I had to do [...] but someone else could do them I guess.
>
> ML: Was that, how was that for you relinquishing those things?
>
> I had been so, I had been so ill, that there was no question. I couldn't, as I say, I couldn't move my arm to so- I knew there was ... and it was a feeling that would come over me, of such intense tiredness and heaviness, that I knew, if I do this I won't be able to do anything for maybe a week? After. So it was just no question.
>
> (Pat)

Given the pervasive and taken-for-granted assumption that women will perform the bulk of care-giving and domestic work, and the accompanying sanctions against women's self-interest, it is not surprising that women so often get to the point of crisis before they 'let go' of the practices of femininity and take up self-care. Self-care is wrapped in moral overtones, often leaving women feeling bad (morally) for the very behaviours that might help make them feel better (physically and psychologically). As Joan said, in reflecting on her prolonged experience of depression,

> I started thinking about that when I was thinking about depression too and thinking about all the women in my life and watching the women in my life who just thought they had to handle stuff and di::d. And never taking the time to say '>Oh my God my life's too much<.' If those are my role models, it's no wonder that I got to the point I:: got to. Never

saying 'That's too much, I'm just going to stop here for a minute.' You know it takes having a meltdown to make you stop.

(Joan)

For these women, conscious attention to their own well-being was described as taken up only after it became a physical imperative. For others, self-care was similarly described as a solitary life-line in a sea of chaos. For instance, Caroline recounted having learned that regular exercise helped her to feel better and became essential to surviving a crippling work schedule. In reference to her work, she said:

I would work late, work through my noon a lot of times, or if I didn't walk in the morning, then I would go to the gym at noon, I kind of mixed them up. So, I always got my hour [of exercise] in, every day.
ML: How did you manage that? I mean, it sounds like you were just so busy, but somehow you managed to keep that there?
Yeah, I did. That was my only sanity I think. That was my only sanity. That was my only one hour to myself and I wasn't giving that up, and it was so hectic at work, and of course, I'm used to running a tight ship, and having everything just so. Well, everything wasn't just so anymore. It was **everywhere**. Like, files were out of control.

(Caroline)

When asked to account for how she managed to prioritize exercise, Caroline responds that it was her only means of coping with an overwhelming situation. Use of repetition here ('That was my only sanity. That was my only sanity. That was my only one hour to myself') serves to highlight her situation as desperate, and justify the comparatively minute allotment of time for herself ('only one hour'). She presents herself on the cusp of crisis, suggesting that without her 'one hour' she would lose her tenuous grasp on sanity. In keeping with the 'self-care through crisis' narrative, attention to herself is presented as a necessity, something she had to do in order to survive.

In examining participants' use of the crisis narrative, I wish to acknowledge both the phenomenological experience of the crises recounted, and the discursive effect of their recounting. I hope to honour participants' experiences of pain and distress while also exploring the rhetorical effects of their talk. Therefore, again, I am not questioning the reality of participants' experiences of crises and pain when I explore the discursive effects of their narratives. Here, the 'self-care through crisis' narrative has the effect of positioning self-care as essential for survival, thereby deflecting the suggestion that it is a selfish, indulgent activity. In this line of accounting, self-care is constructed as the product of the situation, not the speaker: women have to take care of themselves, not because they want to but because they have to. Therefore, the crisis narrative serves to justify self-care while protecting the speaker's identity from scrutiny.

Given the rhetorical power of the crisis narrative, it is perhaps not surprising that it is drawn on with such regularity. Moreover, it is important to consider the positioning of women who are *not* at the point of crisis in their lives – those who may be exhausted, disheartened, or depleted, but not to the point where they can no longer function. How do they justify attention to their own needs and pleasures? For many women (and many mothers in particular), the answer may be that they do not. Given the dominance of the 'good' woman identity, many women may feel unable to justify and therefore take up self-nurturing practices without a line of accounting that holds cultural currency. That is, without the imperative of a crisis, attempts to self-care may be readily construed as selfish.

The equation of women's self-care with selfishness looms large in participants' accounts and abounds in the popular media. For instance, in a seemingly progressive move, *The Oprah Magazine*, published by the American talk show host Oprah Winfrey, dedicated an issue to 'How to take good care of yourself: A guide to restoring health, heart and spirit' (2004). The self-care through crisis narrative figured prominently in this issue. For instance, the series of articles on self-care was introduced with a picture of a doctor's prescription pad scrawled with the words 'Take good care of yourself'. Further, the articles were peppered with pictures of colourful pills inscribed 'Take Care'. The first article introduced by the by-line, 'Scattered? Paralyzed? Approaching meltdown?' went on to describe how self-care was the appropriate 'prescription' for these 'diagnoses'. This presentation may be rhetorically powerful since it draws on the authority of the medical model to legitimize women's distress as severe (diagnoses) and construct self-care as an imperative, a prescription. However, it appears that whenever women's self-care is at issue, the threat of selfishness is never far. While the magazine purported to encourage women to nurture themselves, one of the featured articles was described on the cover with the line, 'Putting yourself first: When it's selfish, when it's essential'. Thus the message for women remains: when in crisis, and when essential to survival, self-care is permissible; otherwise, it is selfish.

Of course a fundamental problem with the crisis narrative is that it is available only to those women in the throes of crisis. Within the limits of this line of accounting, consideration of one's own health is permissible only when health is lost. Further, the effectiveness of the crisis narrative is time-limited; it runs thin with repeated use and becomes significantly less effective as a way of justifying self-care in the long term. Evelyn explored the difficulties and limits of the crisis narrative when she discussed her family's reaction to her experience of depression. She noted that concessions were made in her family only when she was thoroughly incapacitated.

> But it it's very interesting and all the time I might feel like ... terrible like really ... um in the times that I was sort of going dow::n and the times that I was coming up, I was still expected ah as the mo::ther to still truck the kids around. I was still expected to get out of bed haul on my jeans and truck the kids around because my husband was out working. Um you know like there was no give on anybody's part? Like so that is I think a woman's thing and I think that's universal. Like it didn't matter how crappy I felt. When I was incapacitated there was no question. But in the- when I was sort of going down and coming up stages uh the fact that I felt miserable, and awful and and tired all the time, and no con- that didn't matter to anybody. I was still expected to you know try to have meals on the table and I was still expected to truck kids and I was still expected to function as a mother. Whereas, I sort of feel when a man they always say when a man has a head cold he goes to bed for a month. Well it didn't matter for me as a woman. I was still expected to per**form** ah motherly woman things. Like meals, uh nobody still kicked in to do laundry, you know, nobody it was just expected. As a woman thing. That those things still was **my::** duties and as soon as I was home from hospital again they they got done when I was in hospital, obviously, ah you know they knew I was in so it all got done. But as soon as I come through the door? **My::** duties again. So it was just quite interesting.
>
> (Evelyn)

In this excerpt, Evelyn states that despite her experience of depression, her family's expectations of her domestic practices remained unchanged. Once the crisis had passed, she was expected to return to 'normal' and resume her focus on the family. She describes this situation as a gendered problem when she refers to it as a 'universal' 'woman's thing' and contrasts the 'give' differentially allotted to men and women who are ill ('when a man has a head cold he goes to bed for a month. Well it didn't matter for me as a woman'). Thus, not only do women often forgo self-care until their distress culminates in crisis, but the legitimacy afforded to self-care by crisis is often insufficient for the long term, and women are often expected to resume their lives as wives, mothers, and daughters once the crisis has passed.

Moreover, when a woman draws on the crisis narrative repeatedly over time, she risks not only the dismissal of her distress but her identity. Again, the 'reality' and legitimacy of one's condition is readily called into question in cases of chronic illness or disability, particularly when the problem is emotional or psychological (Good et al., 1992; Radley & Billig, 1996). 'Good' patients are expected to do what is required for recovery (e.g., follow doctor's orders, rest, self-care, etc.), and then 'get better' and 'return to normal'. When individuals fail to 'get over it' swiftly or completely, it is the person's character and not the condition that often comes into view as problematic (Kirmayer, 1988). Further, the conditions of a woman's life that might contribute to her distress are eclipsed by this individualistic understanding. The woman, her pain, and the conditions of her life become readily dismissed in the context of a society that already constructs women as over-emotional and over-reactive. Consequently, rather than garner support and compassion, the chronic sufferer is often dismissed as manipulative, histrionic, malingering, weak, or personality disordered (Lafrance, 2007a).

While a crisis narrative enables women to negotiate the negative construction of their identities, participants' talk of self-care may be considered particularly precarious. It can be argued that all talk is precarious and that discourses used to defend can also be drawn on with contrasting effect (Widdicombe & Woffitt, 1990). However, discourses are intimately connected to the ways in which society is socially, politically and economically governed (Burr, 1995). As such, certain discourses have more power or cultural currency than others. The discourse of the 'good' woman requires women to prioritize the needs of others, not themselves. Accordingly, self-care is a violation of this dominant social identity. As a result, those who speak of this activity are on precarious footing in constructing their identities in valued ways. In talking with women about self-care, I came to view selfishness as the default understanding which always loomed close to the surface. In the following extended excerpt, Dianne discusses how she learned to take care of herself through her experience of crisis and depression. In this exchange, I suggest that it is common for women to adopt and enjoy self-care after experiencing depression. My understanding disrupts Dianne's formulation that self-care was brought on by crisis, opening a 'crack in the discourse' and leaving her threatened and understandably defensive.

> And I'm going to be doing more and more. Because I think that's where I need to start and that's what my counsellor has been telling me. I need to be more assertive and to take better care of myself. To do things for myself and to be strong enough that to live with the after-effects or the consequences.

ML: Yeah, yeah. It's interesting to me, it's interesting to me that you are now taking care of yourself and it seems to be in a very positive way. It seems that you've learned so much from it and you're enjoying the activities that you have, you have planned for yourself so that you don't go, you don't become depressed. I'm not even sure what my question is but just that you wouldn't have done these things. You wouldn't have taken care of yourself in such a good way had you not become depressed.

Uh huh. Yes exactly, so that's the good coming out of it.

ML: Yeah

Maybe you know somebody else could have done those things without being depressed but me, maybe I needed, like for some people they need an illness to become aware of certain things or to do something. Me, maybe, for me it was the depression.

ML: Uh huh. I think that's very common with women.

Uh huh

ML: Yeah

Yeah. Well do you think then that we u::se the depression for that?

ML: No

That it's conscious? ((angry tone of voice))

ML: No

No? ((angry tone of voice))

ML: No >but it's just that's what I'm hearing a lot from women that they, they didn't take care of themselves or they, I mean none of us do really but it really took a crisis a really feeling going into that depression before they realized the value in it and that they really had to just kind of you do or you die kind of thing.<

Exactly, it's a matter of survival.

ML: Yeah and the importance gets placed on that in a different way, if that makes sense.

I don't know if the other women told you at first that they would resist it. Like my friends would tell me, 'Listen you need to get out more, you need to do things for yourself.' And I would, well sometimes I would say 'Oh yes, I need to.' But deeply I wasn't thinking, no no I don't need that.

ML: Yeah, yeah

I was really resisting it.
ML: Yeah, I've heard that too. So that's interesting a a common path.
Well good.

(Dianne)

In this exchange, Dianne positions self-care as an imperative, something she had to do in the face of the depths of her despair. She explains that she took up self-care only in response to her depression, and on the advice of her counsellor. Together, these explanations situate her self-care as a forced choice, well outside the purview of her character. That is, the fact that she takes care of herself is presented as having nothing to do with who she is, and later is presented as incongruous with who she is ('I was really resisting it'). While I was talking with Dianne, I began to piece together the pattern in women's accounts wherein they spoke of self-care as emerging through crisis. I reflected on this observation in my fumbling line of questioning when I suggested that it is common for women to take up and enjoy self-care. However, my comment is responded to with anger as it scratches the surface of the apparently ever-present doubt about the legitimacy of women's distress and their self-care. My questioning appears to raise the suggestion that women 'u::se' depression as a 'conscious', presumably manipulative excuse to indulge in nurturing themselves. My rushed and apologetic account serves to repair and I am able to discursively navigate this accusation by reinstating the narrative of self-care through crisis ('do or die'). Dianne's response echoes this position, 'Exactly, it's a matter of survival' and is furthered by stating that she in fact resisted self-care. Positioning self-care as an unwanted activity further inoculates against the suggestion that she was personally motivated to take up the practice, and that she used depression as an excuse. Therefore, although the crisis narrative can be rhetorically powerful, when women talk about self-care, they appear to face significant risks in terms of the legitimacy of their identity and their despair.

The tomboy identity

Thus far, women's talk of self-care has been explored as intimately linked to discourses of femininity. Because women are socially constructed to be other-focused, attention to the self is readily viewed as selfish, unfeminine, and unacceptable. A second way in which participants navigated hegemonic discourses of femininity through complicity was to transpose them altogether and adopt a male identity. Pat, Caroline, and Jacqueline all positioned themselves within the male identity of the tomboy. This rhetorical strategy was interesting not only because it provides further support for the argument that discourses of femininity pose a central threat to women's engagements in self-focused behaviour, but also because these instances in

136

the text represented rare occasions in which participants talked of *enjoying* leisure and self-care. Across women's accounts, leisure and self-care were most often described as ways of managing crises, for instance by warding off depression, stress, and illness. When participants *did* talk about experiencing leisure as pleasure, they tended to do so in the context of childhood experiences, most notably when they played as 'one of the boys'. For instance, Pat described growing up as an active child in a community of boys. She said, 'I remember growing up as a child, I was, I had a brother, and we had more boys in our neighbourhood or farming community, than we had girls it seemed, so I was able to run, and I ran with them'. For her, being fit and active was central to her discussion of self-care.

> ML: And it seems to me that you have very different relationship, very **positive** relationship with your body through activity.
>
> Yes, and I'm sure that that goes way back to when I was young and being active was fun.
>
> ML: Yeah
>
> And it just, we did so many fun things and it all involved, that you had to be fit, or you just couldn't do them, and I didn't want to lose that opportunity of being able to do the really fun things. Because my brother um, had a canoe, so we would canoe, we'd go snowshoeing and winter camping things, so
>
> ML: Yeah
>
> I thought, well, why would a person have to give this up, just because they get older? You could still ... do those things.
>
> (Pat)

Caroline described her introduction to leisure in a very similar way. Again, physical activities such as canoeing and wilderness hiking were at the focus of Caroline's account of self-care. She described learning to love physical play as a child, and notably as a 'tomboy'.

> Like I say, I was always a tomboy, so I mean, there was hunting, **loved** to hunt, loved to fish, still do today. Love to, and ah, going out in the woods. I- I don't like to shoot anything, I just like to go out in the woods, but I love to shoot a gun. Like target practice, but I don't want to kill anything.
>
> ML: Right
>
> And um, fall is probably my favourite time of year. And, but canoeing, and swimming, and, and I guess you know with the boys, you would go to the bridge, and you'd have to jump off the bridge, cause there was just that peer pressure, that

you had to do what they did. So, I always, I don't know, I
guess I was more of a daredevil that way, because of
hanging around with them, and if you fell down you didn't cry,
because the boys didn't do that.

(Caroline)

In this excerpt, Caroline's enjoyment and choice of physical activity are
explained through positioning herself as a 'tomboy'. Both engaging in
leisure and enjoying leisure as play are consistent with a child positioning,
particularly within the positioning of a male child. Caroline stood out
among the interviews as drawing most heavily on a male identity. In fact,
she introduced herself as a 'tomboy' at the very beginning of our interview,
and referenced herself in this way throughout our exchange.

*ML: Okay, why don't we:: just begin, ju- can you tell me a
little bit about yourself?*
Ah, I am forty-five, be forty-six in [month], raised [in area],
with eight children, one of eight. Five brothers, two sisters
a::nd one of the sisters, is quite a bit younger than me, the
two last kids come **much** later, so really, the whole time I
was growing up it was just me and my sister and then the
boys, so I was actually a tomboy. She was the- girly girl and I
was the tomboy. ((laughing))

(Caroline)

By adopting a tomboy identity, Caroline simultaneously rejects the 'good'
girl/woman identity, and positions herself in a higher status. Her contrast
between the 'girly girl' and the 'tomboy' serves to highlight the power
differential between masculinity and femininity, situating herself within the
relative power of the male role. Instances of talk later in her interview
further illustrate how one's gendered position (as a tomboy vs as a woman)
shapes what activities can be legitimately performed (e.g., self-care, leisure,
play), and how such activities are experienced. In particular, Caroline
contrasts enjoying physical activity as a child (and a tomboy) with how her
understanding and experience of physical activity shifted when she grew
older in a woman's body.

Well ... as far as kind of looking after myself, ah, as far as
exercise, and food, and stuff like that, I didn't even really
think about that until I was about twenty-five. Any time
before that, any type of exercise I did, I never thought of it-
exercising for my health, it was always ... I wanted to go
skating cause I liked to skate.

138

ML: It was fun.
It was fun. It was p- of course, that is what you do when you are a kid. You know, you only do these things cause it's fun. You don't think, 'Oh, I'm gonna go out and burn X amount of calories'. ((laughing))

(Caroline)

When I first started [daily exercise regimen] at twenty-five, I didn't do it for fun. I didn't think it was fun, I just thought I'd better start doing something for my **health**, and **as** I got doing it, I got addicted to it, and it became fun again. At first it was a chore for me.

ML: Can you remember that time of why, err- not why, but how you came to that decision or- that I- I have to do this for health? Cause if it wasn't fun ...

I think it was, I think it was because I saw that I **had** to work hard to get my weight down?

ML: OK

and, I was bound that I wasn't gonna let that go back on.

ML: Yeah

So, I kept my weight, really, really too light for me, for a long time, but see when you're single, I wouldn't eat a piece of chocolate if my life depended on it. And like- we'd go to- all these guys I worked with would say, 'let's go to the [pub]' whatever, they would have the french fries and all that, and I'd have the salad, maybe a piece of chicken. [...] So, I ah, I was **very** careful. Once I lost my weight, I was very careful about what I ate. I exercised every day. It was like, I had to get- it's like going out of the house without brushing your teeth- you just- you don't feel right all day. If I don't get my exercise, even now, if I don't get my exercise in, it's like my day doesn't go right. I'm not in as good a mood, I just, I feel like there is something missing. Like you didn't brush your teeth when you left the house. But then, I got pregnant, man, did I ever gain a lot of weight- forty-two or forty-five pounds when I got pregnant. And he was small. That was the worst part of it. He was three weeks early, he was a preemie, little, little, little. So, then, after I had him, I struggled, and I still struggle.

ML: Struggle?
To keep- I never did get back to where I was.

(Caroline)

In the first excerpt, Caroline describes engaging in physical activity for no reason other than enjoyment. She situates exercise for weight loss as a child as unfathomable ('I didn't even really **think** about that until I was about twenty-five') and ridiculous ('You don't think, "Oh, I'm gonna go out and burn X amount of calories" ((laughing))'). However, what is ridiculous for the tomboy-child becomes a serious enterprise for the woman-adult. The age of twenty-five is presented as a turning point in her story; the time at which she developed a rounded female form, and when exercise became work ('work hard', 'a chore') instead of play. Therefore, in contrast to the pleasure of movement and play she experienced as a child and a tomboy, physical activity became a means of disciplining her developing female form. A central way in which femininity is performed is through the intentional shaping of the female body (Bordo, 1993), and Caroline emphasizes her exceptional performance through her description of her dieting as extreme ('I kept my weight, really, really too light'). The gendered nature of eating (or not eating) is further developed when she compares men's careless consumption to the 'hard work' and self-discipline required of her as a person in a woman's body ('they would have the french fries and all that, and I'd have the salad'). Moreover, attention to her female form becomes even more salient when she highlights the fact that she was an unmarried woman. Her statement, 'but see when you're single, I wouldn't eat a piece of chocolate if my life depended on it' is based on the assumption that being single is unacceptable and that unattached women must do everything in their power to remedy this shameful position. She explains that through rigorous self-monitoring and self-discipline she worked to achieve an acceptable body in a process that has now become routinized. Despite her intense efforts at self-discipline, however, her material body limits the shape that can be achieved. Therefore, this account serves as a reminder that we can position ourselves in various ways (e.g., as a tomboy), but our discursive positioning will always be inextricably linked to materiality (e.g., living in a female body, pregnancy).

Caroline's account also highlights the discursive tension that arises when one adopts a masculine identity (tomboy) but engages in traditionally feminine behaviour (dieting). Both Caroline and Jacqueline prided themselves on their athletic prowess as being equal to a man's, but both also spoke about struggling with their weight.

Okay, um, I've always battled weight. That's probably been my biggest- and I used to say by the time I'm fifty I'm going to be fit as a fiddle and I'm gonna drop all this weight and everything will be fine. Well, fifty-one came, and fifty-two came, and fifty-three came, and when I hit fifty-four [...] I kind of thought, okay, this is the way I'm gonna be, and that's fine. And it never really stopped me, like I was an avid canoer, and when the men ran out of men they'd come for me to go, cause I could keep up with them and that sort of thing. [...] I like a slimmer body, more than I do a fatter one but I mean, it never, like you'll hear some people, 'Well, I won't go here' or 'I won't put a bathing suit on', or 'I won't' you know whatever, 'cause I'm overweight'. I don't think it ever stopped me in any of those ways, and I still felt that I could dress and look as nice as anyone else, although I weighed two hundred and some pounds ((laughter)). But I think the big difference is in my energy level. When I weigh less I have more energy.

(Jacqueline)

I read about Weight Watchers in the newspaper, and thought, ah::, 'I just want to get this weight off' and I wasn't gonna starve myself. I decided I wasn't gonna do that. I don't know why I decided that, but I did.

ML: Why did you want to get the weight off?

I just felt uncomfortable.

ML: Yeah

I just felt uncomfortable. I felt I didn't, look good in my clothes and again, still very outgoing, and never stayed home because of it ... I **never** did that. I wasn't, I was never a closet eater type thing [...] A lot of people are less social when they're- when they're heavy, because they're self-conscious, like for example, if everybody said, let's go to the beach, well, I would haul on a bathing suit and I would go to the beach.

ML: What's the difference there? Between your being able to haul it on go to the beach, and other people.

Well, did you ever see those commercials on TV, and you've got this skinny woman, a::nd, you got the heavy man, and he's saying, hmm, 'I'm looking pretty good', and she's saying, ah:::, 'does this make me look fat?' Maybe cause I was raised around boys and they don't **worry** about that

stuff so much. Maybe I even worry about that. Even though I
didn't feel comfortable, and I didn't feel gr- that I looked my
best, cause I knew what- I had been thinner, so I knew what
better looked like, and, but it still didn't stop me. [...] Now,
mind you I wouldn't wear as tight of **clothes** or whatever, but
I would still, and I wouldn't wear a two piece, I wouldn't be
floating around the beach with a bikini on, I'd have a one
piece on, and probably something with tummy control in it,
you know, ((laughing)) whatever, I'd adapt.
ML: Yeah
but >I wouldn't stay home<. I wouldn't stay home and I know
a couple of my friends, one of them has varicose veins,
sh- nice looking girl, she- she wears long pants all the time. I
said, like in that heat, heat, heat these long pants, and I said,
'there's no way', and she said, 'oh yeah if you had them,
you- you would wear long pants too'. I said 'no, I wouldn't. I
just know myself.'

(Caroline)

In these excerpts, both Jacqueline and Caroline speak from a male/tomboy
identity, but their concern with their weight is at odds with this positioning.
Thus, speakers appear faced with an 'ideological dilemma' (Billig, Condor,
Edwards, Gane, Middleton, & Radley, 1988), stuck between masculinity
and femininity as two unsatisfactory and irreconcilable subject positions.
Both reconcile this dilemma with a discursive strategy that at once maintains their rejection of traditional femininity, while also maintaining a
footing within both masculine and feminine frames. Both speakers acknowledge their desire for a slimmer body, however, they qualify this desire and
their discomfort in their own bodies with the claim that despite their weight
dissatisfaction, they never let it stop them ('And it never really stopped me',
'I don't think it ever stopped me' (Jaqueline), 'never stayed home because of
it', 'but it still didn't stop me', 'but I wouldn't stay home' (Caroline)). Social
comparison is again at work in these accounts, serving to position speakers
as more secure and independent than other women who curtail their activity
because of weight concerns. Thus, although both women report dissatisfaction with their figures, they are able to maintain their resistance of
traditional femininity in their claim that while they are women who diet,
they are not 'that kind of woman' (i.e., the insecure, pathetic type). This
device enables a straddling of masculine and feminine identity positions.
Despite their commitment to not being limited by the social construction of
femininity, both live within a cultural context that focuses on women's
bodies and requires thinness for beauty. As Caroline states, while she

142

doesn't let her weight 'stop' her, neither would she wear a bikini in public – she both resists and adapts.

To speak from a tomboy identity enables women to justify leisure, play, and self-care as well as *the enjoyment* of these activities. However, materiality and discourse are inextricably linked, limiting a woman's access to a masculine identity and the legitimacy it affords. Furthermore, I contend that while the effect of this way of accounting is desirable, the means (claiming a masculine identity) is not. Although the co-option of a masculine identity clearly affords greater power, what is ultimately required is greater power for women to speak and be in ways of their choosing.

Self-care is like an oxygen-mask: 'you can't take care of others if you don't take care of yourself'

Thus far, I have argued that as a result of hegemonic discourses of femininity, women risk being positioned as selfish and contemptible when they relinquish practices of femininity and attend to their own health, needs, and pleasures. Supporting this thesis is the finding that a third dominant way in which participants talked about self-care was to define it as *consistent* with the 'good' woman identity, arguing that self-nurturance enables one to become a better, more effective care-giver. In this line of accounting, self-care is constructed as motivated by the care of others, not the self. That is, self-care is constructed as decidedly *unselfish*. For instance, participants routinely talked about paying close attention to their health and well-being when pregnant or in the context of caring for their children. In the following excerpt, Charlotte describes 'taking care of myself' through nutrition, a newly acquired behaviour intended to model appropriate eating habits to her child.

> I'm actually taking care of myself now. I never used to care.
> If I ate, I ate, I was-
> *ML: How do you take care of yourself?*
> I actually make sure I eat once a day if we can afford it. [...]
> Um, I try to actually eat vegetables ... ((laughter)) That's a
> big thing!
> *ML: How did you come to that?*
> Um, I realized that [my daughter] wasn't going to eat it if I
> didn't.
>
> (Charlotte)

Similarly, Elizabeth stated that while she normally struggles to take care of herself, she took very good care of herself both times she was pregnant.

Suddenly it [self-care] takes on a different importance when it isn't just you. When you're carrying another person ... that becomes a much higher priority. Eating the right food, getting enough rest, you know doing the preparatory exercises and all of that good stuff.

ML: Good. So those two times

Yes, I would say were ah, were very significant. And I suppose if you unpack that it's well, 'Isn't it enough to take care of your body for yourself? Do you only take care of your body when you're carrying a baby?'

ML: How do you answer that?

Well, I'm sure it was part of what shaped my, my attitude. Because I- I really, I really wanted to be a mother and I wanted to do this right. And this was before the period that ah smoking in public places was banned, and I remember going to a meeting one time [...] and the room was just full of cigarette smoke, and having to ask the man to put his cigarette out. Now, if I had not been pregnant, I probably would have just put up with it. But there was no way I was gonna do that carrying a child. [...] So in other words, I'm not just being selfish, I'm being **un**selfish to ask you to put, put out your cigarette.

ML: Ah. Tell me about that.

((laughter)) So, stupid isn't it, that at that time, because it wasn't generally accepted that people shouldn't be smoking in public.

ML: Right

That I was interfering with his rights. I'm not interfering with your rights on my behalf, I'm interfering with your rights on my child's behalf. My unborn child.

ML: Yes. That makes all the difference doesn't it? So those were two really pristine times it sounds like, in your life, where you really prioritized your well-being at all costs.

And then as soon as you're actually dealing with having a new infant in the house you go back to ... putting your needs ((laughter)) very much at the bottom of the pile because you've got this baby to look after.

(Elizabeth)

As illustrated in Elizabeth's account, taking care of herself when pregnant signified her fitness as a 'good' mother. As she said, when motivated by the needs of her child, self-care takes on a 'different importance' and became 'a much higher priority'. Elizabeth's story of the man with the cigarette paints a picture of a woman who would not act to protect her own health – to do so would be to 'interfere with the rights of others' and be 'selfish'. However, as a pregnant woman, she acquires the right to demand a healthy and safe environment – not for herself, but for her child. Again, self-care for women comes into view as acceptable when done for the benefit of others, but not the self.

The discursive strategy whereby women are encouraged to look after their own health in order to better care for their family was coined 'the oxygen-mask theory' by the talk show host, Oprah Winfrey (Winfrey, 2002). As the analogy goes, passengers in an aeroplane are instructed to secure their own oxygen-mask before attending to dependants. They are warned that if they do not heed this advice, they may not have sufficient oxygen to care for both themselves and their charge, leaving both in peril. This discursive strategy is framed by crisis thereby constructing self-care as an imperative – something women have to do. Further, self-care is equated with oxygen and constructed as essential for survival. Indeed, in this light, self-care is constructed as morally responsible, countering the suggestion of selfish motivation. In her magazine column, Oprah Winfrey explained:

> None of us is built to run nonstop. That's why, when you don't give yourself the time and care you need, your body rebels in the form of sickness and exhaustion. Taking care of yourself so you can better care for others is an idea many women I talk to still can't embrace. But think of it in terms of the oxygen-mask theory: if you don't put on your mask first, you won't be able to save anyone else.
>
> (Winfrey, 2002)

The rhetorical device of the oxygen-mask is frequently mobilized in articles aimed at promoting women's and care-giver's self-care. For instance, a headline in one of Canada's leading newspapers read, 'You can't care for your spouse unless you look after yourself' (Maté, 2006). Further, advice in a woman's magazine encourages women to

> Commit to taking care of yourself. Get more rest if you need it, and take time to do the things you enjoy: reading a book, taking a walk. Many times women are afraid they will be perceived as selfish by taking time for themselves . . . but you can't be there for your family, your employees, or your friends if you're not there for yourself.
>
> (Homemakers Magazine, 2003, p. 37)

Consistent with these depictions in the media, the oxygen-mask device was drawn on with similar effect by participants describing their attempts to encourage other women to self-care. Daphne noted that she often offers to baby-sit her neighbours' children in order to give them time for themselves. However, she stated that women do not take her up on her offer. Lamenting their refusals, she stated, 'If you don't nurture yourself, you're gonna, you know, it's like the glass, you could only give out so much water before the glass is empty'. Similarly, Jacqueline, a nurse who works with women with substance addictions, described her frustration in working with female patients who fail to take care of their own needs.

> I preach to other people that you can't take care of other people if you don't take care of your fir- yourself first. Like really, passive people, I'd just like to take them and shake them and say, 'it's okay to look after you, cause how can you look after someone else if you don't take care of you first?'
>
> (Jacqueline)

Interestingly, the oxygen-mask device was frequently drawn on in conjunction with social comparison whereby speakers positioned themselves in relation to other women. As discussed previously, the rhetorical device of social comparison is a way of constructing one's identity (Widdicombe & Wooffitt, 1990; Wood & Kroger, 2000). By comparing oneself (favourably) with others, one's own positioning can be built up as acceptable, legitimate, and desirable. Here, those who fail to take proper care of themselves are positioned as misguided, weak, self-defeating, or pathetic ('Many times women are afraid they will be perceived as selfish' (Homemakers Magazine, 2003, p. 37); 'an idea many women I talk to still can't embrace' (Winfrey, 2002); 'Like really, passive people, I'd just like to take them and shake them' (Jacqueline)). In contrast, the speakers' endorsements of self-care practices are positioned as reasonable and justified. In the following excerpt, Tanya tells the story of a woman so depleted by care-giving that she required extensive medical attention. Through the telling of this narrative, Tanya defends her own actions of letting go of exclusive care for others, and taking up care for the self.

> This friend that I walk with at lunch time, she has been sick since Christmas time, with this cough, and she's had, **x-rays,** and allergy tests and she can't get rid of this cough, and she looks after her- her father's in a home, ... sh- she is **so** focussed on helping other people and she has a daughter and a couple of grandchildren. It's like she is an extension of

their life, and-and she is fifty-three years old, an- and I said to her yesterday, she's been **so, so, so** sick, and um, I said, 'you have got to focus on yourself and- and let your other family members fend- ya know, fend for themselves for a while, you've got to get better.' [...] But she is so guilty, she would feel **so** guilty. When she wants a day off, she checks in with the rest of her family, to say, 'I'm gonna be home, I'm just taking a day off.' And I can't get my head wrapped around that at all. She just ca::nnot seem to take, even a day's vacation to be by herself and enjoy her pool. She has to um, invite other family members. She's **al::ways**, always, got to be, um, looking after, making sure they're okay, and she's, oh, I've seen what it's done to her.

ML: *How did she respond when you said-*

She doesn't ah, understand it. She cannot gra::sp what I'm- she really, I don't think she- she gets, gets it at all. I- I think she would think of it as being ah, selfish and not a good mother, daughter, grandmother, [...]

ML: *How do you respond to that?*

I try to ah, talk positively about it, and encourage her, you know, and you know, 'you- you've gotta, if you don't look after yourself, >you're not gonna have the energy to play with your grandkids<' and you know, 'you've been sick since Christmas'. She ended up in the hospital this past weekend. I mean, my heart goes out to her [...], she's a- a wonderful, loving person, but way::: too much.

(Tanya)

In this account, Tanya tells the story of a friend who selflessly works to care for others to the detriment of her own health. This behaviour is clearly gendered and equated with being 'good mother, daughter, grandmother'. The discursive consequences of stepping outside the selfless 'good' woman identity is also clearly delineated as 'selfish' and something that makes women feel 'guilty'. In positioning herself in contrast with her friend, self-lessness and self-sacrifice are constructed as self-defeating, passive, and incomprehensible ('I can't get my head wrapped around that at all'). Through extreme case formulation, Tanya builds up as excessive both her friend's behaviour ('sh- she is **so** focussed on helping other people'; 'she is an extension of their life'; 'She's **al::ways**, always, got to be, um, looking after') and her debilitation ('she's been **so, so, so** sick'). Tanya's suggestion that her friend take time for herself is thus positioned as reasonable, and ultimately something that will enable her to better care for her family. Hegemonic discourses of femininity loom large in this account and are negotiated with the mobilization of the oxygen-mask device. Tanya said in quick and decisive tones, 'if you don't look after yourself >you're not gonna have the energy to play with your grandkids<'. In this way, self-care is constructed as driven by the needs of others, and therefore within the boundaries of proper femininity.

The finding that women's self-care is motivated and limited by their care for others echoes findings from a qualitative study on women's management of diabetes that was conducted in England. Julie Hepworth (1999) interviewed 16 women with diabetes, with the aim of exploring how women construct diabetes management, and how social and familial structures figure into their health practices. She found that the women she interviewed often failed to manage their diabetes properly because they put the food preferences of their husbands and children ahead of their own dietary needs. She noted: '[a]ll women were expected to maintain sameness in food provision for men in order to meet men's preferences' (1999, p. 263); as a result, the women's own health was put at risk. As one of the participants in her study stated,

> I am not going to cook differently for the rest of the family than for myself. Because I have a teeneage son who goes to work. He wants fried chips. I cook up fried chips and I'm not going to cook up something different for myself. That is way beyond me. It is just too much. I'll just have a few of his fried chips and things like that.
>
> (Hepworth, 1999, p. 263)

However, the women Hepworth interviewed described being better able to manage their diabetes when they had gestational diabetes or when their husbands also had diabetes. In these instances, attention to a woman's own health became justified, couched in terms of care for others. For instance, the following two excerpts are from interviews with women who spoke of caring for their health when pregnant.

> I was very . . . I didn't eat one thing that I wasn't supposed to eat. I was very religious. I ate when I was supposed to eat, what I was supposed to eat, and how much and it wasn't until Shane was born that I thought OK, enough.
>
> (Hepworth, 1999, p. 263)

> Only for him, that was the sole reason. If I wasn't pregnant I wouldn't have worried about it. But that was the only reason.
>
> (Hepworth, 1999, p. 263)

Similarly, women whose husbands also had diabetes often spoke of their own diabetes management in terms of meeting their husbands' needs.

> We always go to the podiatrist for our feet and the eye specialist for our eyes.
>
> (Hepworth, 1999, p. 262)

> My husband was not a sweet tooth either so that is all right. We always loved veggies so that is all right too. I haven't got much difficulty with the cooking.
>
> (Hepworth, 1999, p. 262)

> His diet is quite strict. He has got to have a lot of carbohydrate. We like salads in the summer time. We occasionally have spaghetti. I virtually have what he has, other than I don't eat fruit.
>
> (Hepworth, 1999, p. 263)

Notably, across the previous three extracts, diabetes management is spoken of as a shared activity ('We always go to the podiatrist for our feet and the eye specialist for our eyes', 'We always loved veggies', 'We like salads'). As Hepworth (1999) points out in relation to these women's accounts, 'there is a conflation of the husband's health interests with [hers], and an expectation that she will meet her husband's needs before her own are addressed' (p. 263). Thus, when care for the self is couched in terms of care for others, it is positioned as an activity consistent with the 'good' woman ideal, and therefore becomes acceptable.

Hepworth summarized her findings by concluding that her 'study demonstrates the particular difficulties that women face in initiating and maintaining changes for diabetes self-care. Women's needs become secondary to the organization of the household and the eating patterns of others' (1999, p. 264). However, when attention to one's own needs is framed in terms of care for others, it becomes justified and may be more likely adopted in everyday practice.

The notion that women are better equipped to care for others when they care for themselves can be mobilized to encourage women to attend to their own health and needs. For instance, in a study of mothers' experiences of physical activity, Lewis and Ridge (2005) found differences between those who did and those who did not participate in regular exercise. Mothers who were not physically active tended to construct such activity as 'selfish', while those who managed to engage in regular activity constructed it as a way of coping with motherhood, thereby enabling them to be 'better mothers'.[3] The authors concluded that physical activity 'has much more positive meanings for women when it is constructed as something which can help them cope better with the challenges of being a mother and contributing to the well-being of the family' (p. 2299). Further, they argued that

> a crucial point made by women is that, for mothers, physical activity is often underpinned by the 'ethic of care'. That is, physical activity is not necessarily about 'time for self' and thereby in conflict with their notions of being a good mother. Physical activity is often quite consciously constructed around the needs of others and this provides a satisfying resolution to the tensions they experience between self-care and the care of others.
>
> (Lewis & Ridge, 2005, p. 2299)

Thus, the idea that self-care enhances women's ability to care for others appears to resonate with women and provides a satisfactory justification for women's self-care. However, while this strategy may be used to promote positive change, it also maintains the hegemony of discourses of femininity and the expectation of women's perpetual self-sacrifice.

The interweaving of discursive resources

Thus far, I have elaborated on three different ways of accounting that justify women's self-care through complicity with discourses of femininity: the crisis narrative, the tomboy identity, and the equation of self-care with better care for others. Before offering a critique of these strategies, I want to illustrate the flexibility of discourse. Discursive resources are not monolithic entities that operate in isolation. Rather, they are fluid and flexible and can be drawn on in conjunction with or in opposition to other strategies as people 'try on' different ways of accounting. The following excerpt from Charlotte's interview demonstrates both the fluidity of discourse and the dangers for women in claiming self-care. She begins by drawing on a crisis narrative justifying time for herself ('mommy time'). Later in the excerpt, she adopts the argument that her self-care results in better care for her daughter. Throughout her talk of self-care, she defends against being positioned as an unfit mother. Again, this excerpt illustrates how the mere mention of self-care raises a host of problems for the speaker's identity as a loving, caring, and competent mother.

> Mommy time is, I need sanity time. Even before [having daughter]. I need time for **me**.
> ML: So mommy time is sanity time.
> Yeah. It's time just for me, where I:: do something I want to do, be it, read a chapter in a book, have a bath, >which I can't do when she's awake, but, ah, unless she comes in

with me, uh, and I like the water too hot<, um, it's time
where, if I want to break out the barbeque potato chips, I can
have potato chips and dip without- she's not allowed to have
chips. I'm a bossy mom, picky on food, um, things like that.
So it was strictly **selfish::** time.
ML: Selfish?
Totally selfish. It was all for me! Sometimes I'd give myself
a facial, or a manicure, no nail polish, cause of the fumes,
but just totally for **me**.
ML: Yeah, OK
Most times it was just shaving my legs. ((laughter))

(Charlotte)

Charlotte begins by drawing on the crisis narrative, insisting that she needs
time for herself in order to maintain her sanity. She then goes on to list her
self-care activities ('read a chapter in a book, have a bath') but then
interrupts her list. She switches from a slow listing speed, to a faster-paced
repair, addressing the problem of how she cares for her toddler child when
she is taking a bath. Thus, in describing her self-care, her own care-giving
comes into question. She accounts for this problem by stating that she does
not take a bath when the child is awake, unless the child comes in with her.
This qualification seems to pose another problem (hot water could hurt her
child) and she repairs again, abandons the topic of the bath, and resumes
her list. However, the next item on her list, indulging in barbeque chips,
also poses problems for fitness as a mother. She clarifies that she eats the
chips but would not allow her child to do so. She then states that she is in
fact, a 'bossy mom' who is 'picky on food', highlighting herself as a particularly strict mother who monitors her child's behaviour closely. She tries
one more time to pick up her list of indulgences, but runs into trouble yet
again – she states that she gives herself a manicure, but qualifies that she
does not use nail polish because of the fumes it would release. Notably,
each of her claims of self-care is coupled with a discursive move that
defends her as a caring and capable mother. Once again, self-care for
women comes into view as a particularly threatening thing to acknowledge
and put into practice.

Threaded throughout Charlotte's account is the idea that self-care was an
indulgent activity meant just for her. She emphasizes and repeats the words
'me' and 'I' ('I need time for **me**. [. . .] It's time just for me, where **I::** do
something **I** want to do') and in an interesting discursive move, culminates
in calling her activities 'selfish'. By squarely positioning her behaviour as
'strictly' and 'totally selfish', she irreverently accepts being characterized as
such, thereby minimizing and deflecting the weight of this accusation. This

151

is a rare instance in the text whereby a woman defended self-care by defiantly situating her behaviour as selfish, a finding which may reflect both the power of the accusation and the precariousness of the strategy.

There are, however, numerous examples of how this strategy is mobilized in the media to invite women to 'indulge' in self-care. For instance, a magazine advertisement for Botox$^©$ shows a smiling woman headed by the caption: 'Three good reasons. Me, myself and I'. Similarly, an advertisement for women's (pink) razors is presented like an advice column. It invites women to 'break out of their comfort zone' and do things for themselves. The first caption of the ad reads, 'Be selfish – Do things that bring happiness and a sense of self-satisfaction to your life at least once a month'. By encouraging women to become defiantly selfish, presumably by doing something for themselves 'once a month', permission is granted for attending to their own needs. This discursive strategy may serve to deflect feelings of guilt so often expressed by participants in their accounts of self-care. The social construction of women as solely concerned for the well-being of others is also captured in an advertisement for women's vitamins. The ad shows the smiling face of a woman who appears to have just emerged from a swim at the beach. The caption across the centre of the page reads, 'Initially you might feel guilty having so many nutrients all to yourself'. According to the cultural ideal of the 'good' woman, doing anything for yourself (including taking a vitamin) may be reason for guilt. As a final example, a recent advertisement for women's running shoes shows the caption, 'I'll keep running because it lets me be selfish. It's the thing I do that's just for me, and nobody else. FYI, I never thought this being-selfish-thing could take so much discipline.' This campaign may be particularly effective as it highlights the discursive tension inherent in women's self-care – it presents being selfish as both desired and unwanted. By suggesting that a woman would need to force herself into 'this being-selfish-thing' through rigorous 'discipline', the activity, the product, and the woman's identity are all preemptively defended. Thus, this advertisement works by both endorsing and rejecting the assumption that women's self-care is selfish.

While in the previous excerpt, Charlotte resists the selfless 'good' woman identity by defiantly situating herself as 'selfish', her next discursive move serves to situate herself as a 'good' woman. As our interaction continued, Charlotte drew on a third discursive resource in accounting for her self-care, as the appropriate modelling of independence for her child. On the heels of claiming selfishness, she shifts the discourse yet again and situates self-care as motivated by the opposite of selfishness – the care of her daughter.

ML: Yeah. What- . . . are there times that i- it's easier to do mommy time?

Now that she's a little older, I don't usually have to do mommy time, I don't have to specify it with her. Like it used to be, I would tell her, 'this is what it is, it's mommy time', and if she'd fuss during the time, I'd say, 'it's mommy time ... it's independent time, you play your play, I play my play.' Um, now ... as you can see, she's very used to, playing on her own
ML: *Yeah, she's a very independent player.*
But she loves to play **with**, as well. And, we do a lot of both. Um, I'm raising her to be really independent, because I've never been.

(Charlotte)

In this account, Charlotte argues that taking time for herself models independence to her child, helping her to grow into a strong, independent girl. She qualifies that her daughter is already quite independent, but expresses an appropriate balance between playing alone and playing with others. Thus, Charlotte's self-care is positioned as good for her child.

While all lines of accounting described thus far defend self-care in different ways, all address the fundamental problem that for women, and especially for mothers, to take care of the self is to neglect others and to be selfish; to care for the self is to be a bad woman. However, although these discursive resources serve to defend speakers' identities and actions, they operate in complicity with discourses of femininity, and as such pose a set of interlocking 'discursive dangers'.

The discursive dangers of justifying self-care as consistent with discourses of femininity

First, in reference to the 'oxygen-mask theory' in particular, encouraging women to take better care of themselves in order to better care for others invites a whole new realm of demands on a woman's time and energies. Without challenging discourses of femininity and the assumption that a woman should be unfailingly present to the needs of family and household, self-care can become simply another thing to add to her long list of 'things-to-do'. Finding time to self-care can then become yet another pressure in women's already hectic lives (Drew & Paradice, 1996) and another measure of their performance. Therefore, depending on how it is mobilized, the suggestion that women take care of themselves can ultimately have the effect of being oppressive rather than liberating.

Second, the discursive strategy of equating 'care for self' with 'care for others' works by reifying women's caring work as their *raison d'être*. It is notable that the discursive strategy used so often by women to legitimize their self-care depends on the very gendered assumptions that render their

153

self-care illegitimate in the first place. While this discursive device may appeal to women, it maintains the assumption that caring for others is the ultimate eventuality. This discursive strategy is effective *because* it maintains the hegemony of traditional discourses of femininity. Therefore, while this rhetorical move may assist a woman to effect positive change in her life, it operates in collusion with discourses of femininity which are ultimately harmful to all women.

Third, as with all individualistic constructions of self-care, this line of accounting risks oversimplifying women's distress and eclipsing the conditions of their lives. Rather than bring inequity and oppression into view, this discursive strategy presents women's distress as a personal affair – both in cause and in cure. That is, if a woman is distressed, depressed, or incapacitated, then she must be failing to take proper care of herself. Consequently, the conditions of her life are ignored (e.g., the work of childcare and maintaining households, the second shift, care for elderly parents, pay inequity, etc.) and the solutions for resolving her distress are trivialized (e.g., go for a walk, take a bath). The trivialization of women's lives and distress is frequently reflected in advertising campaigns aimed at encouraging women to 'indulge' in self-care products and services. For instance, an American advertisement for bubble bath first launched in 1985 depicted a woman pulled in all directions – a dog tracking mud on the carpet, children making a mess, dinner burning on the stove, and a ringing phone beckoning her attention. Overwhelmed, she cried, 'Calgone, take me away!'. She was then shown magically disrobed and transported to the tub where she relaxed, apparently without a care in the world. In this advertisement, the product was presented as something that helped women better cope with the stressors in their day, ultimately enabling them to better perform as mothers and housewives. A bath was presented as equal to the challenge of relieving the stress of a woman's daily life.

The catch phrase 'Calgone, take me away' became so popular that it was adopted as the logo for Calgone products, one that remains in place over twenty years later (www.takemeaway.com). This phrase infiltrated common discourse in North America as a shorthand for women to express being overwhelmed by the constant demands of caring for children and households – a gendered division of labour that also remains largely in place over twenty years later. To gauge the current use of this colloquialism, I conducted an internet search of the key phrase 'Calgone take me away'. This search revealed over 163,000 results and was frequently referenced in blog spots posted by mothers sharing stories of their daily lives consumed by the work of caring for children and households.

> I usually can't wait to go on vacation but not this time. [My husband] will get away from his job and will be able to relax. But for me, my job is coming with us [. . .] [My son] will love the beach

and water I have no doubt about that. Where is my time away? While he is napping? Three full hours, if I am lucky? Calgone take me away. I wish that my mom was coming with us. Then, I would truly have the best of both worlds. My baby would be with me and I could enjoy myself and relax knowing that he was taken care of. I know that when we get there everything will fall into place. [My son] will adjust well and we will all be able to enjoy the beach and recharge. Or at least that is what I am telling myself in my daily affirmation.[4]

My day so far . . . [My son] and [daughter] got up this morning, and so far they have taken about half of the diapers out of the bins on their changing table and spread them all on the floor, taken my wooden calendar and knocked it down with all the little wood pieces all falling out, [my son] opened the dishwasher and then also hit cancel during a cycle so I had to do them twice, and at lunch [daughter] thinks its a great idea to dump her lunch plate upside down. I can't help but look forward to nap time. Even then you are never guaranteed that they will sleep. Calgone, take me away![5]

I am having one of those Calgone take me away days. It is a holiday here so all the kids are home from school and [husband] had his first all day training session at the restaurant. So I decided to take the kids to the beach today to burn some energy. So at the beach they fought b/c one push another in the water, Then we had the usual she has the sand bucket that I want argument, followed by 20 I'm thirsty, I'm hungry's, and [son] being cranky and well past nap time. So I tried to tune it all out by concentrating on the beautiful scenery . . . When I over heard a new fight developing over, get this . . . Touching each others sand! That's it! I lost it! 'Look around! Do you see all this sand on the beach? You are surrounded by sand and you guys are fighting over it? GET IN THE CAR WE ARE GOING HOME!' So after a long lecture in the car on the way home I tell them they are going straight to the bath, putting their pj's on and going in their rooms for a quiet time. As I tell myself . . . Only a few more minutes and I can have some peace and quiet. So they are all clean and [son] is down for his long awaited nap, [husband] calls. I should say, [husband] calls again. The first time he called to say that he would be two hours late. This next call was two hours later to say that his tire was flat and he needed me to drive downtown and pick him up. AGHHHHHHHHHHHH! So I wake [son] up from his nap, haul all the kids and myself in our pyjama's into the car to pick him up, and come home to cook dinner, do laundry, mop the floors where

[son] thought it would be fun to throw his lasagne, help my husband change his tire, and make an appointment to get that fitting for my straight jacket I am going to be needing. A mothers job is never done. One of those things where you work 24 hours a day 7 days a week, with no pay and little appreciation. Not that I am complaining . . . After all they are really cute when they are sleeping.[6]

Across these excerpts, women describe the unending, demanding, and at times frustrating work of childcare and housekeeping. This work is clearly positioned as the province of women. As the author of the first excerpt wrote, '[My husband] will get away from his job and will be able to relax. But for me my job is coming with us'. And the third wrote, 'A mothers job is never done'. In these excerpts, women express and explain their frustration and exhaustion through a listing of the day's calamities that allow no reprieve. The phrase 'Calgone take me away!' is thus used to signify both the desire for respite and the apparent futility of this wish ('Where is my time away? While he is napping? Three full hours if I am lucky? Calgone take me away' (excerpt #1); 'I can't help but look forward to nap time. Even then you are never guaranteed that they will sleep. Calgone take me away!' (excerpt #2)). With discourses of femininity uninterrupted, writers lament their experience, but see no room for change, no hope for respite. Echoing the original advertisement, real solutions to women's distress are nowhere in sight.

A further problem with the promotion of self-care as consistent with discourses of femininity is that this idea encourages women to conform to society's values through self-regulation. Drawing on the concept of the panopticon, Foucault (1977) explained how individuals come to adopt and reproduce the values of a social system through self-surveillance. Conformity is ensured as individuals come to police their own thoughts, emotions, and behaviours. In this frame, self-care can be seen as practices for regulating the self in accordance with role of the 'good' citizen/patient, in general (a person who obeys health experts' advice to adopt 'healthy' lifestyles), and the 'good' woman in particular. For instance, in describing her self-care practices, Charlotte discussed the importance of attending a public service agency that supports mothers through parenting education and therapy for issues such as self-esteem. Patsy described losing weight and paying attention to her appearance, and Caroline spoke of joining Weight Watchers. While all of these activities were described as self-care and fostering speakers' well-being, they can also be understood as means of self-discipline. That is, the 'good' woman identity can be *performed through* self-care. Notably, each of these self-care activities involves women's status as care-givers or objects of beauty, thereby upholding the standards by which women are measured.

So I contacted them [public service agency], and said, look, I want someone to come in, like she comes in twice a month, to, tell me what to do next. Am I pushing [daughter] too far, too fast, am I holding her back, what can I do, how can I do it for **her**? [...] If she does throw a temper tantrum, I let her. And, you know, I don't worry that people are gonna say, 'Oh, you're a terrible mom', or, I don't worry about that now. It's like, I know what I'm doing, I've had experts tell me that what I'm doing doesn't seem to be **screwing** her up.

(Charlotte)

ML: So what led you to throw yourself into all these kinds of things [self-care activities]?
Um, wanting to turn back the clock.
ML: Tell me about that.
Well, I'm forty-eight, a::nd have gray hair under this dye ((laughing)) and I just wasn't very happy with the aging process. I felt like I'm, you know, getting, not dumpy looking, but I'm getting heavier looking with every pound it's harder to do things. And I didn't feel very good about myself, so I thought like I have to, you know, eat better, and get active, so it's **definitely** a conscious decision.

(Patsy)

Yeah, I went to a dietician, that was to help me to, t- to-because of going to Weight Watchers, that was my first introduction on how to eat properly – portion control, it taught me portion control. What a half a cup of pasta really looks like ((laughter)) and no, it's not a plateful! So, they taught me portion control, they taught me how much calories in each food, they taught me about the different food groups, and that I should have a mixture.

(Caroline)

Across these women's accounts, self-care comes into view as practices for regulating and managing their femininity. For Charlotte, attendance at the public service agency both demonstrates and defends her fitness as a mother. She presents herself through the eyes of 'the experts' who have the authority to judge her ability to care for her child. Caroline and Patsy both spoke about managing their bodies through weight loss. The title and purpose of the organization Weight Watchers provides a poignant example of disciplinary power (McSeveny, Doherty, & Grainger, 2005). Women's bodies are monitored ('watched') to ensure their conformity to the traditional ideal of feminine beauty. Thus, the anticipation of the gaze of others incites women to police their own bodies. With an understanding of disciplinary power, institutionalized supports of mothering practices and women's investments in dieting and beautification all come into view as the internalization of patriarchy's gaze and powerful mechanisms for the social control of women's behaviour (Bordo, 1993).

In conclusion, a central way in which participants spoke about and legitimized their leisure and self-care was to accommodate and collude with discourses of femininity. Three main discursive devices were identified as operating in this manner by excusing (crisis narrative), transposing (co-opting a masculine identity) or adopting (oxygen-mask device) discourses of femininity. These discursive devices figured prominently in the interviews and may be rhetorically powerful for addressing the negative identity implications that accompany women's investments in themselves. While these may be effective discursive devices for encouraging women to relinquish practices of femininity and begin to nurture themselves, they operate in collusion with hegemonic regimes of knowledge. Their prominence across accounts once again suggests the dominance of discourses of femininity for shaping women's self-care behaviour, and signals a need for alternative and more empowering means of supporting women's efforts to nurture themselves. In the second part of this analysis, I explore other ways of accounting that emerged in participants' interviews; ways that are potentially more useful and empowering for women. In this second approach, self-care is defended through the resistance or transcendence of hegemonic constructions of idealized femininity and articulated through three different ways of accounting: through a narrative of personal transformation, the normalization of equality and self-nurturance, and the identification with an earth-centred spirituality.[7]

TALKING ABOUT SELF-CARE: RESISTING AND TRANSCENDING DISCOURSES OF FEMININITY

Narrative of personal transformation

It was particularly interesting to discover a narrative of personal transformation at the heart of women's accounts of both recovery from depression and self-care. As described in Chapter 3, women frequently described having fundamentally changed themselves through recovering from depression. Some participants described their former selves as 'victims' or 'doormats' – passive, servile, and dependent; sacrificing themselves in order to please others and secure relationships. Former selves were also frequently described as having been overly concerned with domestic perfection. Participants referred to their past selves as 'good' women to a fault – 'perfectionists' and 'control freaks', consumed with the endless task of maintaining clean and orderly households. By repositioning the 'good' woman in these ways, participants were able to resist this otherwise revered identity and step into a more empowered and assertive identity.

Notably, many participants in the self-care study also drew on a narrative of personal transformation to account for how they came to take up self-care. For instance, Tanya stated that she used to be more 'submissive', sometimes feeling like her husband's 'shadow'. However, she described evolving into a very different person who can now take care of herself. She said, 'I think I've developed into a, just different kind of person from what I started out as. I grew into a, more, I can do this by myself [type person]'. Similarly, Charlotte said that she used to be 'a doormat', who would do anything to please others. Charlotte also described herself as having been like a mirrored 'disco ball', reflecting a different self to everyone who looked at her so she could be whatever was wanted of her. She said, '[I was like] a disco ball, mirrors to every little place but nothing inside. That's the way I felt a lot of the times. You know, everybody who looked at me saw something different.'

Like Charlotte, other women I interviewed contrasted their past selves with their 'true selves' in a discursive formulation that justifies their rejection of their former identities. Participants described having grown into stronger, more independent women who now ensure that their needs and desires are addressed. Again, they often described coming to resist the 'good' woman/victim identity by 'standing up' for themselves and asserting their right to self-care.

> you've got to take charge, really, ah::, and you'll be so much better off, and, yeah, it's a, and to take care of yourself, and recognize when you're not doing that. When you're giving more than you're getting back and, and realizing that you know, sometimes you have to stand up for yourself. And for me that has always been something that was hard because in relationships I tend to be the one to give give give and I understand, and I don't want to hurt feelings, and **now**, I'm getting to a point in my life where it's like, hey, you know, this is not okay anymore. I don't want this. I don't want this to be part of my life, you know, this is me.
>
> (Isabelle)

Here, Isabelle characterizes her former self as having been caring to a fault. Her account echoes that of one of the participants in the recovery study who described her former self by saying, 'I was a giver and I got taken over and over and over and over agai::n' (Susan). By repositioning their caring as excessive, both Isabelle and Susan are able to justify reorienting toward their own needs. This narrative enables resistance of the cultural expectation that women should be unfailingly self-sacrificing and caring.

In keeping with the narrative of personal transformation drawn on by participants in the recovery study, Marta, Tanya, and Daphne also referred to themselves as 'control freaks' and 'perfectionists' who worked to maintain household order at the expense of their own health. For them, 'letting go' of the need for domestic perfection, and taking time for themselves were central for their health and well-being.

> I'm a bit of a perfectionist. Um, I have ... gotten better over the years for myself. I was um, you know, a woman who looked after everybody and everything first, typical. U::m, and then I just, would read things, [...] and hear things, go to a few seminars, and you know, I have a few friends that are kind of interested in things like that too, so I tag along with them, and, I just thought, >well makes perfect sense.<
> ML: What does?
> Just ye::ah, looking- looking after yourself, and taking time for yourself, and **why::** not? Because, if- if you think about it, um::, other people in your life do that, and they do just fine. Their life goes on, and- and they might not have um, a perfectly clean floor at home, and um, even other women, that ah, don't keep their house as neat as I do, but they're perfectly happy.
> ML: Mmmhmm
> So I thought ... maybe I should just pull back a bit from the perfectionist and having everything done, and the, you know, the groceries always, looked after, and you know what? I was the only one putting that strain on myself.
>
> (Tanya)

> When I stopped to look at my, you know, my life and my first marriage, it was like, where did I get this notion that I had to clean? Well, that's what I grew up with, you know a lot of the self-worth, it was, a lot of what I grew up with was you know, um, you cleaned for what other people thought. You dressed

for what other people thought and this was just hammered and hammered in, and then it was like, I spent so much time cleaning, and that was it. My life was, it was limited. You know, I mean, I did a few things, but that was it. ... No way. I'm not doing that.

ML: How did you come to that, because that's quite revolutionary.

Um, I don't know exactly when it sort of all kind of came together. I think it was over time, you know, like slowly, kind of letting things go.

(Daphne)

Similarly, Marta described herself as a 'perfectionist' who had tried in vain to 'keep a house perfectly clean, keep every piece of laundry done, keep [. . .] everybody orchestrated, and and lined up for appointments and all that'. She described how the pressures in her life culminated, leading her to finally question her values and assumptions.

I remember, again, all part of this discovery time in my late twenties, early, yeah, late twenties, cause I remember sitting at my kitchen table, and I speak about this quite often, so I've kept that memory alive, but I remember that moment distinctively. I was sitting at my kitchen table, my kids had gone to school, or- or the oldest one had gone to kinder-garten, and the little one was still at home, and I was sitting there with a coffee and a cigarette probably, and going through the list of, I should do the laundry, I have to go there, I have to do that, and I should do this, you know, going through the list for the day or the week or whatever it was, and feeling **really** overwhelmed and thinking, '<holy cow>'. And, honest to God, it was like this light bulb that went off and says, **who** says that I should do, and I have to do all this. It's me who's saying that. **Why** am I doing that to myself? It's like I have this choke chain around my neck, and I keep yanking on it. You know? **Why!**

(Marta)

In this excerpt, Marta vividly depicts a story of how she came to question and reject her adherence to the traditional female role. Through listing ('I should do the laundry, I have to go there, I have to do that, and I should do this') she highlights the endless demands on her time. In contrast to the bleakness of her despair, insight is described 'like this light bulb that went off', illuminating an awareness that she alone is responsible for her expectations and her actions. She explains that she came to realize that she overwhelmed *herself* through a process of self-discipline, vividly portrayed with the metaphor of the choke chain. In situating the pressure to be the 'good' woman as an internal, personally held belief, Marta also claims the power to 'let go' of these demands and to give up her hold on the 'choke chain'.

While the women I interviewed described a shift in personality toward independence, assertiveness, and self-nurturance, it is important to note that this did not preclude caring and nurturing for others. Indeed, the personal transformation so often described by participants was in some instances sparked by the birth of a child. For instance, Charlotte (who portrayed herself as having been like a mirrored disco ball) described experiencing a dramatic change in her sense of self when she recently became a mother.

> I didn't know the real me, so I made, sort of mirrors for what other people needed to see, or I thought. So it's only now, real recent that I'm actually coming to, finding out ... who me **is**, and trying to figure it out, what to do with it. That's why I had anxiety attacks, cause I didn't know how to behave.
> ML: Mmm
> I didn't know what was expected, so I didn't know **how** to fit in. [...] Now I don't, and I don't care. I have friends who know me, who like me, [...] and they, you know, it's like fine, I screw up, fine. ((laughing)) We all screw up. I don't have to be perfect anymore. I always used to have to be the perfect this or that, or the other thing, without knowing ... without structure behind, anything's gonna fall, without a proper foundation ... ya know [...]
> ML: So, again, how did, how did that shift happen?
> I had a baby. ((laughing)) Literally it was. [...] I, actually being pregnant made **a lot** of changes in me growth-wise, a::nd, in the last year.
>
> (Charlotte)

What I aim to problematize in this analysis is not caring and connectedness with others, but the taken-for-granted equation of motherwork with self-sacrifice and abnegation. Indeed, motherhood is very often a joyful experience. Further, it can be a source of strength and an important catalyst for positive change in a woman's life (Greaves et al., 2002; Thomas, 2004;

Varcoe & Doane, 2007). For instance, pregnancy and childbirth have been found to be significant and positive turning points for many women who are in abusive relationships or struggling with addiction (Greaves et al., 2002). As described by a participant in a study of African-American women's talk about mothering (Thomas, 2004), becoming a mother can be empowering and can spark a shift in a woman's subjectivity toward strength and positive self-regard.

> It used to be, my self-esteem was flat line . . . Now I take a stand. I'm involved with my son's school – I have to protect him! . . . My [six-year-old] son sees me study. He'll lay on the bed beside me when I'm studying, and I'll say, 'When it's your time to go [to college], maybe you'll appreciate it . . . My being in school is gonna do you a world of good!' I can't let myself feel guilty. I'm making a better life for us! . . . I wish I could tell young girls that when they have a baby, they will change. You may be a passive wimp, but you'll become a lioness. You'll protect this baby!
>
> (Thomas, 2004, pp. 222–3)

It is notable that the narrative of personal transformation was drawn on with remarkable consistency across women's accounts of both recovery and self-care. Given that women's well-being was at the heart of both studies, it is perhaps not surprising that this resource was central to both sets of interviews. This narrative enables women to resist the 'good' woman identity, defend acts of self-care, and position their identities in more positive and empowering ways. That is, women described becoming well when they began to resist living their lives as the 'good' woman. The importance of resisting idealized notions of femininity has also emerged in other research on women's health. For instance, Jane Ussher (2006) interviewed women at various stages of the reproductive life cycle. In contrast to the pejorative stereotypes that abound about women in menopause, mid-life, and beyond, Ussher found that many described themselves as living well. She described these women as moving away from self-silencing and self-negation, attending to their own needs rather than holding an exclusive focus on the needs of others. Interestingly, the accounts of these women bear striking resemblance to those of the women I interviewed in both the recovery and self-care studies. For instance, one of her Australian interviewees, Amy, commented:

> You spend the first half of your life trying to be fairly perfect, you try to fit that mould . . . be doing all the right things and keeping everyone happy . . . and always trying to keep things in balance. Maybe you get to 50 and you think, well bugger it, you've done all

that work and all that effort and you think, gee, have I ever really given myself enough pleasure and consideration?

(Ussher, 2006, p. 155)

Ussher (2006) also cites other research on women's experiences of menopause and mid-life. Again, these excerpts are strikingly similar to women's accounts of both recovery from depression and the adoption of self-care practices.

Your first third of your life, I found I did everything to please my family. Went all out. It was expected of me. I was happy to do it. I was a very good daughter. Then I spent the next third of my life pleasing my family. And I said to my husband, 'If I can't get out of life what *I* want now, I'm going to go it alone'.

(Daly, 1997; cited in Ussher, 2006, p. 155)

My motto this year was to be fully alive, take risks, and I did that. I had a wonderful affair with a 39 year old. I got a tattoo. I played. I laughed. I cried. I feel like a wonderful 17 year old enjoying life. . . . My inner voice is awake after being under general anaesthesia for years. Often I can hear that voice. For years I sacrificed for others – NO MORE. I'm sick of taking care of others; I don't even want a houseplant.

(McQuaide, 1998; cited in Ussher, 2006, p. 156)

Recurrent features of women's recovery narratives are also at work in these accounts, legitimizing speakers' identities and actions. The use of extreme case formulation (e.g., 'doing all the right things and keeping everyone happy'; 'I did everything to please my family. Went all out'; 'For years I sacrificed for others') has the effect of both protecting speakers' identities (as 'good' women) and presenting their practices as unsustainable and warranting renunciation. The depiction of their former identities as imposed and restrictive ('a mould'; 'trying to be fairly perfect'; trying to be 'a very good daughter'), and in contrast to their true selves ('my inner voice') serve to further justify their resistance. In these accounts, speakers equate 'letting go' of practices of femininity with justice. Having spent the bulk of their lives caring for others, they justify taking their turn to care for themselves. Therefore, this typical discursive pattern may be more indicative of women's talk of health and well-being in general, rather than unique to narratives of recovery from depression or self-care. Like the women who talked of recovery from depression, these women's accounts of health revolve around throwing off the myths of idealized femininity. As Ussher (2006) noted,

It appears that for many women, it is only when they can leave these myths behind, or realize that they can't sustain them any more, or when women feel that they have paid their dues, and can turn to their own needs for the first time in their life, that they reach a position of equilibrium and peace.

(p. 159)

If women's equilibrium and peace are central goals of feminism, then finding discursive ways for women to unbind themselves from the depressing and oppressive 'shackles of archetypal femininity' (Ussher, 2006, p. 155) is required. A narrative of personal transformation enables this shift in priorities and is particularly useful if the narrative is politicized and used to trouble idealized notions of femininity. While few participants endorsed a feminist identity (Kate and Joan, both participants in the recovery study), there was evidence of the influence of feminism in the talk of many. As I will explore in the next section, some women positioned self-care in the context of gender equality. These speakers noted that the equal division of labour in their relationships played a significant role in their ability to attend to their own needs and desires.

Equity: 'the new normal'

As described earlier in this chapter, women's ability to nurture themselves is dependent upon their intersubjectivity and the nature of their interpersonal relationships, with more equitable relationships fostering greater self-care (Ussher & Perz, 2008; Ussher et al., 2007). Several participants who were involved in heterosexual partnerships discussed having unusually equitable relationships with their husbands and boyfriends. Indeed, having a partner who shares domestic duties and respects a woman's investment in her own interests was described by these women as imperative for self-care. Interestingly, these women frequently described having grown up with parents who were unusually progressive and subscribed to a non-traditional division of labour in the home.[8]

> My father always made breakfast on Sundays and when we went camping he did a lot of the cooking the meals then but he was ... like, she [mother], she was a really hard worker and- and she managed the money. A::h, and, so he wasn't a typical [...] But I don't know, I guess just it's always been that way. So I've never questioned that it should be any other way, and when I hear other people talk about that their husbands are retired and they, you know, 'They won't do

anything', or 'They make work', or 'I'm trying to do this, and they won't get out of my hair'- it's kind of like, well, 'Why are you doing it in the first place?' Like to me, it just, it's just so normal that we both have our things to do. I always said that when we had meals, I made the mess and he cleaned them up.

(Jacqueline)

Now, my father was an exception to the rule. Back in those days most men did nothing. My father did. He always did. [...] I do remember him changing diapers with them [siblings], and feeding them and everything. So, he was an involved father, <for that day> and I think there's more involved fathers now, so working- cause most women are working. Like, back then, a lot of women didn't, a:nd, **but** there's still an awful lot, and I see it **all** the time [...] I'll hear women say, like, 'Oh my husband's really good because' ah, they both work out, but 'he does the dishes every night and sweeps the kitchen floor.' I say, 'Is that all?' ((laughing)) Like my husband does as much as I do, but see women's expec- tations aren't ... like, I expect him, even- even if he didn't, he does, I don't have to say it to him, like a lot of people say, 'How did you get [husband] trained?' Well, I didn't train [husband]. He came that way, but if he didn't come that way, I would expect him ... if I'm gonna work full time, I expect him to do his share, I just do. But other women don't expect that. Other women, and I see it, not, I don't think it's as much now, but I still see it quite a bit, where women will work all day, and come home, they'll make the supper, they'll look after the kids, they'll do the lessons, and get the kids into bed, and then if there's any time for themselves they have it, and if they don't they don't.

(Caroline)

These two excerpts follow a similar discursive pattern whereby speakers establish equity between husbands and wives as 'the new normal', and, by contrast, women's subservience as outdated. Both describe their fathers as unusually involved in caring and domestic work ('he wasn't a typical' (Jacqueline); 'my father was an exception to the rule' (Caroline)). The division of labour in the speaker's current household is then positioned as a normal modelling of one's childhood experience. Although constructed as normal, 'letting go' of housework is still positioned as resistance to the traditional female role.

Both Jacqueline and Caroline contrast the way they govern their lives with that of other women who do the majority of the work in the home. As described earlier, social comparison used in this way serves to position women who subscribe to traditional gender roles as servile and unassertive while speakers are positioned positively in contrast. An equal distribution of household labour is therefore presented as both normal, unremarkable (according to the speaker's own standards) and radical (according to the standards of society). While clearly informed by a feminist analysis, these women did not explicitly adopt a feminist identity, but rather tempered their resistance as a learned standard. That is, instead of identifying traditional gender roles as oppressive and unacceptable, here they are positioned as simply outside one's experience. Never having direct exposure to the old standard, speakers claim to have never learned any other way. Therefore, through this pattern of accounting, speakers are able to take up rather resistant and radical practice, but without being positioned as such. They are able to construct themselves and their actions according to the principle of gender equity, but without the negative implications for identity that appear to accompany the identity of the feminist (see Chapter 3 for an exploration of the feminist identity).

Although a feminist identity is not adopted outright, the feminist principle of gender equality is at the heart of this discursive device, and both participants' constructions of the feminist identity and 'the new normal' overlap in their effect of defending women's self-care. Notably, they also shared discursive features and were constructed in remarkably consistent ways. For instance, the first excerpt below is from my interview with Joan, the participant in the recovery study who self-identified as a feminist. The second excerpt is from my interview with Jacqueline, a participant in the self-care study who described having an equitable marital relationship, just as her parents did:

> when I was back in university I didn't know where our vacuum cleaner was. Like my family did all of that because I was on a mission and I was busy doing things and I felt hey I did it for thirteen years you people might have to do it for the next thirteen you know ((laughs)) that's how it's gonna be.
>
> (Joan)

> And see I'm very fortunate in that way. I would **never** have to ask him [ask husband to do housework]. Like now that he's retired, I can't tell you where the vacuum cleaner is kept. Dinner is made when I go home at night. He's retired and I'm

> not- so we've changed roles. We've always **shared** them,
> very, very much so. When the kids were little if they'd call me
> to go to work, before he'd go to bed, he'd have all of the
> wash done, everything in its place, and vacuuming done and
> so when I'd get home the next day, there'd be nothing to do.
>
> (Jacqueline)

In analysing patterns across accounts, I noticed the similarity between Joan's and Jacqueline's statements that they didn't know where their vacuum cleaners were kept. While the repetition of this statement may be regarded as merely coincidental, from a discursive perspective they are interesting, not only for their content, but their effect. These claims work up speakers' resistance to discourses of femininity as extreme and defiantly radical – not only did they not do housework, they didn't even know where the equipment was kept. Through these statements, speakers position themselves as operating completely outside the realm of domesticity. Thus, both the adoption of a feminist identity (here, structured through a narrative of personal transformation) and the construction of gender equality as the 'new normal' serve the same effect of opening up spaces in which women's attention to their own pleasures and needs are defended within a frame of justice. These ways of accounting are consistent with feminist visions of equality and were mobilized in women's accounts as viable ways of talking/being.

A final discursive device appeared in participants' accounts as a way of negotiating dominant constructions of proper femininity. In this line of accounting, participants constructed leisure as an expression of earth-centred spirituality. In this discursive frame, speakers equate self-care with spiritual practice thereby transcending traditional formulations of femininity.

Wilderness women: self-care as practices of eco-spirituality

In analysing participants' accounts of self-care, I found a set of instances in which women talked in a very different way about self-care and inner-directed energies. Most often, when women spoke of self-care in the form of exercise, they described being motivated by losing weight. For instance, as discussed earlier, Jacqueline spoke about 'battling her weight' her whole life and Caroline talked of weight management as a persistent 'struggle'. In contrast to the 'battle' with one's body so typically presented, some women talked of physical activity as an expression of a deep-seated spiritual need. These instances stood out as being free of what I came to think of as 'discursive tension'; there appeared to be no ideological dilemmas to account for, and notably, no references to gender. In these moments, women spoke about transcendent experiences in nature, constructing themselves as 'wilderness' women.

> I guess it's always been a very very big part of who I was. Like, even growing up, I mean we played outside, connecting with nature. I always felt so good out there. U::m, I need to, I need to be out there. I just need uh, it just takes me, it really does. I mean, just sitting there on the mountain and listening to the birds and you know how you can sort of, that calm that comes over you.
>
> (Isabelle)

> My husband and I went [...] whale watching or kayaking, sea kayaking, we have a sea kayak, a tandem. And so we went around Campobello Island [...] saw all kinds of beautiful seals, we saw eight different eagles and hawks that day, um, gorgeous, you know, the big huge gray seals, the harbour seals, and we got to go fairly close, we didn't want to disrupt them too much, and we actually, a minke whale that arched up, my God is it ever loud when you're not even that close, oh, fantastic, and that to me, was the ultimate in terms of, where everything comes together in space and time and within your being. It's just a total sense of being connected, everything's connected- the mind, the body, the spirit, the emotions are connected, and you're connected to your environment. So to me the ultimate is the inner connection with the connection to the environment around, and it's just ... ... kind of a sense of peace and awe at the same time. Hard to put into words sort of what that's like.
>
> (Daphne)

> I think your overall wellness is definitely tied in ... to sort of where you are mentally as well as physically. And me personally I'm not like a religious person per se? But I know that sort of ... being outside is definitely, it definitely touches sort of a spiritual end of things. I don't know how to explain it exact(h)ly. Like, I think being outside under a tree is, sort of the same- is a very powerful spiritual sort of experience just as perhaps sitting in a church pew is for other people?
>
> (Jillian)

In these excerpts, participants talked about their experiences of nature as the foundation of their well-being. The call to be in nature is described as fundamental to their sense of self (e.g., 'it's always been a very very big part of who I was', Isabelle) and their experiences are depicted as both personal and profound. Presenting the need to be in nature as a part of who they are both emphasizes its importance in their lives and justifies their participation in outdoor activities. Across these accounts, descriptions of being in nature are presented in mystical language, denoting speakers' difficulty in expressing these experiences. For instance, Daphne noted that it is 'Hard to put into words', and Jillian stated, 'I don't know how to explain it exact(h)ly'. Without trying to explain it, Isabelle talked about 'that calm that comes over you', leaving it up to me as the audience to either understand based on my own experience or not. By situating their experiences as those which cannot be explained but only understood through personal experience, these moments are elevated above the every-day – they are special and rare, and can only be known by those similarly called to commune with nature. In addition, by equating sitting under a tree with sitting in a church pew, Jillian works up her need to be in the woods as a significant and legitimate *spiritual* practice, thereby further justifying this act of self-care.

In contrast to the heavily gendered talk of self-care present in most of the interviews, it was notable that women's talk of eco-spirituality did not involve gendered references. Moreover, there were no references to feeling selfish or guilty in these instances in the text. Perhaps being positioned as a higher spiritual experience innoculates against the usual threats to identity that tend to accompany women's accounts of time for themselves. While the moral imperative of the 'good' woman tends to impel women to focus on others before themselves, a spiritual discourse may carry the weight of a higher calling, enabling women to distribute their energies accordingly. Indeed, drawing on a wilderness woman identity not only justifies self-care as acceptable, but essential. As Jillian stated, being in the wilderness is one of the 'most important things' in her life.

> U::m for me I like to be outside **a lot** so that's **re:ally** important I know like sort of mid March I start to get **re:ally** anxious for summer and- playing in the wilderness ((laughing)) Or even like last summer even like I mean it's not bad to go down to the river and run along the river but I **definitely** miss being sort of in a more wilderness setting. Cause I know that's really important for me being outside, it's key. I know it's one of my most important things I would say.
>
> (Jillian)

The availability of this subject position enables women to justify and engage in outdoor activities. It allows time for exploration, play, and reflection. Although not prominent among the accounts of participants in this study, presumably a more traditional religious discourse would also provide women legitimate solitary space for prayer and reflection. My own grandmother, for instance, was a devoutly Catholic woman and mother of seven. She attended church several times a week and was known to sit alone in the pews quietly, sometimes tearfully. I imagine that for her, going to church may have been her only means of respite. However, unlike the identity positionings for women within many religious traditions, the wilderness woman identity appears to retain a certain subversive edge. For instance, when I asked Daphne what she has to give up in order to find time to engage in self-nurturing activities such as kayaking, she responded without hesitation, 'Housework, man! That goes'. Further, her account worked to pit the energy invested in housecleaning against energy invested in *living*, situating the former as meaningless and misguided. She said, 'Cleaning? Forget it. I mean my God, I'd rather be outside kayaking'. Thus, a 'wilderness' woman identity can be mobilized with the effect of both transcending and resisting hegemonic constructions of femininity.

Often fuelled by a rejection of the injustices defended in the name of religion, many in the West have turned away from traditional religions in favour of more secular spiritualities; a movement reflected in the common disclaimer, 'I'm spiritual but not religious'. As a result, the Western world has witnessed the exponential growth of a range of spiritual practices including eco-spirituality, Goddess-centred spirituality, yoga, and Western adaptations of Buddhism including mindfulness practice and meditation. These spiritual lineages tend to eschew or reject the patriarchal foundations of many Judeo-Christian and Islamic traditions, providing means of both spiritual practice and political resistance to injustices such as environmental degradation, sexism, and heterosexism. Moreover, these spiritual traditions offer spaces for women to honour and nurture their own pleasures, sensualities, embodiment, and well-being.

Such 'alternative' spiritual traditions have grown not only across popular culture, but have also emerged in academic and professional realms. For instance, 'mindfulness-based practice' has been taken up in psychology and medicine to address health concerns including chronic pain (Kabat-Zinn, 1990), 'Borderline Personality Disorder' (Linehan, 1993), and depression (Williams, Teasdale, Segal, & Kabat-Zinn, 2007). This movement into the popular consciousness and the accompanying proliferation of yoga studios, meditation centres, and spiritual retreats may offer new spaces for identity construction for women (and men) that may promote a healthy and respectful balance between care for the self and care for others. They may provide justifiable space and time for women to be still and silent – experiences women so rarely describe in their stories of their daily life.

CONCLUSION

The purpose of this chapter was to explore women's accounts of their experiences of self-care. Defined broadly as relinquishing an exclusive focus on caring and domestic practices and attending to one's own needs, desires, and pleasures, self-care was elaborated as a practice that is both central to women's well-being and threatening to their identities. The material and discursive constraints to women's self-care were explored, including a lack of time, freedom, money, and safety as well as the discursive meaning of self-care for women whereby self-care is equated with selfishness and immorality. Given the pervasive constraints on women's health practices, I questioned how it is that women *do* manage to attend to their own needs and well-being. I probed deeper into the accounts of women who self-identify as taking care of themselves in their everyday lives and identified two central patterns mobilized across these interviews. In the first, discourses of femininity are accepted and accommodated. I identified three main discursive devices as operating in this manner by excusing (crisis narrative), transposing (co-opting a masculine identity), or adopting (oxygen-mask device) discourses of femininity. While these discursive devices figured prominently in the interviews I conducted, and may be rhetorically powerful for addressing the negative identity implications that accompany women's investments in themselves, they operate in collusion with patriarchal power and are thus problematic from a feminist perspective. In the second, potentially more emancipatory pattern in the text, discourses of femininity were resisted or transcended through the mobilization of another set of discursive devices: through a narrative of personal transformation, the normalization of equality and self-nurturance, and the identification with an earth-centred spirituality. While these devices differed in content, they had the common effect of defending against the apparently ever-present threat of being positioned as uncaring, selfish, bad women. That is, they shared the common effect of 'managing the monstrous feminine' (Ussher, 2006).

Notes

1 Because most of the research on women's participation in activities for enjoyment and health is rooted in the leisure studies literature, I will use 'self-care' and 'leisure' interchangeably.
2 While improving women's ability to self-care is important, the notion of self-care as a health care priority clearly pales in comparison to the systemic problems women experience in terms of oppression, poverty and violence. Against the backdrop of these global crises, any initiative aimed at facilitating women's self-care can be construed as an elitist enterprise as self-care is only reliably available to those with sufficient resources. Self-care and leisure are only possible after the basic necessities of living have been met and secured. Before a woman is able to invest in her own health and well-being, there must be adequate food, shelter, and safety for herself and her children. Many women worldwide are denied such

economic security and safety, and rectifying these inequities must be at the forefront of global peace and health initiatives (UNDP, 1997; WHO, 2000a). However, attention to self-care does not deny the critical importance of eradicating women's material marginalization. Instead, I propose the need to attend across the multitude of constraints on women's health. Indeed, a difficulty in attending to one's own health and well-being has been found among women from across a range of sociodemographic backgrounds (Crespo et al., 1999; Miller & Brown, 2005; Thrane, 2000). And, women's struggle to self-care has negative consequences for the quality of their physical and emotional well-being (Hull, 1990; Shaw, 1994; Thrane, 2000). Thus, the exploration of women's self-care here is meant to supplement, not supplant structural understandings of the determinants of women's health. Self-care is approached as another facet of women's health that warrants attention.

3 It is interesting to note that both the oxygen-mask theory and the crisis metaphor were at work in the accounts of participants in this study. For instance, participants spoke of physical activity as a means of 'staying sane' in the face of the demands of motherhood.

4 'Baby carrot: our little carrot in the garden', 31 July 2006, retrieved on 29 September 2006 from <www.ababycarrot.com/blogs/category/announcements/>.

5 'A day in the life of me . . .', 24 May 2006, retrieved on 29 September 2006 from <http://kyleeb.blogspot.com/2006_05_01_kyleeb_archive.html>.

6 'Alyssa's world', 11 October 2004, retrieved on 29 September 2006 from <http://alyssaturner.blogspot.com/2004_10_01_archive.html>.

7 The second part of this analysis focuses on women's resistance to discourses of femininity. While the adoption of a tomboy identity can be seen as a form of resistance, I regard it as inconsistent with this second pattern in the text. From a feminist perspective, the resistance involved in co-opting a masculine identity is undesirable as it leaves patriarchy uninterrupted and maintains the power differential between male and female subject positions. Also, the distinction between these two broad patterns in the data does not suggest these were distinct in individual women's accounts. Participants drew on a range and combination of accounting devices. The distinction drawn here is in terms of the utility of these different ways of accounting, not their use.

8 Variations on this pattern of construction were also present. For instance, Daphne spoke of learning more equitable divisions of labour from her younger and more 'progressive' husband, and Tanya spoke of instilling this standard in her daughter. Regardless of the way in which equity in relationships was modelled, the resource of the 'new normal' had the consistent effect of justifying women's resistance to traditional gender roles.

CHAPTER 5

CONCLUSION: IMPLICATIONS FOR USEFULNESS[1]

In the preceding chapters, I explored women's accounts of depression, recovery from depression, and self-care. Adopting a feminist critical-realist perspective, I endeavoured to produce an analysis that attends to both the material and embodied aspects of women's experiences (including rape, abuse, poverty, domestic and care-giving labour, as well as the toll of these on women's bodies), and to the ways in which these, and indeed all experience are socially constructed through discourse. By grounding the analysis in women's stories, I hoped to generate a compassionate under-standing of women's despair, healing, and well-being that would resonate with the women I spoke with, while also developing a critical analysis of the ways in which their accounts are shaped by discourse.

When participants talked about depression, they talked of their lives as women – as targets of abuse and sexual violation, subjects of economic marginalization, keepers of relationships, managers of households, care-givers of children, nursemaids to the elderly and infirm – as mothers, daughters, and wives. These experiences are shaped and regulated by dis-courses of femininity (and masculinity) that construct men as inherently dominant, instrumental, and independent and women as subservient, relational, and nurturing. These hegemonic constructions both reflect and support political, social, economic, and interpersonal systems that condone, uphold, and indeed celebrate violence against women, women's orientation to relationships and self-sacrifice, as well as their taken-for-granted work in the home. Thus, the pursuit of the 'good' woman ideal and women's everyday experiences are rendered unproblematic and invisible as sources of women's distress. At the same time, the splitting of women into the 'good' woman or the bad (the Madonna or whore, the mother or monster) results in the situation whereby women who step outside the confines of the 'good' woman identity are readily vilified, marginalized, and silenced. Moreover, the dominant understanding of depression as a biomedical problem further eclipses women's oppression, while frequently subverting their expressions of distress as 'not real'. Thus, it was argued that women who are depressed face pervasive delegitimation and silencing forged by both discourses of femininity and biomedicine. These interlocking discourses were similarly implicated in the silencing of a host of health problems that are particularly common among women. While different in their own ways, experiences of pain and distress such as depression, chronic fatigue, fibromyalgia, and migraine all share being both marked and exacerbated by over-extension that typically characterizes women's lives. They also share pervasive delegitimation. Thus, the effect of this interlocking set of discourses is to marginalize and silence women's pain. This silencing in turn maintains the status quo and the hegemony of both patriarchy and its bedfellow biomedicine.[2]

While women's talk of depression was entwined in discourses of femininity and marked by expressions of shame, guilt, and inadequacy, their talk of recovery involved the rupture or resistance of these discourses. That is, while women can be seen to be *silenced* in depression, recovery can be understood as a process through which women *talk back*. Women's accounts of becoming well centred on the importance of having their distress validated, relinquishing an exclusively other-orientation, and beginning to attend to their own needs, desires, and interests. Two central patterns of accounting were identified that supported these aims. In the first, participants reasserted the legitimacy of depression within the medical model. Although arguably problematic from a feminist standpoint, this way of accounting can serve to legitimize women's pain as 'real' and protect them from being blamed for their own distress. Moreover, it can provide a fissure in discourses of femininity and a means through which women can take care of themselves without being vilified as selfish, bad women. While I critiqued this way of accounting on several fronts, an exploration of its discursive effects serves as a reminder that when women are encouraged to forgo a medical explanation of their distress, they may also be faced with the promise of relinquishing a valued means of legitimation, however limited this may be.

In the second, and sometimes overlapping pattern of accounting, participants talked of recovery as a personally transformative experience. They described recovery as a process through which they resisted or rejected the suffocating confines of the 'good' woman identity and began to pay better attention to their own health and happiness. Repositioning the 'good' woman in different ways, speakers opened up spaces for resistance. This is not to suggest that women turned away from relationships and abandoned all care-work, but rather that they began to problematize and resist self-sacrifice and an exclusively other-orientation. In women's narratives of living well after depression, they described a critical need for self-care, including 'standing up' for themselves, 'letting go' of caring, cooking, and cleaning, and 'saying no' to others' demands. Thus, women tended to describe recovery as either a re-naming of their experiences in medical terms, or as a re-authoring of their identities within a narrative of personal transformation. In either case, the importance of self-care (as opposed to self-negation) for women's well-being came to the fore.

While the interruption and resistance of discourses of femininity has been linked to healing and well-being (Lafrance, 2003; Schreiber 1996a; Ussher, 2006), women's accounts of both recovery and self-care indicate that this is not an easy or unproblematic endeavour. A detailed analysis of women's talk revealed a central bind whereby self-care was described as important for their well-being but threatening to their identities as women. Throughout their narratives, women struggled with a dominant discursive context that equates women's 'self-care' with 'selfishness'. And, as women's accounts repeatedly suggested, there is little worse than being a selfish woman. Thus, the struggle to recover and maintain health can be seen to involve not only a pushing through the phenomenological weight of depression, but also the struggle for women to legitimize, take up, and maintain activities that promote their health and well-being. An understanding of what it *means* to women to attend to their own needs elucidates the common difficulty for women to engage in health-promoting behaviours. This pervasive struggle in meaning highlights the need for alternative ways of understanding that do not vilify women's attention to themselves.

In Chapter 4, I explored a variety of discursive resources drawn on in women's accounts that enabled them to negotiate the negative implications for identity associated with women's self-care, with some ways of accounting arguably more useful for feminist projects than others. For instance, I described a discourse of equity ('the new normal') as having more potential for empowerment than the equation of women's self-care with an increased capacity for caring for others (the oxygen-mask device). In this final chapter, I will revisit the research findings and discuss how they might be useful in efforts to support women's health and well-being.

Although discourse analysis has been widely adopted as a vehicle for critique and deconstruction, discourse analysts have been reluctant to suggest ways in which their findings might be drawn on in intervention strategies (Willig, 1999a). The assumptions underlying discourse analytic methods appear to pose a variety of problems for those wishing to 'apply' their findings. For instance, as David Harper (1999) points out, the concept of application does not fit easily within a social constructionist epistemology, since 'it implies a mechanistic, naive, lineal and reductionistic view in suggesting that ideas from "research" be taken out of context and *applied* to a context of "practice" without any problematizing of these terms' (p.128). Further problems arise when we consider that social constructionists reject the possibility that knowledge can ever be unbound from culture and power. When we abandon the concept of value-free 'Truth', how are we to suggest that one way of understanding should be promoted over another? Moreover, given discourse analysts' assumptions about the flexibility of language, they cannot be assured that their findings will not be used in oppressive and disempowering ways. Regardless of the intentions of the researchers, analytic findings can be misused and abused to reify limiting discourses and promote the interests of the more powerful (Cromby & Standen, 1996; Widdicombe, 1995). Given these issues, discourse analysts have tended to avoid speaking beyond the data, and suggesting ways in which their findings might be applied.

In her edited text *Applied discourse analysis: Social and psychological interventions*, Carla Willig (1999a) addresses these and other critiques of an applied discourse analysis. While acknowledging the criticisms and cautions of application, Willig and her co-contributers argue that discourse analysis already is an important form of intervention in that it represents a challenge to 'what is' (Willig, 1999a; Pujol, 1999).

> Discourse analysis is an attractive research tool for critical psychologists because it allows us to question and challenge dominant constructions of psychologically relevant concepts (e.g. 'mental illness', 'intelligence', 'personality'). By deconstructing such categories, we can demonstrate that things could be different, that our customary ways of categorizing and ordering phenomena are reified and interest-driven rather than simple reflections of 'reality'. By revealing the constructed nature of psychological phenomena, we create a space for making available alternatives to what has become psychological common sense.
>
> (Willig, 1999c, p. 2)

As explored in my discussion of epistemology (Appendix A), taking a relativist epistemological stance means that one cannot assert that one way of understanding is more *true* than another. However, as Harper (1999) suggests, this does not preclude us from arguing that some ways of understanding may be *better* than others. Harper acknowledges that this assertion brings up even more questions about 'who judges whether something is useful' (1999, p. 128). However, he regards as more useful those interventions that deconstruct and challenge dichotomous clinical categories (such as individual/social; pathology/normality; form/content; professional/service user) and those that trace 'the influence of power and the production of gender, race, age, class, sexuality and so on' (p. 128). He notes that interventions are never perfect and always involve problematic assumptions. However, some interventions may be more useful than others for supporting the views of service users and for problematizing harmful institutionalized assumptions (such as those inherent in biomedicine). Given the flexibility of language and the risk that research findings can be abused, it becomes important for researchers to engage in ongoing critical reflexivity with the meanings made and the ways in which they are used. This means, for instance, that researchers who aim to work with others in a practical sense can not simply 'apply' their work and walk away (Willig, 1999c). Instead, they must engage in ongoing collective and reflexive work as the interventions unfold, change, and are taken up in different ways with different effects (Willig, 1999c). That is, an exploration of implications for usefulness calls researchers to attend to the contextual and shifting location of their suggestions.

Critical deconstruction is an essential and important enterprise, but like Willig, Harper, and others, I do not want to rest at the level of deconstruction without offering possibilities for reconstruction. As Kenneth Gergen stated, '(i)f all texts are deconstructed, and the deconstructions themselves are deconstructed, you are left with silence' (Misra, 1993, p. 413). This is not to suggest replacing one set of hegemonic truths with another, but rather opening up richer formulations and potentially more empowering outcomes. To develop critical understandings without suggesting how these might be translated into useful and empowering practice is to critique from the sidelines, often only to an elite group of academic colleagues who are already converted (Harper, 1999; Willig, 1999a). There are risks to the application of research findings. However, I agree with Willig (1999d) when she concludes:

> On balance, then, it seems to me that the risks of abstention from involvement in social and psychological practice are greater than its benefits. Even in our roles as discourse analysts, abstention means collusion with the status quo (see also Willig, 1998). We need to mobilize our skills as discourse analysts in order to intervene in the struggle over how language constitutes our world(s).
>
> (p. 158)

In the sections that follow, I will trace what I feel to be some of the central points of my analysis, and how these insights might be useful to researchers, educators, health practitioners, those suffering from depression and other forms of marginalized distress, and those who support them including friends and family. To a large extent, these points are grounded in a rich repository of feminist scholarship, and it might be argued that I need not have done this research to develop many of these suggestions. What this analysis does bring, however, is a grounding in (some) women's words, as well as a richness and depth of understanding of the multitude of ways in which women's experiences are shaped by discourse. By beginning analysis from women's own accounts and tracing the influences of power throughout, new insights, detail, and evidence about women's pain, healing, and lives in general come to the fore.

THE VALUE IN ATTENDING TO STORIES OF RECOVERY AND WELL-BEING

I began this exploration by arguing that recovery from depression has been an area of study that has been largely overlooked. Often reduced to being understood as a 'treatment outcome' or 'spontaneous remission', the experience of recovery has failed to capture the interest and attention of researchers. I argued that a central reason for this oversight may be that depression is considered a 'recurrent disorder' and that as a result many may not 'qualify' as 'properly recovered'. Indeed, many of the participants in my research expressed trouble with the term 'recovery'; however, they certainly talked at length and in depth about healing, transformation, and well-being. Therefore, the problem with 'recovery' appears not to be with lived experience, but with our preconceived notions of what recovery means.

I could have asked potential participants if they had 'recovered' and recruited only those who met pre-established criteria (for instance, those no longer experiencing the requisite symptoms for diagnosis). However, in directing the research from the agenda of the biomedical establishment, rather than from the perspective of those who have lived through depression, I would have missed hearing a completely different set of stories. By allowing women to narrate their experiences without prefiguring which stories are worthy of hearing, I was able to explore how these women's accounts are already silenced and subverted, and perhaps more importantly, how they resist this marginalization in their talk. Further, the adoption of a discourse analytic approach enabled me to cut through the limiting assumptions about 'what recovery really is'. Instead, it allowed me to explore the ways in which recovery was constructed, understood, and experienced by the women I spoke with. Exploring women's accounts in this way allowed the emergence of new insights about the (il)legitimacy of women's pain, healing, and efforts to live well, as well as an exploration of sites of resistance.

In the introductory chapter, I also argued that researchers have over-looked the concept of recovery because the research agenda in mainstream psychology is primarily driven by a preoccupation with deficit, dysfunction, and pathology. Surely there is much to be gained by attending to the ways in which people heal, live well, and flourish. The emerging positive psychology movement, with its focus on happiness, excellence, and health provides new directions for psychological research (Csikszentmihalyi & Csikszentmihalyi, 2006; Peterson, 2006; Snyder & Lopez, 2007). Conducted from this more positive analytic frame, discourse analysts can use their work to open up new and enriching understandings of the ways in which people live healthy, vibrant, fulfilling lives. For instance, recent works in critical health psychology have provided compelling examinations of the discursive formulations that both undermine *and* facilitate health beha-viours such as smoking cessation (Gillies, 1999; Gillies & Willig; 1997;

Parry, Fowkes, & Thomson, 2001) and condom use (Willig, 1995, 1997). One value of these programmes of inquiry is that researchers can identify subject positions occurring in people's talk and then explore the implications of these positions for intervention. For instance, the discourse of addiction has been identified as disempowering in that it strips smokers of agency (Gillies, 1999; Gillies & Willig, 1997). Further, discourses of marriage and romance operate to construct *not* using a condom as an expression of trust or passion, and clearly work in opposition to the negotiation of condom use in relationships (Gavey & McPhillips, 1999; Willig, 1995). Such programmes of study bring forth important insights that can inform health-promotion initiatives by directing interventions away from the use of limiting discourses. Moreover, by exploring the accounts of those who have managed to quit smoking or successfully negotiate condom use, researchers can identify those discourses and subject positions that may best support people's efforts to engage practices of their choosing.

Therefore, discourse analysis can be used to open up new ways of understanding that may be more liberating for those seeking change. However, as Willig (1999a) points out, there is also a danger of becoming too ideological, as language alone can not drive social change. 'For example, talk of a "classless society" does not do away with the systemic social divisions which characterize capitalist economies' (Willig, 1999d, p. 155). Thus, '[a]n "applied discourse analysis" which does not attend to the institutional basis of discourse and subjectivity runs the risk of overestimating its ability to effect change and of blaming individual speakers for failing to shake off limiting discourses' (Willig, 1999d, p. 149). Discourse is grounded in the ways in which society is socially, politically, and economically governed (Parker, 1992). Discourse and materiality operate in synchrony. Accordingly, efforts to promote recovery and well-being among women require simultaneous attention to these interlocking realms of experience. We need to attend to discourse and the ways in which it shapes subjectivity, as well as to the contexts of materiality, embodiment, and power. As Ussher (1991) stated, '[w]e need to operate on the level of the political and of the individual: at the level of discursive practices, and individual solutions for misery. The two must go hand in hand if we are to move forward' (p. 293).

In summary, attention to people's stories of recovery, healing, and wellbeing have been largely absent in the psychological literature. In addition, the terms 'recovery' and 'self-care' – concepts of healing and health – do not appear to resonate with women, and without a language to understand these experiences, they remain marginalized. There is a need to develop alternative discourses that 'speak' to women's experiences of well-being following depression and to their efforts to nurture themselves. Further, there is a need to hear these alternative stories. No one narrative can capture all experience (White & Epston, 1990). Each brings certain features into focus and eclipses others. The dominant 'story' or 'narrative' of depression is that put forward by biomedicine. In this story, depression means illness, chronicity, a body out-of-order, or a body perpetually at risk of relapse. Within this framework, experiences such as a lifting of mood, optimism, hope, or times of joy, may be readily undermined – swallowed up by this totalitizing and pathologizing narrative. Rather than conclude that there are no (or few) legitimate stories of recovery, alternative understandings of healing and well-ness are needed. Participants' stories of living well after depression can be used to foster a sense of hope in those struggling with depressive experiences – stories so often absent in the mainstream. Further, this analysis urges researchers and health-care practitioners to avail themselves of ways of understanding other than symptom remission and the ominous expectation of recurrence. While this is not to deny that a woman may very well experience depression again, it is suggested that she may be better served by understanding her distress and well-being in ways other than in the medical terms of 'illness', 'remission', and 'chronicity'.

DECONSTRUCTING BIO-POWER: THE NEED FOR ALTERNATIVE UNDERSTANDINGS OF PAIN, DISTRESS, AND DIS-EASE

Through a detailed examination of the ways in which participants constructed depression as a medical condition, I came to appreciate the discursive struggle for legitimacy faced by these women. Because participants' accounts had the repeated effect of defending the reality and legitimacy of their pain, depression came into view as an experience that requires such defence. That is, depression, like many other forms of women's distress, can be viewed as a contested experience, because in their repeated defence of depression, participants treated it this way (Wood & Kroger, 2000).

The current dominance of biomedicine forces a variety of illness experiences to the margins of social legitimacy. In their commentary on the social construction of vertigo, Yardley and Beech (1998) state that prevailing discourses surrounding health and illness have deprived sufferers of the language required to construct their experiences in socially legitimate ways.

> The dualist biomedical approach to illness deprives sufferers of the vocabulary they need in order to communicate and understand their experiences . . . In this unsolicited struggle over the meaning of their conditions they are deeply disadvantaged by their deviant status and lack of relevant (medical) authority. In this sense, they can be considered comparable to other socially disempowered groups (e.g., ethnic minorities, lesbians and gay men) who find

181

themselves deprived of 'voice', and are obliged to describe themselves using the language of the dominant group, a language con-
sisting of dichotomies in which the characteristics of the minority
are unfavourably defined by their contrast with the qualities of the
majority (Sampson, 1993).

(Yardley & Beech, 1998, p. 324)

Impelled to use a language that ultimately serves to undermine the legitimacy of their distress, those who suffer marginalized forms of pain are
doubly victimized: once by their embodied experience of pain and dysfunction, and again by a society that denies their pain. When biomedicine is
unable to explain or heal, its predominance is maintained by holding
patients, not the model, accountable for the failure (Kirmayer 1988; Ware,
1992). The blame and shame so often associated with chronic, 'lifestyle',
and 'mental' illnesses are often regarded as a problem of 'stigma'. This
way of accounting off-loads the problem of delegitimation onto an 'ignor-
ant public', and calls for greater public education and awareness of the
legitimacy of these forms of distress (Lafrance, 2007a, 2007b). Ignored by
this approach, however, are the fundamental ontological and epistemological assumptions of the dominant medical discourse that keep marginalization for such conditions in place. Thus, the very notion of 'stigma'
has the effect of reinstating the power of the biomedical model. As long as
naturalism and individualism remain dominant assumptions for establishing the legitimacy of one's experiences and self, efforts to legitimize (or 'de-
stigmatize') experiences such as depression are likely to be forestalled
(Lafrance, 2007a).

Radical changes in the ways in which pain and dis-ease are conceptualized are required. Until that time, however, mental health researchers
and professionals could offer training programmes in critical language
awareness to users of health services, lobbyists, journalists, and others to
support efforts to resist marginalization (Fairclough, 1995; Willig, 1999d).
For instance, users of health services and lobby groups could be trained to
identify discourses and subject positions adopted by themselves and the
professionals and policy makers they work with. Discursive skills could
be mobilized in the deconstruction of discursive formulations that serve to
undermine the legitimacy of sufferers' distress and identities, as well as in
the promotion of alternative ways of understanding. For instance, instead
of promoting depression as 'just like diabetes' (a condition that can be
monitored through blood tests), ways of talking that subvert objectivity as
the marker of truth may be more useful (e.g., 'depression is like electricity;
just because you can't see it doesn't mean it isn't real'). Further, this
analysis highlights the importance for therapists and other health
professionals to validate depressive and other marginalized experiences of
distress as 'real'. Without their troubles being understood as constituting a

'legitimate problem', depressed women may be discursively stranded from taking action toward change. Thus, naming and validating women's pain and distress appear to be essential first steps in movement toward recovery.

The deconstruction of the assumptions of biomedicine must occur from the 'bottom up', but also from the 'top down', and it is important that health-care providers understand the assumptions inherent in the language they speak. Health practitioners-in-training would be well served by foundational courses in epistemology and an understanding of the post-modern critiques of science. Otherwise, the assumptions underlying their practice will remain like water to a fish: taken-for-granted and uncontested truths. These courses could also draw attention to patients' interpretations of their experiences and the promotion of subjectivity as a valid and useful way of knowing.

As previously discussed, the reliance on objectivity to determine the validity of knowledge requires that subjectivity and the symbolic aspects of life are erased. Thus, facets of experience that cannot be measured in objective, quantifiable terms are ignored and marginalized. Submerging the subjective is unhelpful not only because it results in the dismissal and subsequent intensification of many people's pain, but also because it provides a truncated view of illness and health, even for those suffering from what may be understood as 'real biological disease'. After all, '(n)o one ever experiences cancer as the uncontrolled proliferation of abnormal cells. Indeed, we can experience anything at all only through and by means of culturally constructed and socially reproduced structures of metaphor and meaning' (DiGiacomo, 1992, p. 117). Listening to sufferers' accounts requires that understandings of pain, illness, and distress are seen as more than 'problems of the body machine' or 'a temporary break in an otherwise healthy existence' (Radley, 1993, p. 1). Rather, such experiences are shaped by cultural assumptions and practices, and fundamentally disrupt sufferers' worlds and identities (Radley, 1993). From a discursive perspective, illness and distress come into view as inseparable from the moral order of the cultural context and integral to the construction of sufferers' biographies (Kleinman, 1995; Radley, 1993). To encompass this perspective, then, requires educators and practitioners to extend their gaze beyond a focus on biomedical disease and that which can be objectively identified, and toward an 'empathic witnessing' of the person-in-context (Kleinman, 1995; Kleinman & Kleinman, 1997).

> Professionals in the health care system are trained and, when in practice, are rewarded to take as the object of inquiry the disease and the individual's response to it. They frequently minimize the broad social scope of serious illness in the interpersonal space of everyday life. They also fail to engage the cultural significance of suffering as embodied moral critique and opportunity for social

transformation and even transcendence. Yet, suffering is inseparable from these social processes, which are of importance to its experience and treatment. The chief issue for health care researchers and teachers, and especially for those concerned with the intersection of values and medicine, is to figure out strategies by which these aspects of suffering can be more validly understood and engaged in biomedicine and in the wider society.

(Kleinman, 1995, p. 184)

In order to better understand and validate the embodied, subjective, and cultural meanings of suffering, many have called for a radical reformulation of current conceptions of health and illness (Good et al., 1992; Radley, 1993; Stoppard, 2000; Ussher, 1991; Wilkinson, 2000; Yardley, 1996). Such reformulation would require the transcendence of limiting dichotomies such as body/mind, objectivity/subjectivity, and individual/society. Previous attempts to integrate and give equal consideration to the physical, individual, and social contexts have been largely unsuccessful. For instance, the term *psychosomatic*, as originally proposed, refers to a holistic and dialectical model of body and mind (Cohn, 1999; Kirmayer, 1988). However, this understanding remains grounded in Cartesian dualism. The body continues to be divided from the mind, and afflictions of the body are considered 'more real' than afflictions of the mind (Ware, 1993). Further, it has been argued that psychosomatic explanations are often used to shift the blame for medicine's failure to diagnose and heal (Horton-Salway, 2002; Yardley, 1996). Thus, a psychosomatic diagnosis has become used 'not as a means of integrating the psychological and the somatic but rather to indicate a nondiagnosis' (Tishelman & Sachs, 1998, p. 55).

In 1977, Engel proposed the biopsychosocial model as a way of bringing together in harmony the biological, psychological, and social realms of experience. This theory has had a broad impact on conceptualizations of illness and disease. Again, however, this approach remains rooted in the biomedical perspective and the dominance of objectivity (over subjectivity) and the body (over the mind) is maintained (Yardley, 1996). The psychological and social are 'factors duly noted and entered into the equation of the patient's distress, while disease remains the one solid fact about the person' (Kirmayer, 1988, pp. 83–4). Within this formulation, the body remains medicalized and regarded only as a mechanistic vehicle (Stoppard, 2000). Moreover, this approach conceptualizes culture as merely a surface 'coating' on the universal human and fails to encompass how culture infuses the very ways in which we construct our experiences of ourselves and our world (Gordon, 1988; Kitzinger, 1992). In contrast to these modernist frameworks, recent developments in feminist and postmodern scholarship offer new ways of understanding. Critical-realist (Nightingale & Cromby, 1999; Sims-Schouten et al., 2007; Willig, 1999b), material-discursive (Stoppard, 1997,

1998, 2000; Ussher, 1996, 1997; Yardley, 1996, 1997b), and material-discursive-intrapsychic approaches (Ussher, 2002, 2003a, 2006) all represent theoretical frameworks that attend to materiality as well as the ways in which meaning is socially produced. As the postmodern turn continues to expand in influence, I hope that these alternative visions take hold as new and more useful ways of understanding health and illness – ways that might better serve those suffering marginalized forms of distress.

THE 'GOOD' WOMAN IS ALIVE AND UNWELL: THE NEED FOR DECONSTRUCTION AND RESISTANCE OF DISCOURSES OF FEMININITY

It was she who bothered me and wasted my time and so tormented me that at last I killed her. You who come of a younger and happier generation may not have heard of her – you may not know what I mean by the Angel in the House. I will describe her as shortly as I can. She was intensely sympathetic. She was immensely charming. She was utterly unselfish. She excelled in the difficult arts of family life. She sacrificed herself daily. If there was a chicken, she took the leg; if there was a draught, she sat in it – in short she was so constituted that she never had a mind or a wish of her own, but preferred to sympathize always with the minds and wishes of others . . . I turned upon her and caught her by the throat. I did my best to kill her. My excuse, if I were to be had up in a court of law, would be that I acted in self-defence. Had I not killed her she would have killed me.

(Woolf, 1942, pp. 236–8)

Virginia Woolf wrote these words in the 1940s, Dana Jack reminded us of them in the early 1990s (Jack, 1991), and apparently they warrant repeating yet again. Despite Woolf's supposition that those of a 'younger and happier generation' might not know the 'Angel in the House,' the spectre of idealized femininity continues to haunt women today. Although no longer wearing her iconic pearls, heels, and apron, this phantom has modernized, but remains equally pernicious. She morphs in focus from the sexual to the maternal across a (truncated) range of ages. However, across these representations, she is always fraught with contradictions, always unattainable, and therefore always oppressive. As the youthful beauty, she is flawlessly attractive, but effortlessly so. She eats, but remains skeletal. She has a childlike frame, but enlarged breasts. She exudes both innocence and sexuality.[3] In the mother form, she is endlessly pleased and pleasing. She nurtures others, wanting nothing more for herself. Indeed, she is satisfied in her own self-sacrifice. Of course, across all these representations, she is young, white, heterosexual, and able-bodied.

185

The narrow confines of the 'good' woman ideal means that very few women, if any, are able to meet and maintain its standards. Instead, these images of femininity so widely celebrated as perfection, often leave women endlessly striving toward an unattainable ideal while at the same time feeling woefully inadequate. Further, the bifurcation of femininity into the 'good' and the 'bad', the Madonna or the whore, in conjunction with the heterosexual matrix in which femininity is constructed, have the effect of positioning alternative identities for women as abject (such as lesbian women, women without children, and single women) (Ussher, 2006).

For many women, the constant struggle to approximate the ideal (and at the same time resist being positioned as 'other') means engaging in practices that consume their time and energies, often leaving them extended and exhausted. However, the pleasant-natured, 'good' woman ideal and the taken-for-granted nature of her practices (including everything from dieting to childcare) afford little space for women to understand and express feelings of discontent, anger, sadness, or frustration. Instead, women's distress is often rendered incomprehensible, dismissed, and silenced. This point may be best articulated in the words of Barb, one of the women I interviewed, who became depressed when single-handedly caring for her dying mother, while at the same time maintaining the work of wife, mother, and frequent care-giver for her toddler grandchild.

> You know I felt I had to so::lve all these problems, there was nobody else to do it. So it was just an **accumulation** and you know. My doctor asked me once, she said 'Have you ever thought of committing suicide?' I said 'No, but you know I dream about a time when I could wake up in the morning and for two weeks everybody would have disappeared off the face of the earth ((laughs)) just let me be for two weeks. You know, nobody making demands, not even feeding the cat, they're gone, they're fi::ne, but they're gone somewhere'. [...] And she sort of thought that was funny ((laughs)) It was all the pressures, all the demands, even making breakfast for your husband. It was like <everything> got piled on top of the other, you didn't want to do any of them. Yet it bothered you that you didn't do them! Cra::::zy! Really crazy.
>
> (Barb)

As illustrated in Barb's account, discourses of femininity appear to form an unarticulated backdrop against which women judge themselves and are judged (Lafrance & Stoppard, 2006, 2007). These are not simply ideas injected into women's unsuspecting heads, but rather are systems of meaning that infuse the ways in which we construct and understand what it

186

means to be a woman. Thus, practices of femininity remain taken-for-granted and invisible as a source of distress in women's lives. As Barb stated, she longed for respite, but was bothered by her reprieve. While this apparent contradiction may appear 'crazy', it can be understood as a reasonable reaction to the invisible, limiting, and unrelenting requirements of the 'good' woman identity – an identity that is both a measure of a woman's worth and taxing in its production.

This analysis calls for the continued critique of patriarchal power to construct women in limiting and oppressive ways. Given the current ethos of individualism in concert with the persistent backlash against feminism, I have found that the students I work with often endorse the position that women 'have arrived' in terms of gender equality. They often appear to regard themselves as self-determined individuals unencumbered by archaic gender roles. 'The oppression of women is old news', they say; 'we can do anything and be anything we want'. While undeniable advances have been made toward gender equality, I fear a widespread lulling into complacency. In ignoring the sometimes subtle but powerful ways in which we are shaped into gendered ways of being, patriarchal power gradually, imperceptibly, tightens its hold. Thus, persistent critique and resistance by women and men alike of the social construction of femininity and masculinity are required. This critique must include a dismantling of the glorification of women's selflessness and the equation of caring with femininity. Depictions of women as the natural care-givers, and men as somehow less natural or competent care-givers, abound in media representations and in everyday talk (hooks, 2000; Sunderland, 2002). These constructions in turn support and naturalize a social organization whereby nurture-work (such as teaching, nursing, and childcare) is women's work, and accordingly, is undervalued and underpaid, if paid at all (England et al., 2002).

It is as critical now as ever that we publicly challenge gendered assumptions across domains, including education, public policy (e.g., low wages for care-givers, the dismantling of public health care in favour of 'home care'), and the media (e.g., representations of fathers as inept care-givers). As feminist therapists have done for decades, it is also critical that political and societal influences be traced through women's experiences such that they are not led to blame themselves for 'faulty thinking', but rather gain a deeper appreciation of their shared oppression as well as possible avenues for resistance. Discussion and deconstruction of the 'good' mother ideal could also form an important part of pre-natal education and parenting groups, including those that are formed through the internet. Often spaces for the intensification of discourses of femininity, such programmes could be transformed into validating arenas for the expression of a range of feelings and experiences associated with parenting, including exhaustion, distress, ambivalence, frustration, and sadness. In keeping with this suggestion, Daphne, a woman interviewed in the self-care study, proposed the need for publicly funded courses in 'Reality Parenting'. The name she proposed might resonate with parents by capitalizing on the current obsession with 'reality television' in the West, while also working to normalize a range of experiences involved in parenting work. Such forums could allow for the elaboration of other ways of mothering, 'ways that do not deny a mother her agency, autonomy, authenticity, and authority, thereby allowing her both her selfhood and power' (O'Reilly, 2004b, p. 11). Further, transgressive spaces such as 'Reality Parenting' classes could allow for the development of alternative discourses of 'effective parenting' in which both women and men are constructed as equally able to parent and equally valued for their care-work. As bell hooks (2000) has argued,

> There should be a concept of effective parenting that makes no distinction between maternal and paternal care. The model of effective parenting . . . has been applied only to women and has prevented fathers from learning how to parent. They are allowed to conceive of the father's role solely in terms of exercising authority and providing for material needs. They are taught to think of it as a role secondary to the mother's. Until males are taught how to parent using the same model of effective parenting that has been taught to women, they will not participate equally in child care. They will even feel that they should not participate because they have been taught to think they are inadequate or ineffective as child-rearers.
>
> (hooks, 2000, pp. 130–40)

Disrupting the cultural equation of caring with femininity, and developing non-gendered discourses of effective parenting could assist in the recruitment of men in care-work. At the same time however, it can be very problematic, and indeed dangerous for women when the *idea* of 'non-gendered' parenting is upheld without the concomitant *reality* of equal partnership in parenting work (for instance, when family courts force women to 'share' custody of children with men who are neglectful or abusive (Gavey, 2008, personal communication)). Thus, changes in discourse must occur in tandem with a restructuring of material support. Those who provide care must be valued both socially and economically and there is an urgent need for structural changes including the appropriate economic compensation for the work of care-giving, the availability of affordable public day-care that is of high quality, adequate accommodations for parental leave, and job security for those who take it. Envisioning such a social organization, Loretta Brewer (2001) described the need for a

> culture where caring is viewed as a valued human undertaking, where no one suffers as a result of providing care, and where the legitimate needs of all are adequately addressed. Only when both men and women can freely choose to engage in . . . care – and

when they receive the recognition and support they deserve for doing so – will this be possible.

(p. 233)

In inviting social critique, this analysis can also be used to open up spaces for resistance. Women's accounts of recovery, health, and well-being repeatedly involve a discursive rupture or resistance of discourses of femininity whereby women can relinquish an exclusive focus on others and begin to attend to their own needs, desires, and pleasures (Lafrance, 2003; Schreiber, 1996a; Ussher, 2006). Thus, I conceptualized recovery as a site of women's resistance. In this way, I did not regard recovery from depression as a form of individual 'awakening', but rather as a continued discursive struggle to position oneself within a cultural context that glorifies the 'good' woman identity and vilifies women's (particularly mothers') attention to their own needs as 'selfish' (McMahon, 1995). A strength of this analysis is that it explores *how* resistance is discursively formulated in women's accounts, including an analysis of the implications of their talk for meaning and identity. A central way in which participants resisted discourses of femininity was through their use of a narrative of personal transformation. This narrative appeared across the accounts of participants in the recovery and self-care studies, as well as in other research on women's recovery and health (e.g., Schreiber, 1996a; Ussher, 2006). The repeated emergence of this narrative provides support for the position that discourses of femininity constrict women's well-being, and that it can also be reclaimed (at least in part) through resistance. Moreover, the repeated presence of this discursive resource speaks to the cultural availability of this narrative for providing more emancipatory means of self-construction for women. Therapists working with women who are depressed can be attuned to the emergence of this narrative in women's talk, not to impose this narrative, but rather to foster its seeds when they occur as a means of re-authoring the self (Lafrance & Stoppard, 2007). At the same time, however, aspects of this narrative warrant further scrutiny and critique. For instance, authoring one's former self as a 'perfectionist', 'control freak', 'victim' or 'doormat' may allow for the repositioning and resistance of the 'good' woman identity, but ultimately these rest on a unified, pejorative, and individualistic understanding of self. Instead, tracing the ways in which these identities or qualities are socially constructed as a part of femininity, and how women can collectively resist such oppression, is warranted.

The importance of developing new and more useful stories of the self is of central importance in narrative therapy (Brown & Augusta-Scott, 2007; White, 1995, 2000, 2004; White & Epston, 1990). Emerging from postmodern thought, this approach to therapy attends to the ways in which identities and possibilities for action are shaped by the stories we tell ourselves and the stories that are told of us. It is argued that people become immobilized by

189

problem-saturated stories – stories often driven by hegemonic truths about the 'right way to be'. Interrupting these stories and generating alternative ways of understanding is the cornerstone of healing practice.

> Insofar as the desirable outcome of therapy is the generation of alternative stories that incorporate vital and previously neglected aspects of lived experience, and insofar as these stories incorporate alternative knowledges, it can be argued that the identification of and provision of the space for the performance of these knowledges is a central focus of the therapeutic endeavor . . . [T]he externalization of the problem can be utilized en route to the identification and externalization of the unitary knowledge. This is helpful in that it assists persons in challenging the 'truths' that specify their lives – to protest their subjugation to unitary knowlededges.
>
> (White & Epston, 1990, p. 31)

Through a narrative of personal transformation, women can be seen to 'protest their subjugation', resist hegemonic constructions of femininity, and construct alternative, more liberating senses of self. These new understandings can then allow new possibilities for action. As Michael White pointed out, '[s]tories about life and identity are not equal to each other in their constitutive effects. It is clearly apparent that some stories sponsor a broader range of options for action in life than do others' (2004, p. 90). Thus, narratives that afford and legitimize women's attention to their own needs and pleasures can be seen as more empowering and useful in efforts to support women's health.

Insights from this analysis can inform the ways in which narrative therapists approach the meaning-making in women's stories of depression and despair. For instance, in their germinal text, *Narrative means to therapeutic ends*, Michael White and David Epston (1990) made frequent references to their work with women who have felt consumed by guilt, responsibility for others, self-loathing, and perfectionism. While the externalization of such problems is useful as a means of separating the person from the problem, and therefore opening up space for agency and resistance, a deeper appreciation of the social and gendered nature of these problems is required. The types of questions frequently used in narrative therapy might assist in tracing the patriarchal origins of such experiences (e.g., 'How have you been recruited into perfectionism, guilt, self-loathing etc.?') and highlighting women's resistance (e.g., 'Are there times in which you have ignored or resisted the pull to sacrifice yourself for others?').

In addition, narrative therapy points to the importance of inviting others to witness, support, and strengthen the new ways in which people narrate their lives. These 're-membering' practices can be fostered as sites of solidarity whereby women can connect with the histories and qualities of others (such as mothers, grandmothers, sisters, or friends) in challenging patriarchal norms and forging new understandings of self (O'Grady, 2005). They can also involve connecting women to communities of resistance. For instance, the 'Red Hat Society', popular in Canada and the United States, is a community that calls for older women to focus on fun and friendship. This organization (or 'dis-organization' as they call it) aims to defy the expectation that women should invest in the comfort and pleasure of others at the expense of themselves. As described on their official website, this group was formed as

> an opportunity for those who have shouldered various responsibilities at home and in the community their whole lives, to say goodbye to burdensome responsibilities and obligations for a little while. This is the place to have fun and enjoy yourself. The refrain of the popular Red Hat Society theme song by Mike Harline puts it rather bluntly 'All my life, I've done for you. Now it's my turn to do for me'.
>
> (Red Hat Society, 2007)

'The Raging Grannies' provides another, much more politicized forum for women's resistance and solidarity. Originating in Vancouver, Canada, the 'Raging Grannies' is an international movement of older women who engage in peaceful protest around issues relating to women's rights, peace, the environment, and social justice (Caissie, 2006; Narushima, 2001). These women publicly perform protest songs and skits while dressed in garb that mocks stereotypes of older women. Through satire, humour, and persistence, these women subvert efforts to dismiss and undermine their voices, and exert their power in meaningful ways. As feminist therapists have long argued, it is important for individual women to join together in solidarity in order to put the political nature of women's problems at the forefront, and to work toward social and political change. From a narrative perspective, the joining of women in fun or protest takes on the additional significance of nurturing and strengthening the re-storying of women's lives. After all, 'we do not, and cannot create our stories by ourselves' (Brown & Augusta-Scott, 2007, p. xix). The struggles women face in constructing a valued identity and recovering and maintaining well-being require a supportive social context, and are best supported through solidarity (O'Grady, 2005).

UNDERSTANDING WOMEN'S STRUGGLE TO SELF-CARE

Finally, this analysis sheds light on the recurrent finding that women often express ambivalence or a rejection of the need to care for themselves

(Harrington et al., 1992; Henderson, 1991; Miller & Brown, 2005). Because they are so basic, health-related activities such as rest, nutrition, exercise, time alone and the like can easily be taken-for-granted by therapists and other health professionals. When women fail to take up these suggestions, they can be readily positioned as defiant or deficient – as insufficiently motivated to change, unassertive, irrational, or masochistic. However, the cultural equation of women's self-care with selfishness renders these seemingly innocuous behaviours as potentially dangerous for women to take up. Without an understanding of the meaning of women's self-care, therapists and other health professionals run the risk of overlooking a potentially pervasive impediment to women's well-being.

The challenge for many therapists and health-care professionals is finding ways to assist women to attend to their own health needs (O'Grady, 2005). For instance, Jacqueline, a participant in the self-care study and a psychiatric nurse working in addictions, noted that the pull to prioritize the needs of others often interferes with women's ability to care for themselves.

> The reasons that I wanted visiting hours to stop here [inpatient unit for women and addictions], among other reasons, like people taking drugs in and that sort of thing, was the fact that men would bring the children in, and say, 'Look, I'm having a hard time with these children', and the women would have that guilt, and leave and go home with the kids. Like they weren't able to look after what they needed first. [...] Where I **never** heard tell of a woman calling and saying, 'Look, I can't look after the kids. You have to go home'. So, it- it is, I think, more difficult for women to nurture themselves than it is for men.
>
> (Jacqueline)

In her work on gender, Foucault, and therapy, Helen O'Grady (2005) also addressed the problem of how to encourage women to find space and time for themselves. Indeed, she asserted that increased care for the self is an antidote to women's self-policing. Toward this end, she suggested that therapists might capitalize on

> the idea that greater care for the self enhances relations of integrity with others often resonates for women. This is reflected in claims such as: 'If I don't start taking care of myself, I'm not going to be much use to my children/partner/family, etc.' Even though this sort of motivation might appear suspect because it sits too comfortably

within predominantly other-oriented training, it nonetheless provides a valuable entry point for enhanced relations of care for the self.

(O'Grady, 2005, p. 90)

While drawing on this line of accounting (explored in Chapter 3 as the oxygen-mask device) might provide a valuable entry point to introduce the idea of self-care, I would argue that ongoing and reflexive dialogue about justice, equity, and the social construction of femininity is essential. I offered similar cautions in regard to other discursive resources such as the 'crisis narrative' and the promotion of a 'tomboy' identity. I then explored potentially more liberating means of constructing self-care, including the narrative of personal transformation, positioning self-care as a reflection of equity ('the new normal'), and in terms of participants' connections with spiritual communities (such as eco-spirituality, yoga, mindfulness-based-practice, etc.). Again, I am not suggesting imposing these ideas or positionings on the women who seek therapeutic services, but rather my aim is to highlight the possibilities and implications of various ways of accounting. A greater appreciation of these ways of accounting might inform the work of health practitioners and assist them to better support women's efforts toward health and well-being.

CONCLUSION

The implications for usefulness of this research suggest change at both individual and sociopolitical levels; changes both in discourse and institutional practices and policy. They call for a transformation and expansion in the ways in which femininity is socially understood, performed, and celebrated. As previously discussed, language alone cannot drive social change (Willig, 1999a). However, changes in language, in discourse, can open up new possibilities for practice, just as changes in institutions or technologies give birth to new ways of speaking. What I heard in women's accounts were recurring challenges to the legitimacy of their depressive experiences, identities, and practices of recovery and self-care. What I also heard were the ways in which women mapped out a language of resistance enabling them to take up new and varied ways of being. The goal of this analysis is not to suggest replacing one delimited set of practices of femininity (selflessness and an other-orientation) with another (self-care), but rather to open up legitimate space for women to live in ways of their choosing. By attending to and highlighting these moments of resistance, women's health and happiness in their various forms might be better understood and fostered.

Notes

1 This term is taken from Harper (1999).
2 Further evidence of how discourses of femininity and biomedicine are implicated in the delegitimation of distress is provided by a study of doctors' and nurses' accounts of men's health in the context of medical practice (Seymour-Smith, Wetherell, & Phoenix, 2002). Interpretative repertoires drawn on by health providers constructed men as serious users of the health service, while women, in contrast, were constructed as presenting with 'routine', 'trivial' or 'hypochondriacal' complaints. Even when men were discussed as having presented with less serious problems, the claim 'my wife ordered me to come' was frequently used, thereby maintaining hegemonic masculinity and blaming women for wasting doctors' time. The authors explore how, in these ways, gender is centrally involved in the social construction of legitimate health complaints, and constructions of 'the proper patient'.
3 This image of the 'sexy virgin' is perpetrated by the advertising and pornography industries alike, campaigns that ultimately support the sexualization and abuse of girls. Childhood sexual abuse and the trafficking of girls in the sex trade around the world are just some of the realities that stem from both the devaluation and sexualization of girls and women.

APPENDIX A

A BRIEF DISCUSSION OF EPISTEMOLOGY, SOCIAL CONSTRUCTIONISM, AND DISCOURSE

Although not often acknowledged, all researchers begin inquiry from some perspective on the nature of reality (ontology) and how one develops knowledge within that view (epistemology) (Schwandt, 1997; Sexton, 1997). For the most part, research in psychology has assumed a modernist epistemological stance. This position necessitates a belief in a knowable and objective world that exists independent of any observer (Sexton, 1997). Within this paradigm, research is aimed at discovering the 'true' nature of reality, often by isolating certain variables (such as aggression, intelligence, or attitudes) and eliminating confounding variables (such as experimenter subjectivity) (Burr, 1995; Gergen, 1992). Through reliance on an empirical method, it is believed that the accumulation of knowledge will lead to reliable, value-neutral, and universal laws of the nature of reality. In other words, empirical psychology endeavours to be 'progressive' in that it is aimed at the discovery of universal properties of human behaviour that are consistent across time, place, person, and culture (Gergen, 1992; Ryan, 1999).

The publication of Kuhn's *The structure of scientific revolutions* in 1962 delivered a blow to the 'progressive' foundation of modern science, and was a critical element in 'the postmodern turn' (Gergen, 1992; Ryan, 1999). Kuhn proposed that what scientists consider to be increments in knowledge are actually shifts in perspective. He argued that the application of the scientific method does not lead to the linear accumulation of knowledge, but rather to shifts in world view. The notion of 'truth' became contextualized and the essential elements of postmodernism in psychology began to emerge. There was (and continues to be) increasing talk of epistemology among Western psychologists, of the values inherent in psychological research, and of the social and political foundations upon which scientific knowledge rests (Gergen, 1992). The twentieth-century French intellectuals Derrida and Foucault highlighted the constructed and contextual nature of meaning and offered radically different conceptions of language and power. In addition, feminist influences both within and outside psychology brought to the fore the impossibility of value-neutral research and knowledge

(Bohan, 1992; Hollway, 1989; Ussher, 1991). Instead, psychology was critiqued as harbouring and promoting sexist, racist, and heterosexist views of the human condition (Teo, 2005). In view of such problems with the modernist project, many scholars began to turn away from positivist science, and embrace postmodern perspectives that allowed them to attend to the multiple, shifting, and at times discordant voices of those they engaged with in research. While there is no single way of defining post-modernism (this would actually be inconsistent with postmodernism, which emphasizes plurality), it can be thought of in terms of its rejection of the modernist ideas of ultimate truth, in the form of grand theories, and of structuralism, the idea that the world is composed of underlying rules or structures (Burr, 1995; Polkinghorne, 1992).

> In a sense, the essence of postmodernism is a reversal of the form of epistemology that originally came to define modernism. At bottom is the conviction that reality is created or constructed, that the only meaningful knowledge is restricted to the particular, is time-limited, and pertains only to specific circumstances. Any attempt to locate or define the universal, the timeless, and the general, regardless of specific knowers, will end in failure.
>
> (Ryan, 1999, p. 491)

In the sections that follow, I will better situate my research by first elaborating on the epistemological perspective taken. In particular, I have adopted a critical-realist position (Bhaskar, 1978, 1989; Parker, 1992) within a social constructionist epistemology (Burr, 1995; Gergen, 1985).

SOCIAL CONSTRUCTIONISM

Social constructionism involves systems of thought that emerged within postmodernism and, in keeping with the postmodern spirit, it defies simplistic and static definition. Instead, Burr (1995) suggests that what links social constructionist writers together is a kind of 'family resemblance'. While there is no one feature common to all social constructionists, we might group under this heading any position which is founded on one or more of four basic assumptions (Burr, 1995). First, social constructionism invites a critical stance toward taken-for-granted knowledge (Burr, 1995; Potter, 1996a). It rejects the assumptions that the world reveals its 'true' nature to observers, and that observation, and resulting knowledge, can be objective, unbiased, and value-free (Gergen, 1985). Therefore, social con-structionism involves the rejection of the modernist assumptions of empiric-ism (the belief that valid knowledge can only be derived through an adherence to objective and scientific observation and experimentation) and positivism (the belief that what is perceived under scientific observation is the way the world actually is) (Burr, 1995; Nightingale & Cromby, 1999). Social constructionism calls into question the very categories we use to understand our world. All ways of understanding, including basic assumptions such as the division of people into categories 'male' and 'female', are understood as not simply 'the way things are' but as socially and politically negotiated constructions (Burr, 1995; Kitzinger, 1992). Therefore, social constructionism is 'centrally concerned with understanding how the language we use, and the taken-for-granted categories we employ about the world, construct our experience in ways which we then reify as "natural", "universal", and "the way things have to be"' (Kitzinger, 1992, p. 224).

The second theme that runs through social constructionist thought is the focus on the historical and cultural specificity of all knowledge (Burr, 1995; Martin & Sugarman, 2000; Stam, 1990). The ways in which we understand our experience and the concepts we use are considered to be products of the specific culture and time in which we live (Gergen, 1973, 1985). Therefore, knowledge is dependent upon the social, political, and economic forces operating at the time, as are the criteria by which certain ways of understanding are deemed valid (or not) (Gergen, 1992). In this way, knowledge can be considered a kind of cultural artifact, and as a result no one way of understanding is any better (in the sense of being more 'true') than any other (Burr, 1995).

Third, social constructionism holds that all knowledge, including scientific knowledge, is constructed rather than revealed (Banister, Burman, Parker, Taylor, & Tindall, 1994; Burr, 1995). 'From this perspective, knowledge is not something people possess somewhere in their heads, but rather, something people do together' (Gergen, 1985, p. 270). What is regarded as 'truth' at any one time is not the product of objective observation, but of the social processes and interactions in which people engage on a daily basis (Hayes & Oppenheim, 1997). 'When people talk to each other, the world gets constructed' (Burr, 1995, p. 7). Therefore, the categories we use to understand our world (e.g., gender, intelligence) are not viewed as naturally occurring (or the way things have to be) but rather as socially constructed accomplishments that become reproduced and elaborated in our everyday interactions.

The fourth and final assumption of social constructionism involves the interconnectedness of knowledge and action. Each different way of understanding, or construction, has ramifications for action in the social world (Burr, 1995; Gergen, 1985). Or, stated the other way, certain ways of acting are appropriate given certain ways of understanding. For instance, understanding 'depression' as a biological disorder would necessitate certain kinds of action (e.g., drug therapy) and may preclude others (e.g., initiating changes in one's life or going to counselling).

The role of language

To summarize, social constructionism takes a critical stance toward our taken-for-granted ways of understanding. Instead of regarding knowledge as simply the 'way things are', all ways of understanding are considered to be the products of cultural and historical contexts, and prevalent forms of knowledge are viewed as being sustained by social processes. Finally, social constructionists emphasize the implications for action that come with different ways of understanding our world (Burr, 1995; Cromby & Nightingale, 1999). If, as social constructionists assert, the nature of the world is created rather than discovered, how then does that 'construction' take place? To answer this question, social constructionists point to the role of language. Traditionally, language has been viewed as a passive vehicle that serves to express our internal thoughts, emotions, and experiences (Burr, 1995; Stam, 1990). The nature of the world and ourselves comes first and are then expressed to others through the labels and concepts available in language. For social constructionists, language takes on a more active role. Rather than thinking of language as a 'bag of labels which we can choose from in trying to describe our internal states (thoughts, feelings, etc.)' (Burr, 1995, p. 33), language is thought of as enabling us to structure and understand ourselves and our world. 'Language does not mimic reality; rather language constitutes reality, with each language constructing specific aspects of reality, each in its own way' (Hayes & Oppenheim, 1997, p. 25). From a social constructionist perspective, then, the structure of our language determines the structure of our experience.

Discourse

To acknowledge the active or performative role of language as well as the socially mediated nature of knowledge, constructionist writers have taken up the term 'discourse'. Discourse can be thought of as 'a system of statements which construct an object' (Parker, 1992, p. 5). It refers to 'a set of meanings, metaphors, representations, images, stories, statements and so on that in some way together produce particular versions of events' (Burr, 1995, p. 48). Therefore, the discourses available to an individual shape the ways in which she or he understands and experiences the world.

> Discourses do not simply describe the social world, but categorise it, they bring phenomena into sight. A strong form of the argument would be that discourses allow us to see things that are not 'really' there, and that once an object has been elaborated in a discourse it is difficult not to refer to it as if it were real.
>
> (Parker, 1992, pp. 4–5)

Any one object, event, or person may be surrounded by a number of different discourses, each with a different representation and different implications for action. For instance, Burr (1995) gives the British example of foxhunting as an object with at least two different discourses. The 'foxhunting as pest control' discourse invokes the notion that foxhunting is a necessary part of maintaining ecological balance. Farmers might draw on this discourse to defend their hunting practice as a natural response to overpopulation. A different discourse could be 'foxhunting as the contravention of basic morality'. Animal activists lobbying the government to stop the hunt might draw on this discourse by arguing that foxhunting is a cruel disregard for animals' right to life. A number of other discourses are equally possible (e.g., 'foxhunting as healthy outdoor sport' or 'foxhunting as pastime of the idle rich'). Burr explains:

> The point is that numerous discourses surround any object and each strives to represent or 'construct' it in a different way. Each discourse brings different aspects into focus, raises different issues for consideration, and has different implications for what we should do. So discourses, through what is said, written, or otherwise represented, serve to construct the phenomena of our world for us, and different discourses construct these things (like 'foxhunting') in different ways, each discourse portraying the object as having a very different 'nature' from the next. Each discourse claims to say what the object really is, that is, claims to be the truth.
>
> (Burr, 1995, p. 49)

Discourse and power

Postmodern psychologists have taken up Foucault's work on power/knowledge (e.g., 1977, 1980a) in their examination of discourse. According to these scholars, the discourses available within a culture are not random constructions, but are intimately connected to the ways in which society is socially, politically, and economically governed (Burr, 1995; Parker, 1997). Therefore, prevalent discourses tend to reflect the interests of powerful groups in society. For instance, capitalist economy offers the discourse of the 'independent individual' which brings with it all the implications inherent in this way of understanding people (e.g., notions of the 'survival of the fittest' and an assumed meritocracy which serve to promote those who 'have' and further oppress those who 'have not'). Discourses of femininity in Western patriarchal culture portray women as gentle and nurturing and therefore unsuited to the competitive realm of business. Understanding the 'nature' of women in this way relegates women to duties of care while at the same time justifying this station as 'natural'. However, all of this is not to say that prevalent discourses are destined to remain as such. For example, we have seen marked shifts in discourses of 'the family' and 'femininity' alongside economic, political, and social changes brought about by the feminist movement (Burr, 1995). Therefore, discourses, like the cultural contexts in which they are constructed, are in a constant state of flux.

The realism–relativism debate

Thus far I have described social constructionism as a relatively coherent system of thought. However, like all positions, there are unresolved and contentious issues that continue to be debated. One of the most hotly debated issues is what has become known as the realism–relativism debate (Cromby & Nightingale, 1999; Edwards et al., 1995; Parker, 1999). At the heart of social constructionism is the denial of the existence of 'objective truth' and an emphasis on the constructed nature of knowledge. The almost exclusive focus on language in social constructionist thought has led some to advocate a relativist position (Edwards et al., 1995). According to this relativist position, since all experience is necessarily mediated through language, then language is all there is (Hayes & Oppenheim, 1997). This position embraces ontological idealism, which is the idea that 'the only reality that things have is the reality they are given in the symbolic realm of language' (Burr, 1995, p. 86). Or, in Derrida's now famous phrase, 'There is nothing outside of the text' (Derrida, 1976, p. 158). In contrast to this relativist position, those taking a realist position accept the 'reality' of an external world which exists independent of our representations of it (Cromby & Nightingale, 1999). The realist camp repudiates the relativist's exclusive focus on language at the expense of acknowledging extra-discursive forces such as embodiment, materiality, and power (Cromby & Nightingale, 1999).[1]

Critical realism

The position I have adopted within the realism-relativism continuum is that of critical-realism (Bhaskar, 1978, 1989; Parker, 1992), a position based in a realist ontology while also accepting a relativist epistemology (Willig, 1999b).[2] That is, while I acknowledge the reality of a material world, I maintain that our understandings of this world and the things in it are necessarily mediated through discourse. In order to arrest constructionism's 'slide into relativism', Parker (1992) proposes that we conceptualize 'things' as being endowed with material reality (e.g., our bodies and brains as well as the physical and organizational properties of our environments (Burr, 1985)) while at the same time, acknowledging that we cannot have direct knowledge of these things, since thought is necessarily constructive and interpretive. The ways in which we 'know' are always bound in the social, political, and moral contexts operating within the time and place of knowledge construction. Therefore, this position allows recognition that 'things exist', while calling for respect for 'the different and provisional culturally bounded explanations of the nature of things' (Parker, 1992, p. 30). From a critical-realist perspective, then, 'there is a reality that exists outside of discourse, and this reality provides the raw material from which we may structure our understanding of the world, through discourse' (Burr, 1995, p. 88). Material structures and discourses are inextricably linked and all ways of understanding are loaded with moral and political implications (Willig, 1999a, 1999b).

In adopting a critical-realist perspective on women's depression then, I acknowledge the reality of women's bodies and their pain, but hold that all understandings of these are inseparable from the social and political contexts from which they emerge.

Validating knowledge claims

The acceptance of a critical-realist perspective requires a certain scepticism regarding all knowledge and its production. This position raises problems, however, for researchers who wish to promote the value of their findings. If we can no longer hold onto 'Truth' as the golden standard for 'good' knowledge, how can we promote certain ways of understanding as 'better' than others? Does the adoption of a relativist epistemology mean that everyone's views are equally valid and that, essentially, *anything goes*? Some have argued that a relativist position strips away any basis upon which to assert that one representation is more valid than another (Edwards et al., 1995). However, others, such as Parker (1992, 1999), have argued that the denial of absolute truth need not necessitate a slide into the perspective that there are only ever competing stories. In a similar vein, as Stam (1990, p. 249) has pointed out, 'Constructionists have not claimed that we cannot know; only that knowledge is inevitably of a certain kind'.

In the absence of a belief in 'Truth', we can still argue for the merit of some knowledges over others by shifting to a view of 'usefulness'. That is, if our experiences of the world are constructed through discourse, then one role of research is to critically examine and open up different ways of understanding that are more useful and empowering to those involved. The purpose of research is to promote knowledge that 'works' instead of purporting to discover knowledge that is universally true. For Harper (1999, p. 128), usefulness does not imply 'a technical utility in the sense of developing new treatment technologies, but refer(s) to whether a particular idea or intervention leads to richer understanding(s) and to just and socially responsible outcomes'. This focus on pragmatism can be illustrated in the following analogies. Positivist psychologists might look for knowledge that 'matches' reality in the same sense that one might look for paint that matches a paint chip. In the constructionist approach, rather than looking for knowledge that 'matches' reality, we might instead look for 'fit'. This conception can also be illustrated in the idea of a key fitting a lock. In this analogy, 'fit' describes the capacity of the key rather than the characteristic of the lock. While there may be a number of differently shaped keys that can open a door, a key 'fits' if it opens the lock (Von Glaserfeld, 1981/1984, cited in Chiari & Nuzzo, 1996). Similarly, Polkinghorne (1992) has proposed that postmodern psychology should be guided by, and adhere to, the tenet of neopragmatism:

> Neopragmatism shifts the focus of knowledge generation from attempts to describe the real as it is in itself (theoretical knowledge and 'knowing that') to programs to collect descriptions of actions that have effectively accompanied intended ends (practical knowledge and 'knowing how'). Pragmatic knowing concentrates on understanding *how* to, for example, ride a bicycle, rather than knowing *what* laws of nature allow the bicycle to remain upright. The test for pragmatic knowledge is not whether it produces a picture that corresponds to the real. In the postmodern view, we have no way to ascertain whether there is such a correspondence. Instead, the test for pragmatic knowledge is whether it functions successfully in guiding human action to fulfill intended purposes.
>
> (Polkinghorne, 1992, p. 151)

Kenneth Gergen (1992), one of the most influential postmodern writers in contemporary psychology, offers an eloquent summary of the postmodern perspective and an inviting vision for researchers in psychology:

> Postmodernism asks the scientist to join in the hurly-burly of cultural life – to become an active participant in the construction of the culture. For, as we have seen, the primary result of most scholarly inquiry is discourse itself. And, rather than simply recanting the taken-for-granted presumptions of the culture, the psychological scholar is in an optimal role to transform this discourse – and, by implication, the culture itself. Rather than 'telling it like it is' the challenge for the postmodern psychologist is to 'tell it as it may become'.
>
> (Gergen, 1992, p. 27)

In keeping with this postmodern spirit, the aim of the current analysis is to explore women's accounts of recovering from depression, with a view to elaborating potentially more useful and emancipatory ways of talking/ being.

Notes

1 Here, embodiment means to be within a body. It highlights how the experience of selfhood and the material body are inextricably linked and refers to the simultaneous experience of *having* a body and *being* a body. Materiality refers to the ways in which our experiences are always grounded in material reality (e.g. physical bodies, institutions, environments, and technologies) (Nightingale & Cromby, 1999; Yardley, 1996, 1997b).

2 My thinking in terms of the realism–relativism debate is also greatly influenced by a material-discursive perspective which acknowledges the inseparability of material reality and symbolic, discursive meaning (Stoppard, 1997, 1998, 2000; Ussher, 1996, 1997; Yardley, 1996, 1997a, 1997b). Developed in response to the linguistic idealism often associated with discursive approaches, a material-discursive perspective points to 'a continuous dialectic of mutual influence between nature and the socially constructed world' (Yardley, 1996, p. 493). Here, experience is always understood as both 'embodied and social, material and discursive' (Stoppard, 2000, p. 211). The body is therefore understood as both a biological, physical organism and a site for the production of cultural, symbolic, discursive systems of meaning (Stoppard, 2000). Materiality is taken to refer not only to physical bodies but also social structures such as institutions, environments, and technologies (Nightingale & Cromby, 1999; Yardley, 1996, 1997b). Materiality is infused with discursive meaning, and meaning is reproduced and constructed through materiality.

APPENDIX B

ADDITIONAL INFORMATION ABOUT THE RESEARCH PARTICIPANTS AND INTERVIEW PROCESS

Participants in both studies were women living in a semi-rural province in Eastern Canada. Participants ranged in age from 19 to 66 and came from diverse socioeconomic backgrounds, ranging from below the poverty line to upper-middle class. Most were more educated than average Canadians, having some postsecondary education, including professional training courses. Eight of the 33 women had completed all or some high school, while the rest had varying levels of postsecondary education. Reflecting the largely homogeneous population of the area in terms of racial and ethnic background, all participants were White and English-speaking; several were bilingual with French as either a first or second language. Most women were raised in Canada. Three women had immigrated from other countries; one from an Eastern European country, one from Central America and one from England. Almost all spoke of having been in heterosexual relationships. One woman identified as bisexual and spoke of her coming out experience as central to her recovery from depression. At the time of the interviews, most (20) were married or in monogamous relationships, seven were divorced or separated, one was widowed, and five stated that they were not involved in a romantic relationship. Most (28) had children, with ten of these having young or teenage children living in the home at the time of the study.[1]

I conducted all interviews in a rather informal way and endeavoured to create a comfortable space in which the participants could tell their stories. In order to encourage participants to orient to topics of concern to them (as opposed to my preconceived notions (about what they *should* discuss (Anderson & Jack, 1991; Devault, 1990)), I began interviews with a general and open-ended question. For instance, in the recovery study I began by asking, 'I'd like for us to talk about your experiences of getting out of depression. If that's where we're going, where should we begin?'. In the self-care study, I asked, 'I'm interested in women's health and well-being – whatever that means for you. Can you tell me about a time where you would consider yourself to have been healthy or well?'. During the interviews, I paid special attention to inviting participants to expand upon their use of different words, expressions, and ways of accounting (Potter & Wetherell, 1987). While my interview style tended to be more supportive than challenging, I did point out inconsistencies in accounts in order to explore the limits of different ways of accounting. In addition, I attempted to address the same issue on more than one occasion during an interview in order to allow the opportunity for both consistency and variability to emerge in participants' accounts (Potter & Wetherell, 1987; Wood & Kroger, 2000).

Note

1 It has been argued that demographic information should not be presented as I have done here, since the contextual information that the researcher may think is important (e.g., gender, education) may not have been germane to participants in the construction of their accounts (Schegloff, 1997; Wood & Kroger, 2000). Rather, it has been suggested that only those pieces of contextual information to which participants orient to should be presented (Schegloff, 1997). I have chosen to provide demographic information about participants in order to give readers some sense of the women I interviewed. However, this information should not be considered as 'variables' associated with research findings. That is, I am not suggesting that women with particular demographic profiles talk in certain ways.

APPENDIX C

TRANSCRIPT NOTATION

Note: From a discursive perspective, the content and form (what is said and how it is said) of speakers' accounts are inextricably linked (Potter, 1996a). In order to help me and the readers of this work better 'hear' women's accounts in the transcripts, I used a modified version of the transcript notations presented in Potter and Wetherell (1987) and Wood and Kroger (2000) and previously developed by Gail Jefferson.

Pseudonyms are used to refer to individual participants and indicated at the end of each excerpt in round brackets.
    e.g., (Cynthia)

Italics and initials are used to indicate the speech of the interviewer (Michelle Lafrance).
    e.g., *ML: Can you begin by telling me a bit about yourself?*

An equal sign at the end of a speaker's utterance and at the start of the next utterance indicates the absence of a discernible gap.
    e.g., *ML: Where was=*
    = we were talking about

Three periods indicate a discernible pause. More periods prolong the pause.
    e.g., that's one of the things that ... that is ... ... hardest

A dash shows a sharp cutoff of speech.
    e.g., I thought we would go bu-

A colon indicates an extension of the sound or syllable it follows. More colons prolong the stretch.
    e.g., I'm so:: sorry. Re::::lly I am.

Bold font indicates that words are uttered with added emphasis.
    e.g., and I couldn't believe he just **stood** there

Audible inbreaths (.hh) and outbreaths (hh) are inserted in the speech where they occur. More 'h's prolong the sound.

    e.g., .hhh So hhh that's what happened

Square brackets containing information either indicate clarifying information or that some of the transcript has been deliberately omitted to maintain the anonymity of the participant.

    e.g., So I grew up in [province] and went to school to become a [profession]

A series of three periods enclosed within square brackets [...] indicates that material has been left out of the excerpt.

Square brackets also mark overlap between utterances, distinguished by the text within them breaking onto a new line.

    e.g., *ML: What do you [remember*
I remember] thinking that

Double round brackets enclose the transcriber's description of non-speech sounds or other features of the talk or scene.

    e.g., ((crying))
    e.g., ((phone rings))

'Less than' and 'greater than' signs indicate talk that is noticeably faster or slower than the surrounding talk.

    e.g., <slow>
    e.g., >fast<

An 'h' in parentheses indicates laughter within words.

    e.g., Rea(h)lly?

Punctuation marks (e.g. .,?!) are used to mark speech delivery rather than grammar. A period indicates a stopping fall in tone; a comma indicates a continuing intonation; a question mark indicates a rising inflection; an exclamation point indicates an animated or emphatic tone.

REFERENCES

Allgöwer, A., Wardle, J., and Steptoe, A. (2001) 'Depressive symptoms, social support, and personal health behaviors in young men and women', *Health Psychology*, 20 (3), 223–7.

American Psychiatric Association (2000) *Diagnostic and statistical manual of mental disorders*, 4th ed, Text Revision (DSM-IV-TR), Washington, DC: APA.

Anderson, K.J. and Jack, D.C. (1991) 'Learning to listen: Interview techniques and analyses', in S. Berger Gluck and D. Patai (eds), *Women's words: The feminist practice of oral history*, pp. 11–26, New York: Routledge.

Anonymous (1989) 'How I've managed chronic mental illness', *Schizophrenia Bulletin*, 15, 635–40.

Anthony, W.A. (1993) 'Recovery from mental illness: The guiding vision of the mental health service system in the 1990s', *Psychosocial Rehabilitation Journal*, 16 (4), 11–23.

Anthony, W.A. (2004) 'The recovery effect', *Psychiatric Rehabilitation Journal*, 27 (4), 303–4.

Arendell, T. and Estes, C. (1994) 'Older women in the post-Regan era', in E. Fee and N. Krieger (eds), *Women's health, politics, and power*, pp. 333–49, Amityville, NY: Baywood.

Armstrong, T., Bauman, A., and Davies, J. (2000) *Physical activity patterns of Australian adults: Results of the 1999 National Physical Activity Survey*, Canberra, Australia: Australian Institute of Health and Welfare.

Baines, C.T., Evans, P.M., and Neysmith, S.M. (1998) 'Women's caring: Work expanding, state contracting', in C.T. Baines, P.M. Evans, and S.M. Neysmith (eds), *Women's caring: Feminist perspectives on social welfare*, 2nd ed, pp. 1–22, Toronto: Oxford University Press.

Banister, B., Burman, E., Parker, I., Taylor, M., and Tindall, C. (1994) *Qualitative methods in psychology: A research guide*, Buckingham: Open University Press.

Barthes, R. (1982) 'Inaugural lecture, Collège de France', in S. Sontag (ed.), *A Barthes reader*, London: Jonathan Cape.

Baxter, J. (2005) 'To marry or not to marry: Marital status and the household division of labor', *Journal of Family Issues*, 26 (3), 300–21.

Beauboeuf-Lafontant, T. (2007a) '"You have to show strength": An exploration of gender, race, and depression', *Gender & Society*, 21 (1), 28–51.

Beauboeuf-Lafontant, T. (2007b) 'Listening for and past the lies that make us sick:

208

A voice-centered analysis of depression among Black women', paper presented at the Fifth Biennial Conference of the International Society for Critical Health Psychology, Boston, MA.

Beaudet, M.P. (1996) 'Depression', *Health Reports*, 7, 11–24.

Bebbington, P. (1996) 'The origins of sex-differences in depressive disorder – bridging the gap', *International Review of Psychiatry*, 8, 295–332.

Bedini, L.A. (2002) 'Family caregivers and leisure: An oxymoron?', *Parks and Recreation*, 37 (1), 25–9.

Bedini, L.A. and Guinan, D.M. (1996) '"If I could just be selfish . . .": Caregivers' perception of their entitlement to leisure', *Leisure Sciences*, 18, 227–39.

Belle, D. and Doucet, J. (2003) 'Poverty, inequality, and discrimination as sources of depression among U.S. women', *Psychology of Women Quarterly*, 27, 101–13.

Bhaskar, R. (1978) *A realist theory of science*, 2nd ed, Brighton: Harvester Press.

Bhaskar, R. (1989) *Reclaiming reality: A critical introduction to contemporary philosophy*, London: Verso.

Bialeschki, D.M. and Pearce, K.D. (1997). '"I don't want a lifestyle – I want a life": The effect of role negotiations on the leisure of lesbian mothers', *Journal of Leisure Research*, 29 (1), 113–31.

Billig, M., Condor, S., Edwards, D., Gane, M., Middleton, D., and Radley, A. (1988) *Ideological dilemmas: A social psychology of everyday thinking*, Thousand Oaks, CA: Sage Publications.

Billig, M. (1991) *Ideology and opinions: Studies in rhetorical psychology*, London: Sage.

Bittman, M. and Wajcman, J. (2000) 'The rush hour: The character of leisure time and gender equity', *Social Forces*, 79 (1), 165–89.

Blehar, C.M. (2006) Women's mental health research: The emergence of a biomedical field, *Annual Review of Clinical Psychology*, 2, 135–60.

Blum, L.M. and Stracuzzi, N.F. (2004) 'Gender in the prozac nation: Popular discourse and productive femininity', *Gender & Society*, 18 (3), 269–86.

Bohan, J.S. (1992) *Seldom seen, rarely heard: Women's place in psychology*, Boulder, CO: Westview Press.

Boland, R.J. and Keller, M.B. (1996) 'Outcome studies of depression in adulthood', in K.I. Shulman, M. Tohem, and S.P. Kutcher (eds), *Mood disorders across the lifespan*, pp. 217–50, New York: John Wiley.

Bordo, S.R. (1989) 'The body and the reproduction of femininity: A feminist appropriation of Foucault', in A.M. Jagger and S.R. Bordo (eds), *Gender/body/ knowledge: Feminist reconstructions of being and knowing*, London: Rutgers University Press.

Bordo, S. (1993) *Unbearable weight: Feminism, western culture and the body*, Berkeley, CA: University of California Press.

Boston Women's Health Book Collective (2005) *Our bodies, ourselves: A new edition for a new era*, New York: Simon & Schuster.

Boyd, S.C. (2004) *From witches to crack moms: Women, drug law and policy*, Durham, NC: Carolina Academic Press.

Brewer, L. (2001) 'Gender socialization and the cultural construction of elder caregivers', *Journal of Aging Studies*, 15, 217–35.

Broota, A. and Dihr, R. (1990) 'Efficacy of two relaxation techniques in depression', *Journal of Personality and Clinical Studies*, 6 (1), 83–90.

Brown, C. and Augusta-Scott, T. (2007) *Narrative therapy: Making meaning, making lives*, Thousand Oaks, CA: Sage.

Brown, P.R., Brown, W.J., Miller, Y.D., and Hansen, V. (2001) 'Perceived constraints and social support for active leisure among mothers with young children', *Leisure Sciences*, 23, 131–44.

Brown, S.D. (1999) 'Stress as regimen: Critical readings of self-help literature', in C. Willig (ed.), *Applied discourse analysis: Social and psychological interventions*, pp. 22–43, Buckingham: Open University Press.

Burr, V. (1995) *An introduction to social constructionism*, London: Routledge.

Caissie, L.T. (2006) 'The raging grannies: Understanding the role of activism in the lives of older women', unpublished dissertation, University of Waterloo, Canada.

Canadian Research Institute for the Advancement of Women (CRIAW) (2001) *Women, health and action*, retrieved 5 June 2006 from <www.criaw-icref.ca>.

Canadian Research Institute for the Advancement of Women (2002) *Violence against women and girls*, retrieved 5 June 2006, from <www.criaw-icref.ca>.

Caplan, P. (1995) *They say you're crazy: How the world's most powerful psychiatrists decide who's normal*, Reading, MA: Addison-Wesley.

Chesler, P. (1972) *Women and madness*, New York: Avon.

Chiari, G. and Nuzzo, L (1996) 'Psychological constructivisms: A metatheoretical differentiation', *Journal of Constructivist Psychology*, 9, 163–84.

Chrisler, J.C. and Caplan, P. (2002) 'The strange case of Dr. Jekyll and Ms. Hyde: How PMS became a cultural phenomenon and a psychiatric disorder', *Annual Review of Sex Research*, 13, 274–306.

Cleeton, E.R. (2003) 'Are you beginning to see a pattern here? Family and medical discourses shape the story of black infant mortality', *Journal of Sociology & Social Welfare* 30 (1), 41–64.

Cohn, S. (1999) 'Taking time to smell the roses: Accounts of people with chronic fatigue syndrome and their struggle for lefitimisation', *Anthropology & Medicine*, 6 (2), 195–215.

Collins, P.H. (1994) 'Shifting the centre: Race, class, and feminist theorizing about motherhood', in E. Nakano Glenn, G. Chang, and L. Rennie Forcey (eds), *Mothering: Ideology, experience, and agency*, pp. 45–65, New York: Routledge.

Collins, P.H. (2000) *Black feminist thought: Knowledge, consciousness and the politics of empowerment*, 2nd ed, New York: Routledge.

Cody, R. and Lee, C. (1999) 'Development and evaluation of a pilot program to promote exercise among mothers of preschool children', *International Journal of Behavioral Medicine*, 6 (1), 13–29.

Connolly, C.M. and Socola, M.K. (2006) 'Listening to lesbian couples: Communication competence in long term relationships', in J.J. Bigner (ed.), *An introduction to GLBT Family Studies*, pp. 271–96, New York: Howarth Press.

Corrigan, P.W., Gifford, D., Rashid, F., Leary, M., and Okeke, I. (1999) 'Recovery as a psychological construct', *Community Mental Health Journal*, 35 (3), 231–9.

Coryell, W. and Winokur, G. (1992) 'Course and outcome', in E.S. Paykel (ed.), *Handbook of affective disorders*, 2nd ed, pp. 89–108, New York: Guilford.

Crespo, C.J., Ainsworth, B.E., Keteyian, S.J., Heath, G.W., and Smit, E. (1999) 'Prevalence of physical inactivity and its relation to social class in U.S. adults: Results from the Third National Health and Nutrition Examination Survey, 1988–1994', *Medicine & Science in Sports & Exercise*, 31 (12), 1821–7.

Cromby, J. and Nightingale, D.J. (1999) 'What's wrong with social construction-ism?', in D.J. Nightingale and J. Cromby (eds), *Social constructionist psychology: A critical analysis of theory and practice*, pp. 1–19, Buckingham: Open University Press.

Cromby, J. and Standen, P. (1996) 'Psychology in the service of the state', *Psychology Politics Resistance Newsletter*, 3, 6–7.

Csikszentmihalyi, M. and Csikszentmihalyi, I.S. (2006) *A life worth living: Contributions to positive psychology*, New York: Oxford University Press.

Culbertson, F.M. (1997) 'Depression and gender: An international review', *American Psychologist*, 52, 25–31.

Culter, S.E. and Nolen-Hoeksema, S. (1991) 'Accounting for sex differences in depression through female victimization: Childhood sexual abuse', *Sex Roles: A Journal of Research*, 24, 425–38.

Currie, J. (2005) 'The marketization of depression: The prescribing of SSRI antidepressants to women', Toronto: Women and Health Protection, retrieved 28 May 2008, from <www.whp-apsf.ca/pdf/SSRIs.pdf>.

Currie, J. (2004) 'Motherhood, stress and the exercise experience: Freedom or constraint?', *Leisure Studies*, 23 (3), 225–42.

Davidson, L. and Strauss, J.S. (1992) 'Sense of self in recovery from severe mental illness', *British Journal Medical Psychology*, 65, 131–45.

Davidson, L. and Strauss, J.S. (1995) 'Beyond the biopsychosocial model: Integrating disorder, health and recovery', *Psychiatry*, 58, 44–55.

Davidson, L., Harding, C., and Spaniol, L. (2005) *Recovery from severe mental illnesses: Research evidence and implications for practice*, Boston, MA: Center for Psychiatric Rehabilitation/Boston University.

Davies, B. and Harré, R. (1990) 'Positionings: The discursive production of selves', *Journal of Theory and Social Behaviour*, 20, 43–63.

Dean, K. (1992) 'Double burdens of work: The female work and health paradox', *Health Promotion International*, 7 (1), 17–25.

Deegan, P.E. (1988) 'Recovery: The lived experience of rehabilitation', *Psychosocial Rehabilitation Journal*, 11 (4), 11–19.

Deem, R. (1988) 'Feminism and leisure studies: Opening up new directions', in E. Wimbush and M. Talbot (eds), *Relative Freedoms: Women and leisure*, pp. 5–17, Milton Keynes, UK: Open University Press.

Dempsey, K. (1989) 'Women's leisure, men's leisure: A study in subordination and exploitation', *The Australian and New Zealand Journal of Sociology*, 25 (1), 27–45.

Derrida, J. (1976) *Of grammatology*, Baltimore, MD: Johns Hopkins University Press.

Devault, M.L. (1990) 'Talking and listening from women's standpoint: Feminist strategies for interviewing and analysis', *Social Problems*, 37 (1), 96–116.

DiGiacomo, S.M. (1992) 'Metaphor as illness: Postmodern dilemmas in the representation of body, mind and disorder', *Medical Anthropology*, 14, 109–37.

Drew, S. and Paradice, R. (1996) 'Time, women and well-being', *Feminism & Psychology*, 6 (4), 563–8.

Dunne, G. (1999) 'A passion for "sameness"? Sexuality and gender accountability', in E.B. Silva and C. Smart (eds), *The new family?*, pp. 68–83, London: Sage.

Eaton, W.W., Anthony, J.C., Gallo, J., Cai, G., Tien, A., Romanoski, A. et al.

211

(1997) 'Natural history of diagnostic interview schedule/DSM-IV major depression', *Archives of General Psychiatry*, 54, 993–8.

Edge, D. and Rogers, A. (2005) 'Dealing with it: Black Caribbean women's response to adversity and psychological distress associated with pregnancy, childbirth, and early motherhood', *Social Science & Medicine*, 61, 15–25.

Edley, N. and Wetherell, M. (1997) 'Jockeying for position: The construction of masculine identities', *Discourse & Society*, 8, 203–17.

Edley, N. and Wetherell, M. (2001) 'Jekyll and Hyde: Men's constructions of feminism and feminists', *Feminism & Psychology*, 11, 439–57.

Edwards, A.E. (2004) 'Community mothering: The relationship between mothering and the community work of black women', in A. O'Reilly (ed.), *Mother outlaws: Theories and practices of empowered mothering*, pp. 203–13, Toronto: Women's Press.

Edwards, D., Ashmore, M., and Potter, J. (1995) 'Death and furniture: The rhetoric, politics and theology of bottom line arguments against relativism', *History of the Human Sciences*, 8 (2), 25–49.

Eldridge, N.S. and Gilbert, L.A. (1990) 'Correlates of relationship satisfaction in lesbian couples', *Psychology of Women Quarterly*, 14, 43–62.

England, P., Budig, M., and Folbre, N. (2002) 'Wages of virtue: The relative pay of care work', *Social Problems*, 49, (4), 455–74.

Evans, P.M. (1998) 'Gender, poverty, and women's caring', in C.T. Baines, P.M. Evans, and S.M. Neysmith (eds), *Women's caring: Feminist perspectives on social welfare*, 2nd ed, pp. 47–68, Toronto: Oxford University Press.

Fairclough, N. (1995) *Critical discourse analysis: The critical study of language*, Harlow: Addison-Wesley Longman.

Fava, G.A., Ruini, C., and Belaise, C. (2007) 'The concept of recovery in major depression', *Psychological Medicine*, 37 (3), 307–17.

Fergusson, D., Doucette, S., Cranley Glass, K., Shapiro, S., Healy, D., Hebert, P. et al. (2005) 'Association between suicide attempts and selective serotonin reuptake inhibitors: Systematic review of randomised controlled trials', *British Medical Journal*, 330 (7488), 396–403.

Findlay, D.A. and Miller, L.J. (1994) 'Through medical eyes: The medicalization of women's bodies and women's lives', in B.S. Bolaria and H.D. Dickinson (eds), *Health, illness and health care in Canada*, 2nd ed, pp. 276–306, Toronto: Harcourt Brace Canada.

Fisher, D.B. (1994) 'Health care reform based on an empowerment model of recovery by people with psychiatric disabilities', *Hospital and Community Psychiatry*, 45 (9), 913–15.

Fiske, J.A. (1993) 'Child of the state mother of the nation: Aboriginal women and the ideology of motherhood', *Culture*, 13 (1), 17–35.

Folbre, N. and Nelson, J. (2000) 'For love or money – or both?', *Journal of Economic Perspectives*, 14, 123–40.

Foucault, M. (1975) *The birth of the clinic: An archeology of medical perception*, New York: Vintage.

Foucault, M. (1977) *Discipline and punish: The birth of the prison*, New York: Vintage.

Foucault, M. (1980a) *Power/knowledge: Selected interviews and other writings, 1972–1977*, New York: Pantheon.

Foucault, M. (1980b) *The history of sexuality, Vol I: An introduction*, New York: Vintage.

Foucault, M. (1986) *The history of sexuality, Vol. III: The care of the self*, New York: Vintage.

Frank, A.W. (1998) 'Stories of illness as care of the self: A Foucauldian dialogue', *Health*, 2 (3), 329–48.

Frank, E. and Stewart, B.D. (1984) 'Depressive symptoms in rape victims: A revisit', *Journal of Affective Disorders*, 7, 77–82.

Frank, E., Prien, R.F., Jarrett, R.B., Keller, M.B., Kupfer, D.J., Lavori, P.W. et al. (1991) 'Conceptualization and rationale for consensus definitions of terms in major depressive disorder: Remission, recovery, relapse, and recurrence', *Archives of General Psychiatry*, 48, 851–5.

Frese, F.J. and Davis, W.W. (1997) 'The consumer-survivor movement, recovery and consumer professionals', *Professional Psychology: Research and Practice*, 28 (3), 243–5.

Freysinger, V.J. and Flannery, D. (1992) 'Women's leisure: Affiliation, self-determination, empowerment and resistance?', *Society and Leisure*, 15 (1), 303–22.

Friedan, B. (1963) *The feminine mystique*, New York: Dell.

Fullagar, S. (2008) 'Leisure practices as counter-depressants: Emotion-work and emotion-play within women's recovery from depression', *Leisure Sciences*, 30, 35–52.

Gammell, D.J. and Stoppard, J.M. (1999) 'Women's experiences of treatment of depression: Medicalization or empowerment?', *Canadian Psychology*, 40, 112–28.

Gardner, P. (2003) 'Distorted packaging: Marketing depression as illness, drugs as cure', *Journal of Medical Humanities*, 24, 105–30.

Gavey, N. and McPhillips, K. (1999) 'Subject to romance: Heterosexual passivity as an obstacle to women initiating condom use', *Psychology of Women Quarterly*, 23, 349–67.

George, U. (1998) 'Caring and women of colour: Living at the intersecting oppressions of race, class and gender', in C.T. Baines, P.M. Evans, and S.M. Neysmith (eds), *Women's caring: Feminist perspectives on social welfare*, 2nd ed, pp. 69–83, Toronto: Oxford University Press.

Gergen, K.J. (1973) 'Social psychology as history', *Journal of Personality and Social Psychology*, 26 (2), 309–20.

Gergen, K.J. (1985) 'The social constructionist movement in modern psychology', *American Psychologist*, 40 (3), 266–75.

Gergen, K.J. (1992) 'Toward a postmodern psychology', in S. Kvale (ed.), *Psychology and postmodernism*, pp. 17–30, London: Sage.

Gillespie, R. (2000) 'When no means no: Disbelief, disregard and deviance as discourses of voluntary childlessness', *Women's Studies International Forum*, 23 (2), 223–34.

Gillespie, R. (2003) 'Childfree and feminine: Understanding the gender identity of voluntarily childless women', *Gender & Society*, 17 (1), 122–36.

Gillies, V. (1999) 'An analysis of the discursive positions of women smokers: Implications for practical interventions', in C. Willig (ed.), *Applied discourse analysis: Social and psychological interventions*, pp. 66–86, Buckingham: Open University Press.

Gillies, V. and Willig, C. (1997) '"You get the nicotine and that in your blood' – Constructions of addiction and control in women's accounts of cigarette smoking', *Journal of Community & Applied Social Psychology*, 7, 285–301.

Gilligan, C. (1982) *In a different voice: Psychological theory and women's development*, Cambridge, MA: Harvard University Press.

Golding, J.M. (1999) 'Intimate partner violence as a risk factor for mental disorders: A meta-analysis', *Journal of Family Violence*, 14, 99–132.

Good, M.J.D., Brodwin, P.E., Good, B.J., and Kleinman, A. (1992) *Pain as human experience: An anthropological perspective*, Berkeley: University of California Press.

Gordon, D.R. (1988) 'Tenacious assumptions in western medicine', in M. Lock and D. Gordon (eds), *Biomedicine examined*, pp. 19–56, Dordrecht, Holland: Kluwer Academic Publishers.

Gotlib, I.H. and Hammen, C.L. (eds) (2002) *Handbook of depression*, New York: Guilford Press.

Graham, H. (1987) 'Women's poverty and caring', in C. Glendenning and J. Millar (eds), *Women and Poverty in Britain*, pp. 221–40, Brighton: Wheatsheaf.

Greaves, L., Varcoe, C., Poole, N., Morrow, M., Johnson, J., Pederson, A. et al. (2002) *A motherhood issue: Discourses on mothering under duress*, Ottawa: Status of Women Canada.

Green, E., Hebron, S., and Woodward, D. (1987) *Leisure and gender: A study of Sheffield women's leisure experiences*, London: The Sport Council and Economic and Social Research Council.

Green, E., Hebron, S., and Woodward, D. (1990) *Women's leisure, what leisure?*, London: Macmillan Education.

Hamilton, J.A. and Jensvold, M. (1995) 'Sex and gender as critical variables in feminist psychopharmacology research and pharmacology', *Women & Therapy*, 16, 9–30.

Hansson, A., Hillerås, P., and Forsell, Y. (2005) 'What kind of self-care strategies do people report using and is there an association with well-being?', *Social Indicators Research*, 73, 133–9.

Harper, D. (1999) 'Tablet talk and depot discourse: Discourse analysis and psychiatric medication', in C. Willig (ed.), *Applied discourse analysis: Social and psychological interventions*, pp. 125–44, Buckingham: Open University Press.

Harré, R. and Van Langenhove, L. (1991) 'Varieties of positioning', *Journal for the Theory of Social Behaviour*, 20, 391–407.

Harrington, M., Dawson, D., and Bolla, P. (1992) 'Objective and subjective constraints on women's enjoyment of leisure', *Society and Leisure*, 15 (1), 203–21.

Harvey, C.D.H. and Yoshino, S. (2006) 'Social policy for family caregivers of elderly: A Canadian, Japanese, and Australian comparison', *Marriage & Family Review*, 39 (1–2), 142–58.

Hayes, R.L. and Oppenheim, R. (1997) 'Constructivism: Reality is what you make it', in T.L. Sexton and B.L. Griffin (eds), *Constructivist thinking in counselling practice, research and training*, pp. 19–40, New York: Teachers College Press.

Hays, S. (1996) *The cultural contradictions of motherhood*, New Haven, CT: Yale University Press.

Health Canada (2002) *Healthy Canadians: A federal report on comparable health indicators 2002*, Ottawa, ON: Author.

214

Healy, D. (2003) *Let them eat Prozac*, Toronto: James Lorimer & Co.

Healy, D. and Aldred, G. (2005) 'Antidepressant drug use & the risk of suicide', *International Review of Psychiatry*, 17 (3), 163–72.

Heise, L., Ellsberg, M., and Gottemoeller, M. (1999) 'Ending violence against women', *Population Reports, Series L* (11), Baltimore, MD: Population Information Program, Johns Hopkins University School of Public Health.

Henderson, K.A. (1991) 'The contribution of feminism to an understanding of leisure constraint', *Journal of Leisure Research*, 23 (4), 363–77.

Henderson, K.A. (1994) 'Broadening an understanding of women, gender, and leisure', *Journal of Leisure Research*, 26 (1), 1–7.

Henderson, K.A. (1996) 'One size doesn't fit all: The meaning of women's leisure', *Journal of Leisure Research*, 28 (3), 139–54.

Henderson, K.A. and Allen, K.R. (1991) 'The ethic of care: Leisure possibilities and constraints for women', *Society and Leisure*, 14 (1), 97–113.

Henderson, K.A. and Bialeschki, D.M. (1991) 'A sense of entitlement to leisure as constraint and empowerment for women', *Leisure Sciences*, 13, 51–65.

Henderson, K.A. and Bialeschki, D.M. (1993) 'Fear as a constraint to active lifestyles for females', *The Journal of Physical Education, Recreation & Dance*, 64, 44–7.

Henderson, K.A., Bialeschki, D.M., Shaw, S.M., and Fresinger, V.J. (1989) *A leisure of one's own: A feminist perspective on women's leisure*, State College, PA: Venture.

Henderson, K.A., Hodges, S., and Kivel, B.D. (2002) 'Context and dialogue in research on women and leisure', *Journal of Leisure Research*, 34 (3), 253–71.

Henderson, K.A. and Winn, S. (1996) 'Females and physical activity', *Parks & Recreation*, 31 (8), 28–32.

Hepworth, J. (1999) 'Gender and the capacity of women with NIDDM to implement medical advice', *Scandinavian Journal of Public Health*, 27 (4), 260–6.

Herrera, V.M., Koss, M.P., Bailey, J., Yuan, N., and Lichter, E. (2006) 'Survivors of male violence: Research and training initiatives to facilitate recovery from depression and posttraumatic stress disorder', in J. Worrel and C.D. Goodheart (eds), *Handbook of girls' and women's psychological health*, pp. 455–66, New York: Oxford University Press.

Herridge, K.L., Shaw, S.M., and Mannell, R.C. (2003) 'An exploration of women's leisure within heterosexual romantic relationships', *Journal of Leisure Research*, 35 (3), 274–91.

Himmelweit, S. and Sigala, M. (2003) *Internal and external constraints on mothers' employment: Some implications for policy*, ESRC Future of Work Programme, Working paper no 27. London: ESRC.

Hollway, W. (1989) *Subjectivity and method in psychology: Gender, meaning, and science*, London: Sage.

Holroyd, E.E. (2003) 'Chinese family obligations toward chronically ill elderly members: Comparing caregivers in Beijing and Hong Kong', *Qualitative Health Research*, 13 (3), 302–18.

Homemakers Magazine (2003) 'Be your own coach', *Homemakers Magazine*, (September), 37.

hooks, b. (1982) *Ain't I a woman. Black women and feminism*, London: Pluto.

215

hooks, b. (1984) *Feminist theory: From margin to center*, Boston, MA: South End Press.

hooks, b. (1990) *Yearning: Race, gender, and cultural politics*, Boston, MA: South End Press.

hooks, b. (1993) *Sisters of the yam: Black women and self-discovery*, Toronto: Between the lines.

hooks, b. (2000) *Feminist theory: From margins to center*, 2nd ed, Cambridge, MA: South End Press.

Horton-Salway, M. (2001) 'Narrative identities and the management of personal accountability in talk about ME: A discursive psychology approach to illness narrative', *Journal of Health Psychology*, 6 (2), 247–59.

Horton-Salway, M. (2002) 'Bio-psycho-social reasoning in GPs' case narratives: The discursive construction of ME patients' identities', *Health: An Interdisciplinary Journal for the Social Study of Health, Illness and Medicine*, 6 (4), 401–21.

Hu, F.B., Sigal, R.J., Rich-Edwards, J.W., Colditz, G.A., Solomon, C.G., Willet, W.C. et al. (1999) 'Walking compared with vigorous physical activity and risk of type 2 diabetes in women: A prospective study', *Journal of the American Medical Association*, 282 (15), 1433–9.

Hull, R.B. (1990) 'Mood as a product of leisure: Causes and consequences', *Journal of Leisure Research*, 22 (2), 99–111.

Hutchby, I. and Wooffitt, R. (1998) *Conversation analysis: Principles, practices and applications*, Cambridge, UK: Polity Press.

Inaba, A., Thoits, P.A., Ueno, K., Gove, W.R., Evanson, R.J., and Sloan, M. (2005) 'Depression in the United States and Japan: Gender, marital status, and SES patterns', *Social Sciences & Medicine*, 61, 2280–92.

Izuhara, M. (2002) 'Care and inheritance: Japanese and English perspectives on the "generational contract"', *Ageing & Society*, 22, 61–77.

Jack, D.C. (1991) *Silencing the self: Women and depression*, New York: Harper Collins.

Jackson, J.E. (1992) '"After a while no one believes you": Real and unreal pain', in M.J.D. Good, P.E. Brodwin, B.J. Good, and A. Kleinman (eds), *Pain as human experience: An anthropological perspective*, pp. 138–68, Berkeley: University of California Press.

Jackson, S.W. (1986) *Melancholia and depression: From Hippocratic times to modern times*, New Haven, CT: Yale University Press.

James, K. (2000) '"You can *feel* them looking at you": The experiences of adolescent girls at swimming pools', *Journal of Leisure Research*, 32 (2), 262–80.

James, S. (1993) 'Mothering: A possible Black feminist link to social transformation?', in S. James and A. Busia (eds), *Theorizing Black feminisms: The visionary pragmatism of Black women*, pp. 44–54, New York: Routledge.

James, K. and Embrey, L. (2001) '"Anyone could be lurking around!": Constraints on adolescent girls' recreational activities after dark', *World Leisure*, 43 (4), 44–52.

Jenkins, C.D. (2003) *Building better health: A handbook of behavioral change*, Washington, DC: Pan American Health Organization.

Jenkins, J.H., Kleinman, A., and Good, B.J. (1991) 'Cross-cultural studies of depression', in J. Becker and A. Kleinman (eds), *Psychosocial aspects of depression*, pp. 67–99, Hillsdale, NJ: Lawrence Erlbaum Associates.

Kabat-Zinn, J. (1990) *Full catastrophe living: Using the wisdom of your body and mind to face stress, pain, and illness*, New York: Dell.

Keller, M.B. (1996) 'Depression: Consideration for treatment of a recurrent and chronic disorder', *Journal of Psychopharmacology*, 10 (Suppl. 1), 41–4.

Kendler, K.S., Walters, E.E., and Kessler, R.C. (1997) 'The prediction of length of major depressive episode: Results from an epidemiological sample of female twins', *Psychological Medicine*, 27, 107–17.

Kessler, R.C., McGonagle, K.A., Swartz, M., Blazer, D.G., and Nelson, C.B. (1993) 'Sex and depression in the National Comorbidity Survey I: Lifetime prevalence, chronicity and recurrence', *Journal of Affective Disorders*, 29, 85–96.

Kessler, R.C., Sonnega, A., Bromet, E. Hughes, M., and Nelson, C. (1995) 'Post-traumatic stress disorder in the National Comorbidity Survey', *Archives of General Psychiatry*, 52, 1048–60.

Keyes, C.L.M. and Goodman, S.H. (eds) (2006) *Women and depression: A handbook for the social, behavioral, and biomedical sciences*, New York: Cambridge University Press.

Kickbusch, I. (1989) 'Self-care in health promotion', *Social Science and Medicine*, 29 (2), 125–30.

Kiecolt-Glaser, J.K., Dura, J.R., Speicher, C.E., Trask, O.J., and Glaser, R. (1991) 'Spousal caregivers of dementia victims: Longitudinal changes in immunity and health', *Psychosomatic Medicine*, 53 (4), 345–62.

Kirmayer, L.J. (1988) 'Mind and body as metaphors: Hidden values in biomedicine', in M. Lock and D. Gordon (eds), *Biomedicine examined*, pp. 57–93, Dordrecht, Holland: Kluwer Academic Publishers.

Kitzinger, C. (1992) 'The individuated self concept: A critical analysis of social-constructionist writing on individualism', in G.M. Breakwell (ed.), *Social psychology of identity and the self concept*, pp. 221–49, London: Surrey University Press.

Kleinman, A. (1992) 'Pain and resistance: The delegitimation and relegitimation of local worlds', in M.J.D. Good, P.E. Brodwin, B.J. Good and A. Kleinman (eds), *Pain as human experience: An anthropological perspective*, pp. 169–97, Berkeley: University of California Press.

Kleinman, A. (1995) 'The social course of chronic illness: Delegitimation, resistance, and transformation in North American and Chinese societies', in S.K. Toombs, D. Barnard, and R.A. Carson (eds), *Chronic illness: From experience to policy*, pp. 176–88, Bloomington: Indiana University Press.

Kleinman, A., Brodwin, P.E., Good, B.J., and Good, M.J.D. (1992) 'Pain as human experience: An introduction', in M.J.D. Good, P.E. Brodwin, B.J. Good, and A. Kleinman (eds), *Pain as human experience: An anthropological perspective*, pp. 1–28, Berkeley: University of California Press.

Kleinman, A. and Kleinman, J. (1997) 'Moral transformation of health and suffering in Chinese society', in A.M. Brandt and P. Rozin (eds), *Morality and health*, pp. 101–18, New York: Routledge.

Kline, M. (1995) 'Complicating the ideology of motherhood: Child welfare law and First Nation women', in M. Albertson Fineman and I. Karpin (eds), *Mothers in law: Feminist theory and the legal regulation of motherhood*, pp. 118–41, New York: Columbia University Press.

Koss, M.P., Goodman, L.A., Browne, A., Fitzgerald, L.F., Keita, G.P., and Russo,

N.F. (1994) *No safe haven: Male violence against women at home, at work, and in the community*, Washington, DC: American Psychological Association.

Koss, M.P., Koss, P.G., and Woodruff, W.J. (1990) 'Relation of criminal victimization to health perceptions among women medical patients', *Journal of Consulting & Clinical Psychology*, 58 (2), 147–52.

Koss, M.P., Koss, P.G., and Woodruff, W.J. (1991) 'Deleterious effects of criminal victimization on women's health and medical utilization', *Archives of Internal Medicine*, 151, 342–8.

Kramer, E.J., Kwong, K., Lee, E., and Chung, H. (2002) 'Cultural factors influencing the mental health of Asian Americans', *Western Journal of Medicine*, 176, 227–31.

Kuhn, T.S. (1962) *The structure of scientific revolutions*, Chicago: University of Chicago Press.

Lafrance, M.N. (2003) 'Struggling for legitimacy: Women's accounts of recovery from depression', unpublished doctoral dissertation, University of New Brunswick, Canada.

Lafrance, M.N. (2007a) 'A bitter pill: A discursive analysis of women's medicalised accounts of depression', *Journal of Health Psychology*, 12 (1), 127–40.

Lafrance, M.N. (2007b) '"It's just like diabetes": A discursive analysis of medicalized constructions of depression', paper presented at the International Society of Critical Health Psychology, Boston, USA, July.

Lafrance, M.N. and Stoppard, J.M. (2006) 'Constructing a non-depressed self: Women's accounts of recovery from depression', *Feminism & Psychology*, 16 (3), 307–25.

Lafrance, M.N. and Stoppard, J.M. (2007) 'Re-Storying women's depression: A material-discursive approach', in K. Brown and T. Augusta-Scott (eds), *Narrative therapy: Making meaning, making lives*, pp. 23–37, Thousand Oaks, CA: Sage.

Lapsley, H., Nikora, L.W., and Black, R. (2000) 'Women's narratives of recovery from disabling mental health problems: A bicultural project from Aotearoa/New Zealand', in J.M. Ussher (ed.), *Women's health: Contemporary international perspectives*, pp. 415–23, Leicester: British Psychological Society.

Lee, I.M. (2003) 'Physical activity and cancer prevention – data from epidemiologic studies', *Medicine & Science in Sports & Exercise*, 35 (11), 1823–7.

Levand, D.I., Herrick, J.M., and Sung, K. (2000) 'Eldercare in the United States and South Korea', *Journal of Family Issues*, 21 (5), 632–51.

Lewinsohn, P.M., Zeiss, A.M., and Duncan, E.M. (1989) 'Probability of relapse after recovery from an episode of depression', *Journal of Abnormal Psychology*, 98, 107–16.

Lewis, B. and Ridge, D. (2005) 'Mothers reframing physical activity: Family oriented politicism, transgression and contested expertise in Australia', *Social Science & Medicine*, 60, 2295–306.

Lewis, S.E. and Nicholson, P. (1998) 'Talking about early motherhood: Recognising loss and reconstructing depression', *Journal of Reproductive and Infant Psychology*, 16, 177–97.

Liebert, R. and Gavey, N. (2006) '"They took my depression and then medicated me into madness": Co-constructing narratives of SSRI-induced suicidality', *Radical Psychology*, 5, retrieved 27 May 2008, from <www.radpsynet.org/journal/vol5/Liebert-Gavey.html>.

Linehan, M.M. (1993) *Cognitive-behavioral treatment of borderline personality disorder*, New York: Guilford.

Liss, M., Hoffner, C., and Crawford, M. (2000) 'What do feminists believe?', *Psychology of Women Quarterly*, 24, 279–84.

Lupton, D. (2000) '"Where's me dinner?": Food preparation arrangements in rural Australian families', *Journal of Sociology*, 36 (2), 172–86.

Maier, W., Gänsicke, M., Gater, R., Rezaki, M., Tiemens, B., and Urzúa, F. (1999) 'Gender differences in the prevalence of depression: A survey in primary care', *Journal of Affective Disorders*, 53, 241–52.

Malson, H. (1998) *The thin woman: Feminism, post-structuralism and the social psychology of anorexia nervosa*, London: Routledge.

Marecek, J. (1999) 'Trauma talk in feminist clinical practice', in S. Lamb (ed.), *New versions of victims: Feminist struggles with the concept*, pp. 158–82, New York: New York University Press.

Marecek, J. (2006) 'Social suffering, gender, and women's depression', in C.L. Keyes and S.H. Goodman (eds), *Women and depression: A handbook for the social, behavioral, and biomedical sciences*, pp. 283–308, Cambridge: Cambridge University Press.

Martin, J. and Sugarman, J. (2000) 'Between the modern and the postmodern: The possibility of self and progressive understanding in psychology', *American Psychologist*, 55 (4), 397–406.

Maté, G. (2006) 'You can't care for your spouse unless you look after yourself', *The Globe and Mail*, 25 February, Toronto, Canada, F4.

Matthews, A.K., Tartaro, J., and Hughes, T.L. (2003) 'A comparative study of lesbian and heterosexual women in committed relationships', *Journal of Lesbian Studies*, 7 (1), 101–14.

Mattingly, M.J. and Bianchi, S.M. (2003) 'Gender differences in the quantity and quality of free time: The U.S. experience', *Social Forces*, 81 (3), 999–1030.

Mauthner, N.S. (2002) *The darkest days of my life: Stories of postpartum depression*, Cambridge, MA: Harvard University Press.

Mauthner, N.S. (2003) '"Imprisoned in my own prison": A relational understanding of Sonya's story of postpartum depression', in J.M. Stoppard and L.M. McMullen (eds), *Situating sadness: Women and depression in social contexts*, pp. 88–112, New York: New York University Press.

May, C., Doyle, H., and Chew-Graham, C. (1999) 'Medical knowledge and the intractable patient: The case of chronic low back pain', *Social Science & Medicine*, 48, 523–34.

Mazure, C.M., Keita, G.P., and Blehar, M.C. (2002) *Summit on women and depression: Proceedings and recommendations*, American Psychological Association, Washington, DC: American Psychological Association (available online at: <www.apa.org/pi/wpo/women&depression.pdf>).

McGrath, E., Keita, G.P., Strickland, B.R., and Russo, N.F. (1990) *Women and depression: Risk factors and treatment issues*, Washington, DC: American Psychological Association.

McMahon, M. (1995) *Engendering motherhood: Identity and self-transformation in women's lives*, New York: Guilford.

McMahon, M. (1998) 'Between exile and home', in S. Abbey and A. O'Reilly (eds),

Redefining motherhood: Changing identities and patterns, pp. 187–200, Toronto: Second Story Press.

McSeveny, K., Doherty, K., and Grainger, K. (2005) 'Attack of the chip monster: Use of humour in the online confessions of Weight Watchers members', paper presented at the International Society of Critical Health Psychology, Sheffield, England, March.

Meisler, J.G. (1999) 'Chronic pain conditions in women', *Journal of Women's Health*, 8 (3), 313–20.

Miedema, B., Stoppard, J., and Anderson, V. (2000) *Women's bodies, women's lives: Health, well-being and body image*, Toronto: Sumach.

Miller, J.G. (1994) 'Cultural diversity in the morality of caring: Individually oriented versus duty-based interpersonal moral codes', *Cross-Cultural Research*, 28 (1), 3–39.

Miller, J.G. (1997) 'Culture and the self: Uncovering the cultural grounding of psychological theory', in J.G. Snodgrass (ed.), *The self across psychology: Self-recognition, self-awareness, and the self-concept*, pp. 217–30, New York: New York Academy of Sciences.

Miller, J.G. (2002) 'Bringing culture to basic psychological theory – beyond individualism and collectivism: Comment on Oyserman et al. (2002)', *Psychological Bulletin*, 128 (1), 97–109.

Miller, Y.D. and Brown, W.J. (2005) 'Determinants of active leisure for women with young children – an "ethic of care" prevails', *Leisure Sciences*, 27, 405–20.

Misra, G. (1993) 'Psychology from a constructionist perspective: An interview with Kenneth J. Gergen', *New Ideas in Psychology*, 11 (3), 399–414.

Morell, C. (1994) *Unwomanly conduct: The challenges of intentional childlessness*, New York: Routledge.

Morell, C. (2000) 'Saying no: Women's experiences with reproductive refusal', *Feminism & Psychology*, 10 (3), 313–22.

Morton, P. (1991) *Disfigured images: The historical assault on Afro-American women*, Westport, CT: Greenwood Press.

Moynihan, D.P. (1965) *The Negro family: The case for national action*, Office of Policy Planning and Research, Washington, DC: United States Department of Labor.

Mueller, T.I. and Leon, A.C. (1996) 'Recovery, chronicity, and levels of psychopathology in major depression', *Psychiatric Clinics of North America*, 19, 85–102.

Mueller, T.I., Leon, A.C., Keller, M.B., Solomon, D.A., Endicott, J., Coryell, W. et al. (1999) 'Recurrence after recovery from major depressive disorder during 15 years of observational follow-up', *American Journal of Psychiatry*, 156, 1000–6.

Murray, C.J. and Lopez, A.D. (1996) 'Alternative visions of the future: Projecting mortality and disability, 1990–2020', in C.J. Murray and A.D. Lopez (eds), *The global burden of disease: A comprehensive assessment of mortality and disability from diseases, injuries, and risk factors in 1990 and projected to 2020*, pp. 325–95, Boston, MA: Harvard University Press.

Narushima, M. (2001) 'A gaggle of raging grannies: The empowerment of older Canadian women through social activism', *International Journal of Lifelong Education*, 23 (1), 23–42.

National Alliance for Caregiving (NAC) and AARP (2004) *Caregiving in the U.S.*, available: <www.caregiving.org/data/04finalreport.pdf> [retrieved 5 June 2006].

National Family Caregivers Association (NFCA) and National Alliance for Caregiving (NCA) (2002) *Self-awareness in family caregiving: A report on the communications environment*, available: <www.thefamilycaregiver.org/pdfs/CommEnvironmentFINAL.pdf> [retrieved 5 June 2006].

National Family Caregivers Association/Fortis (1998) *Family caregiving demands recognition: Caregiving across the lifecycle: Final Report*, Milwaukee, WI: National Family Caregivers Association/Fortis.

Neale Hurston, Z. (1937) *Their eyes were watching God*, Greenwich, CT: Fawcett.

Nentwich, J.C. (2008) 'New fathers and mothers as gender troublemakers? Exploring discursive constructions of heterosexual parenthood and their subversive potential', *Feminism & Psychology*, 18 (2), 207–30.

Nicholson, P. (1998) *Post-natal depression: Psychology, science and the transition to motherhood*, New York: Routledge.

Nightingale, D.J. and Cromby, J. (eds) (1999) *Social constructionist psychology: A critical analysis of theory and practice*, Buckingham: Open University Press.

Nolen-Hoeksema, S. and Girgus, J. (1994) 'The emergence of gender differences in depression during adolescence', *Psychological Bulletin*, 115, 424–43.

Oakley, A. (1986) 'Beyond the yellow wallpaper', in A. Oakley, *Telling the truth about Jerusalem*, pp. 131–48, Oxford: Blackwell.

Oguma, Y. and Shinoda-Tagawa, T. (2004) 'Physical activity decreases cardiovascular disease risk in women: Review and meta-analysis', *American Journal of Preventive Medicine*, 26 (5), 407–18.

O'Grady, H. (2005) *Woman's relationship with herself: Gender, Foucault and therapy*, New York: Routledge.

O'Reilly, A. (2004a) *Mother outlaws: Theories and practices of empowered mothering*, Toronto: Women's Press.

O'Reilly, A. (2004b) 'Introduction', in A. O'Reilly (ed.), *Mother outlaws: Theories and practices of empowered mothering*, pp. 1–28, Toronto: Women's Press.

O'Reilly, A. (2004c) 'Politics of the heart: African-American womanist thought on mothering', in A. O'Reilly (ed.), *Mother outlaws: Theories and practices of empowered mothering*, pp. 171–91, Toronto: Women's Press.

Parker, I. (1992) *Discourse dynamics : Critical analysis for social and individual psychology*, London and New York: Routledge.

Parker, I. (1997) 'Discursive psychology', in D. Fox and I. Prilleltensky (eds), *Critical psychology: An introduction*, pp. 284–98, London: Sage.

Parker, I. (1999) 'Against relativism in psychology, on balance', *History of the Human Sciences*, 12, 61–78.

Parry, O., Fowkes, F.G.R., and Thomson, C. (2001) 'Accounts of quitting among older ex-smokers with smoking-related disease', *Journal of Health Psychology*, 6 (5), 481–93.

Peden, A.R. (1993) 'Recovering in depressed women: Research with Peplau's theory', *Nursing Science Quarterly*, 6 (3), 140–6.

Percy, C. and Kremer, J. (1995) 'Feminist identification in a troubled society', *Feminism & Psychology*, 5 (2), 201–22.

Perz, J. and Ussher, J.M. (2006) 'Women's experience of premenstrual syndrome: A case of silencing the self', *Journal of Reproductive and Infant Psychology*, 24 (4), 289–303.

Peterson, C. (2006) *A primer in positive psychology*, New York: Oxford University Press.

Pettie, D. and Triolo, A.M. (1999) 'Illness as evolution: The search for identity and meaning in the recovery process', *Psychiatric Rehabilitation Journal*, 22 (3), 255–62.

Phoenix, A. and Woollett, A. (1991) 'Motherhood: Social construction, politics and psychology', in A. Phoenix, A. Wollett, and E. Lloyd (eds), *Motherhood: Meanings, practices and ideologies*, pp. 13–27, London: Sage.

Pilgrim, D. and Bentall, R. (1999) 'The medicalisation of misery: A critical realist analysis of the concept of depression', *Journal of Mental Health*, 8 (3), 261–74.

Polkinghorne, D.E. (1992) 'Postmodern epistemology of practice', in S. Kvale (ed.), *Psychology and postmodernism*, pp. 146–65, London: Sage.

Pomerantz, A. (1986) 'Extreme case formulation: A way of legitimizing claims', *Human Studies*, 9, 219–29.

Pondé, M.P. and Santana, V.S. (2000) 'Participation in leisure activities: Is it a protective factor for women's mental health?', *Journal of Leisure Research*, 32 (4), 457–72.

Potter, J. (1996a) 'Discourse analysis and constructionist approaches: Theoretical backgrounds', in T.E. Richardson (ed.), *Handbook of qualitative research methods for psychology and the social sciences*, pp. 125–40, Leicester: British Psychological Society.

Potter, J. (1996b) *Representing reality: Discourse, rhetoric and social construction*, London: Sage.

Potter, J. and Wetherell, M. (1987) *Discourse and social psychology: Beyond attitudes and behaviour*, London: Sage.

Pujol, J. (1999) 'Deconstructing and reconstructing: Producing a reading of human reproductive technologies', in C. Willig (ed.), *Applied discourse analysis: Social and psychological interventions*, pp. 87–109, Buckingham: Open University Press.

Quinn, J.E.A. and Radtke, L. (2006) 'Dilemmatic negotiations: The (un)tenability of feminist identity', *Psychology of Women Quarterly*, 30 (2), 187–98.

Radley, A. (1993) 'The role of metaphor in adjustment to chronic illness', in A. Radley (ed.), *Worlds of illness: Biographical and cultural perspectives on health and discourse*, pp. 109–23, New York: Routledge.

Radley, A. and Billig, M. (1996) 'Accounts of health and illness: Dilemmas and representations', *Sociology of Health & Illness*, 18 (2), 220–40.

Red Hat Society (2007) <www.redhatsociety.com/info/WhatDoWeDo.html>, retrieved 26 April 2007.

Reiffenberger, D.H. and Amundson, L.H. (1996) 'Fibromyalgia syndrome: A review', *American Family Physician*, 53 (5), 1698–704.

Reitsma-Street, M. (1998) 'Still girls learn to care: Girls policed to care', in C.T. Baines, P.M. Evans, and S.M. Neysmith (eds), *Women's caring: Feminist perspectives on social welfare*, 2nd ed, pp. 87–113, Toronto: Oxford University Press.

Reynolds, J. and Wetherell, M. (2003) 'The discursive climate of singleness: The consequences for women's negotiation of a single identity', *Feminism & Psychology*, 13 (4), 489–510.

Rhodebeck, L.A. (1996) 'The structure of men's and women's feminist orientations: Feminist identity and feminist opinion', *Gender & Society*, 10, 386–403.

Rich, A. (1980) 'Compulsory heterosexuality and lesbian existence', *Signs*, 5, 631–60.

Rich, A. (1986) *Of woman born: Motherhood as experience and institution*, New York: Norton.

Ridge, D. and Ziebland, S. (2006) '"The old me could never have done that": How people give meaning to recovery following depression', *Qualitative Health Research*, 16 (8), 1038–53.

Rogers, A., May, C., and Oliver, D. (2001) 'Experiencing depression, experiencing the depressed: Separate worlds of patients and doctors', *Journal of Mental Health*, 10 (3), 317–33.

Rowe, R., Tilbury, F., Rapley, M., and O'Ferrall, I. (2003) '"About a year before the breakdown I was having symptoms": Sadness, pathology and the Australian newspaper media', *Sociology of Health & Illness*, 25 (6), 680–96.

Ryan, B.A. (1999) 'Does postmodernism mean the end of science in the behavioral sciences, and does it matter anyway?', *Theory & Psychology*, 9 (4), 483–502.

Sampson, E.E. (1993) *Celebrating the other: A dialogic account of human nature*, Hemel Hempstead: Harvester Wheatsheaf.

Sampson, E.E. (1993) 'Identity politics: Challenges to psychology's understanding', *American Psychologist*, 12, 1219–30.

Saunders, B.E., Kilpatrick, D.G., Hanson, R.F., Resnick, H.S., and Walker, M.E. (1999) 'Prevalence, case characteristics, and long-term psychological correlates of child rape among women: A national survey', *Child Maltreatment*, 4, 187–200.

Sayer, L.C. (2005) 'Gender, time and inequality: Trends in women's and men's paid work, unpaid work and free time', *Social Forces*, 84 (1), 285–303.

Schegloff, E.A. (1997) 'Whose text? Whose context?', *Discourse & Society*, 8, 165–87.

Schreiber, R. (1996a) '(Re)Defining my self: Women's process of recovery from depression', *Qualitative Health Research*, 6, 469–91.

Schreiber, R. (1996b) 'Understanding and helping depressed women', *Archives of Psychiatric Nursing*, 10 (3), 165–75.

Schreiber, R. (1998) 'Clueing in: A guide to solving the puzzle of self for women recovering from depression', *Health Care for Women International*, 19, 269–88.

Schreiber, R., Noerager Stern, P., and Wilson, C. (2000) 'Being strong: How black West-Indian Canadian women manage depression and its stigma', *Journal of Nursing Scholarship*, 32 (1), 39–45.

Schulz, R. and Beach, S.R. (1999) Caregiving as a risk factor for mortality: The caregiver health effects study, *Journal of the American Medical Association*, 282 (23), 2215–19.

Schwandt, T.A. (1997) *Qualitative inquiry: A dictionary of terms*, Thousand Oaks, CA: Sage.

Sexton, T.L. (1997) 'Constructivist thinking within the history of ideas: The challenge of a new paradigm', in T.L. Sexton and B.L. Griffin (eds), *Constructivist thinking in counselling practice, research and training*, pp. 3–18, New York: Teachers College Press.

Seymour-Smith, S., Wetherell, M., and Phoenix, A. (2002) '"My wife ordered me to come": A discursive analysis of doctors' and nurses' accounts of men's use of general practitioners', *Journal of Health Psychology*, 7, 253–67.

Shannon, C.S. and Shaw, S.M. (2005) '"If the dishes don't get done today, they'll get done tomorrow"': A breast cancer experience as a catalyst for changes to women's leisure', *Journal of Leisure Research*, 37 (2), 195–215.

Shaw, S.M. (1991) 'Research note: Women's leisure time – using time budget data to examine current trends and future predictions', *Leisure Studies*, 10, 171–81.

Shaw, S.M. (1994) 'Gender, leisure, and constraint: Towards a framework for the analysis of women's leisure', *Journal of Leisure Research*, 26 (1), 8–22.

Shaw, S.M., Bonen, A., and McCabe, J.F. (1991) 'Do more constraints mean less leisure? Examining the relationship between constraints and participation', *Journal of Leisure Research*, 23 (4), 286–300.

Shirley, C. and Wallace, M. (2004) 'Domestic work, family characteristics, and earnings: Reexamining gender and class differences', *The Sociological Quarterly*, 45 (4), 663–90.

Silverman, K. and Carter, R. (2006) 'Anxiety disturbances in girls and women', in J. Worell and C.D. Goodheart (eds), *Handbook of girls' and women's psychological health: Gender and well-being across the lifespan*, pp. 60–8, New York: Oxford University Press.

Sims-Schouten, W., Riley, S.C.E., and Willig, C. (2007) 'Critical realism in discourse analysis: A presentation of a systematic method of analysis using women's talk of motherhood, childcare and female employment as an example', *Theory & Psychology*, 17 (1), 101–24.

Skärsäter, I., Dencker, K., Bergbom, I., Häggström, L., and Fridlund, B. (2003) 'Women's conceptions of coping with major depression in daily life: A qualitative, salutogenic approach', *Issues in Mental Health Nursing*, 24, 419–39.

Snelling, S.J. (1999) 'Women's perspectives on feminism: A Q-methodological study', *Psychology of Women Quarterly*, 23, 247–66.

Snyder, C.R. and Lopez, S.J. (2007) *Positive psychology: The scientific and practical exploration of human strength*, Thousand Oaks, CA: Sage.

Solomon, D.A., Keller, M.B., Leon, A.C., Mueller, T.I., Lavori, P.W., Shea, M.T. et al. (2000) 'Multiple recurrences of major depressive disorder', *American Journal of Psychiatry*, 157 (2), 229–33.

Solomon, D.A., Keller, M.B., Leon, A.C., Mueller, T.I., Shea, M.T., Warshaw, M. et al. (1997) 'Recovery from major depression: A 10-year prospective follow-up across multiple episodes', *Archives of General Psychiatry*, 54, 1001–6.

Spitzer, D., Neufeld, A., Harrison, M., Hughes, K., and Stewart, M. (2003) 'Caregiving in transnational context: "My wings have been cut: Where can I fly?"', *Gender*, 17 (2), 267–86.

Stam, H.J. (1990) 'Rebuilding the ship at sea: The historical and theoretical problems of constructionist epistemologies in psychology', *Canadian Psychology*, 31 (3), 239–53.

Statistics Canada (1995) *Women in Canada: A statistical report*, 3rd ed, Ottawa, ON: Minister of Industry.

Statistics Canada (2006) *Women in Canada: A gender-based report*, 5th ed, Ottawa, ON: Author.

Steen, M. (1996) 'Essential structure and meaning of recovery from clinical depression for middle-adult women: A phenomenological study', *Issues in Mental Health Nursing*, 17, 73–92.

Stoppard, J.M. (1997) 'Women's bodies, women's lives and depression: Towards a reconciliation of material and discursive accounts', in J.M. Ussher (ed.), *Body talk: The material and discursive regulation of sexuality, madness and reproduction*, pp. 10–32, London: Routledge.

Stoppard, J.M. (1998) 'Dis-ordering depression in women: Toward a materialist-discursive account', *Theory & Psychology*, 8 (1), 79–99.

Stoppard, J.M. (1999) 'Why new perspectives are needed for understanding depression in women', *Canadian Psychology /Psychologie Canadienne*, 40 (2), 79–90.

Stoppard, J.M. (2000) *Understanding depression: Feminist social constructionist approaches*, New York: Routledge.

Stoppard, J.M. and McMullen, L.M. (2003) *Situating sadness: Women and depression in social context*, New York: New York University Press.

Sunderland, J. (2002) 'Baby entertainer, bumbling assistant and line manager', in L. Litosseliti and J. Sunderland (eds), *Gender identity and discourse analysis*, pp. 293–324, Amsterdam: John Benjamins Publishing.

Swann, J.M. and Ussher, C.J. (1995) 'A discourse analytic approach to women's experience of premenstrual syndrome', *Journal of Mental Health*, 4, 359–67.

Takeuchi, D.T., Chung, R.C., Lin, K.M., Shen, H., Kurasaki, K., Chun, C.A. et al. (1998) 'Lifetime and twelve month prevalence rates of major depressive episode and dysthemia among Chinese Americans in Los Angeles', *American Journal of Psychiatry*, 155 (10), 1407–14.

Teo, T. (2005) *The critique of psychology: From Kant to postcolonial theory*, New York: Springer.

The Oprah Magazine (2004) July issue, New York.

Thomas, T. (2004) '"You'll become a lioness": African-American women talk about mothering', in A. O'Reilly (ed.), *Mother outlaws: Theories and practices of empowered mothering*, pp. 215–28, Toronto: Women's Press.

Thomsson, H. (1999) 'Yes, I used to exercise, but . . . – A feminist study of exercise in the life of Swedish women', *Journal of Leisure Research*, 31 (1), 35–56.

Thrane, C. (2000) 'Men, women, and leisure time: Scandinavian evidence of gender inequality', *Leisure Sciences*, 22, 109–22.

Tishelman, C. and Sachs, L. (1998) 'The diagnostic process and the boundaries of normality', *Qualitative Health Research*, 8, 48–60.

Toombs, S.K., Barnard, D., and Carson, R.A. (eds) (1995) *Chronic illness: From experience to policy*, Bloomington, IN: Indiana University Press.

Ulrich, M. and Weatherall, A. (2000) 'Motherhood and infertility: Viewing motherhood through the lens of infertility', *Feminism & Psychology*, 10 (3), 323–36.

United Nations Development Program (UNDP) (1995) *Human development report*, New York: Oxford University Press.

United Nations Development Program (UNDP) (1997) *Human development report*, New York: Oxford University Press.

Ussher, J. (1991) *Women's madness: Misogyny or mental illness?*, Amherst: University of Massachusetts Press.

Ussher, J.M. (1996) 'Premenstrual syndrome: Reconciling disciplinary divides through the adoption of a material-discursive epistemologie standpoint', *Annual Review of Sex Research*, 7, 218–51.

Ussher, J.M. (1997) *Body talk: The material and discursive regulation of sexuality, madness and reproduction*, London: Routledge.

Ussher, J.M. (2002) 'Processes of appraisal and coping in the development and maintenance of premenstrual dysphoric disorder', *Journal of Community & Applied Psychology*, 12, 309–22.

Ussher, J.M. (2003a) 'The ongoing silencing of women in families: An analysis and rethinking of premenstrual syndrome and therapy', *Journal of Family Therapy*, 25, 388–405.

Ussher, J.M. (2003b) 'The role of premenstrual dysphoric disorder in the subjectification of women', *Journal of Medical Humanities*, 24 (1/2), 131–46.

Ussher, J.M. (2006) *Managing the monstrous feminine: Regulating the reproductive body*, New York: Routledge.

Ussher, J.M. and Sandoval, M. (2008) 'Gender differences in the construction and experience of cancer care: The consequence of the gendered positionings of carers', *Psychology & Health*, 23 (8), 945–63.

Ussher, J.M. and Perz, J. (2008) 'Empathy, egalitarianism and emotion work in the relational negotiation of PMS: The experience of women in lesbian relationships', *Feminism & Psychology*, 18 (1), 87–111.

Ussher, J.M., Perz, J., and Mooney-Somers, J. (2007) 'The experience and positioning of affect in the context of intersubjectivity: The case of premenstrual syndrome', *International Journal of Critical Psychology*, 21, 145–65.

Varcoe, C. and Hartrick Doane, G.H. (2007) 'Mothering and women's health', in M. Morrow, O. Hankivsky, and C. Varcoe (eds), *Women's health in Canada*, pp. 297–323, Toronto: University of Toronto Press.

Vertinsky, P. (1998) '"Run, Jane, run": Central tensions in the current debate about enhancing women's health through exercise', *Women & Health*, 27 (4), 81–111.

Vidler, H.C. (2005) 'Women making decisions about self-care and recovering from depression', *Women's Studies International Forum*, 28 (4), 289–303.

Vidler, H.C. (2006) 'Improving treatment outcomes for depressed women: Use of a self-help inventory in counselling settings', *Psychotherapy in Australia*, 12 (2), 74–81.

Viinamäki, H., Tanskanen, A., Honkalampi, K., Koivumaa-Honkanen, H., Antikaimen, R., Haatainen, K. et al. (2006) 'Recovery from depression: A two-year follow-up study of general population subjects', *International Journal of Social Psychiatry*, 52 (1), 19–28.

Wane, N.N. (2004) 'Reflections on the mutuality of mothering: Women, children, and othermothering', in A. O'Reilly (ed.), *Mother outlaws: Theories and practices of empowered mothering*, pp. 229–39, Toronto: Women's Press.

Ware, N.C. (1992) 'Suffering and the social construction of illness: The delegitimation of illness experience in chronic fatigue syndrome', *Medical Anthropology Quarterly*, 6, 347–61.

Ware, N.C. (1993) 'Society, mind and body in chronic fatigue: An anthropological view', in *Proceedings of the Ciba Foundation Symposium*, 173, pp. 62–82, New York: Wiley.

Ware, N.C. (1999) 'Toward a model of social course in chronic illness: The example of chronic fatigue syndrome', *Culture, Medicine and Psychiatry*, 23, 303–31.

Ware, N.C. and Kleinman, A. (1992) 'Culture and somatic experience: The social course of illness in neurasthenia and chronic fatigue syndrome', *Psychosomatic Medicine*, 54, 546–60.

Wearing, B. (1984) *The ideology of motherhood: A study of Sydney suburban mothers*, Sydney: George Allen and Unwin.

Wearing, B. (1990) 'Beyond the ideology of motherhood: Leisure as resistance', *Australian and New Zealand Journal of Sociology*, 26 (1), 36–58.

Wearing, B., Wearing, S., and Kelly, K. (1994) 'Adolescent women, identity and smoking: Leisure experience as resistance', *Sociology of Health & Illness*, 16 (5), 626–43.

Weaver, J.J. and Ussher, J.M. (1997) 'How motherhood changes life: A discourse analytic study with mothers of young children', *Journal of Reproductive and Infant Psychology*, 15, 15–68.

Weissman, M.M., Bland, R., Joyce, P.R., Newman, S., Wells, J.E., and Wittchen, H. (1993) 'Sex differences in rates of depression: Cross-national perspectives', *Journal of Affective Disorders*, 29, 77–84.

Wellard, S. (1998) 'Constructions of chronic illness', *International Journal of Nursing Studies*, 35 (1–2), 49–55.

Wetherell, M. (1998) 'Positioning and interpretative repertoires: Conversation analysis and post-structuralism in dialogue', *Discourse & Society*, 9 (3), 387–412.

White, J. and Frabbut, J.M. (2006) 'Violence against girls and women: An integrative developmental perspctive', in J. Worell and C.D. Goodheart (eds), *Handbook of girls' and women's psychological health*, pp. 85–93, New York: Oxford University Press.

White, M. (1995) *Re-authoring lives: Interviews and essays*, Adelaide: Dulwich Centre Publications.

White, M. (2000) *Reflections on narrative practice*, Adelaide: Dulwich Centre Publications.

White, M. (2004) *Narrative practice and exotic lives: Resurrecting diversity in everyday life*, Adelaide: Dulwich Centre Publications.

White, M. and Epston, D. (1990) *Narrative means to therapeutic ends*, New York: Norton.

Whitwell, D. (1999) 'The myth of recovery from mental illness', *Psychiatric Bulletin*, 23, 621–2.

Whyte, L.B. and Shaw, S.M. (1994) 'Women's leisure: An exploratory study of fear of violence as a leisure constraint', *Journal of Applied Recreation Research*, 19 (1), 5–21.

Widdicombe, S. (1995) 'Identity, politics and talk: A case for the mundane and the everyday', in S. Wilkinson and C. Kitzinger (eds), *Feminism and discourse: Psychological perspectives*, pp. 106–27, London: Sage.

Widdicombe, S. and Wooffitt, R. (1990) '"Being" versus "doing" punk: On achieving authenticity as a member', *Journal of Language and Social Psychology*, 9, 257–77.

Wilkinson, S. (2000) 'Women with breast cancer talking causes: Comparing content, biographical and discursive analyses', *Feminism & Psychology*, 10 (4), 431–60.

Williams, M., Teasdale, J., Segal, Z., and Kabat-Zinn, J. (2007) *The mindful way through depression: Freeing yourself from chronic unhappiness*, New York: Guilford.

Willig, C. (1995) '"I wouldn't have married the guy if I'd have to do that": Heterosexual adults' constructions of condom use and their implications for sexual practice', *Journal of Community & Applied Social Psychology*, 5, 75–87.

Willig, C. (1997) 'The limitations of trust in intimate relationships: Constructions of trust and sexual risk taking', *British Journal of Social Psychology*, 36, 211–21.

Willig, C. (1998) 'Social constructionism and revolutionary socialism: A contradiction in terms?', in I. Parker (ed.), *Social constructionism, discourse and realism*, London: Sage.

Willig, C. (ed.) (1999a) *Applied discourse analysis: Social and psychological interventions*, Buckingham: Open University Press.

Willig, C. (1999b) 'Beyond appearances: A critical realist approach to social constructionist work', in D.J. Nightingale and J. Cromby (eds), *Social constructionist psychology: A critical analysis of theory and practice*, pp. 37–51, Buckingham: Open University Press.

Willig, C. (1999c) 'Introduction: Making a difference', in Willig, C. (ed.), Applied *discourse analysis: Social and psychological interventions*, pp. 1–21, Buckingham: Open University Press.

Willig, C. (1999d) 'Conclusion: Opportunities and limitations of "applied discourse analysis"', in C. Willig (ed.), *Applied discourse analysis: Social and psychological interventions*, pp. 145–59, Buckingham: Open University Press.

Willig, C. (2000) 'A discourse–dynamic approach to the study of subjectivity in health psychology', *Theory & Psychology*, 10 (4), 547–70.

Winfrey, O. (2002) 'What I know for sure', *The Oprah Magazine* (October) (retrieved from <www.oprah.com/omagazine/200210/omag_200210_mision.jhml>).

Wood, L.A. and Rennie, H. (1994) 'Formulating rape: The discursive construction of victims and villains', *Discourse & Society*, 5 (1), 125–48.

Wood, L.A. and Kroger, R.O. (2000) *Doing discourse analysis: Methods for studying action in talk and text*, Thousand Oaks, CA: Sage.

Woodward, D., Green, E., and Hebron, S. (1989) 'The sociology of women's leisure and physical recreation: Constraints and opportunities', *International Review for the Sociology of Sport*, 24 (2), 121–36.

Woolf, V. (1942) *The death of the moth and other essays*, New York: Harcourt, Brace and Company.

Woollett, A. (1991) 'Having children: Accounts of childless women and women with reproductive problems', in A. Phoenix, A. Woollett, and E. Lloyd (eds), *Motherhood: Meanings, Practices and Ideologies*, pp. 47–65, London: Sage.

World Health Organization (WHO) (2000a) *Women's mental health: An evidence based review*, retrieved 5 June 2006 from <www.who.int/mental_health/media/en/67.pdf>.

World Health Organization (WHO) (2000b) *Violence against women*, retrieved 23 July 2006 from <www.who.int/mediacentre/factsheets/fs239/en/>.

World Health Organization (WHO) (2001) *The world health report 2001 – Mental health: New understanding, new hope*, available: <www.who.int/whr/2001/en/whr01_en.pdf> [5 June 2006].

World Health Organization (WHO) (2003a) *Consultation document to guide development of a WHO global strategy for diet, physical activity, and health*, retrieved 20 July 2006 from <who.int/dietphysicalactivity/media/en/gscon_doc_en.pdf>.

World Health Organization (WHO) (2003b) 'Diet, nutrition and the prevention of chronic diseases', WHO Technical Report Series No. 916, Geneva: WHO.

Wueve, J., Kang, J.H., Manson, J.E., Breteler, M.M.B., Ware, J.H., and Grodstein, F. (2004) 'Physical activity, including walking, and cognitive function in older women', *Journal of the American Medical Association*, 292 (12), 1454–61.

Yardley, L. (1996) 'Reconciling discursive and materialist perspectives on health and illness: A reconstruction of the biopsychosocial approach', *Theory & Psychology*, 6 (3), 485–508.

Yardley, L. (1997a) 'Disorientation in the (post) modern world', in L. Yardley (ed.), *Material discourses of health and illness*, pp. 109–31, London: Routledge.

Yardley, L. (ed.) (1997b) *Material discourses of health and illness*, London: Routledge.

Yardley, L. and Beech, S. (1998) '"I'm not a doctor": Deconstructing accounts of coping, causes and control of dizziness', *Journal of Health Psychology*, 3, 313–27.

Young, S.L. and Ensing, D.S. (1999) 'Exploring recovery from the perspective of people with psychiatric disabilities', *Psychiatric Rehabilitation Journal*, 22 (3), 219–31.

Zhan, H.J. (2004) 'Through gendered lens: Explaining Chinese caregivers' task performance and care reward', *Journal of Women & Aging*, 16 (1/2) 123–42.

INDEX